From the Ground Up

From the GROUND UP

BRAC's Innovations in the Development of Agriculture in Bangladesh and Beyond

edited by
Mushtaque Chowdhury | Muazzam Husain
Md. A. Saleque | Hugh Brammer

University Press Limited
In association with
brac

The University Press Limited
Red Crescent House (Level 6)
61 Motijheel Commercial Area
Dhaka 1000, Bangladesh
Phone: (+8802) 9565441, 57160710
Mobile: 01917733741
E-mail: info@uplbooks.com.bd
Website: www.uplbooks.com

First published, December 2019

Cover design by Shajedur Rahman

ISBN 978 984 506 282 4

Published by Mohiuddin Ahmed, The University Press Limited, Red Crescent House (Level 6), 61 Motijheel C/A, Dhaka 1000. Book designed by Md. Nazmul Haque. Printed at the Kharimati Ad.Com, 234 New Elephant Road (3rd floor), Dhaka 1205, Bangladesh.

Dedicated to

Sir Fazle Hasan Abed KCMG
the visionary and founder of BRAC

Md. Aminul Alam
who led the expansion of the agricultural programmes across
Bangladesh and beyond
and

Mahabub Hossain
who added new dimensions to BRAC agricultural programmes

Contents

List of Tables, Figures, Map and Photos

Tables

Figures

Map

Photos

Acknowledgements

The idea for this book grew out of the realisation that many of BRAC's game-changing interventions, particularly its contributions to the development of the agriculture sector, have remained largely undocumented and unknown. Even BRAC staff belonging to the current generation are unaware of their organisation's path-breaking innovations of the 1980s and the 1990s. Most of the older generation who worked during the past decades have since retired, and some of the early learning has been forgotten. One of us (Mushtaque Chowdhury) initially discussed this with his colleagues (Md. A. Saleque and others) and proposed the idea of jointly authoring a record of BRAC's seminal role in agricultural development in Bangladesh and its extension to the international context. The idea was enthusiastically welcomed. Soon, he took the proposal to BRAC's founder and the then Chairperson, Sir Fazle Hasan Abed, who immediately gave it his nod of approval. Furthermore, Md. A. Saleque was assigned to coordinate the writing of this book.

Although the initial idea came from an individual, the current product is the combined efforts of many. Firstly, we would like to acknowledge the contributions of the authors of the five key case studies presented in this book: Dr. Jiban Krishna Biswas, the author of Chapter 2, Professor S.D. Chowdhury for Chapter 3, Professor A.K. Fazlul Haque Bhuiyan for Chapter 4, Dr. M. Saifuddin Shah for Chapter 5, and Dr. Md. A. Saleque for Chapter 6. They spent a lot of their valuable time in researching the issues related to their respective chapters. They visited the field and interviewed key people who were either involved with BRAC at various times directly or indirectly or had seen the innovations implemented from a distance.

Senior BRAC staff including Mr. S.N. Kairy, Ms. Tamara Abed, Mr. Mohammad Anisur Rahman, Dr. Sirajul Islam, and Mr. Jobaidul Karim Masud gave invaluable support. We sincerely thank and appreciate the active participation of many of the other staff, namely, Mr. Md.

Azizul Haque, Mr. A.Q.M. Shafiqur Rouf, Mr. Musharaf Hossain, and Mr. Mahabubur Rahman for providing relevant past and present information on BRAC's involvement in the agricultural programme. Special thanks go to some of BRAC's former staff members including Mr. Sudhir Chandra Nath, Mr. Mokarrom Hossain, Mr. Mohammad Ali, Mr. S. Nandi, and Mr. Mizanur Rahman, who contributed substantially to this book by providing valuable information and input from their years of experiences in the field of agriculture.

We acknowledge the tremendous contributions and support of senior officials from the Government of Bangladesh including Mr. Golam Hossain, Former Director General, Bangladesh Fisheries Research Institute (BFRI); Mr. Mokammel Hossain, Former Director General, Department of Fisheries; Mr. Kazi Abdul Fattah, Former Director General, Department of Livestock Services (DLS); Mr. Md Hamidur Rahman, Director General, Department of Agricultural Extension; Mr. Md. Azizur Rahman, Former Deputy Director, DLS, and Mr. Talukdar Saiful Islam, Former Deputy Director, DLS. The authors and editors were also immensely benefited from discussions and exchange of ideas with representatives of different agricultural associations including Mr. Moshiur Rahman, Convener, Bangladesh Poultry Industry Coordination Committee and Mr. Md. Shafiqul Islam, Chairman, Prawn Hatchery Owners Association. Media personality and agriculture expert Mr. Shykh Seraj, Founder Director and Head of News, Channel I, also provided his own perspectives and assessments based on his field observations in Bangladesh and Uganda. These are gratefully acknowledged.

Dr. Kazi M. Badruddoza, one of Bangladesh's foremost experts on agriculture and a most respected scientist, has kindly and graciously written the *Foreword*. We are greatly honoured by his recognition and approval of our book and are deeply grateful to him.

The book is dedicated to three individuals.

First and foremost, to the founder of BRAC Sir Fazle Hasan Abed, the visionary who took up the challenge of bettering the lives of the poor in Bangladesh. Abed bhai, as we call him, is the father of all innovations in BRAC and many of the ideas that BRAC has come to be famous for came from him. Needless to mention, he remains the hopes and aspirations for millions of poor and disadvantaged people around the world.

Mr. Aminul Alam was Abed bhai's right-hand person in implementing at scale the various BRAC innovations, including the agricultural programmes narrated in this book. At the time of his demise in 2010, he was the Executive Director of BRAC's international programmes.

Dr. Mahabub Hossain connected research with programme implementation. He initiated several agricultural development programmes including the "Sharecroppers Credit Support Programme" which was implemented by BRAC with financial support from Bangladesh Bank, the central bank of the country. Until his demise in 2016, he worked as Executive Director of BRAC in Bangladesh.

Much appreciation goes to BRAC and BRAC International for the opportunity for us to be involved in the production of this book. We also thank their staff who offered logistical and other support. Our sincere thanks to the University Press Limited for publishing the book at short notice. We are grateful to Ms. Mahrukh Mohiuddin and Mr. Babul Chandra Dhar of UPL for their patience and support in producing the book.

Although this book is a compilation of many individuals' and groups' observations, experience, and knowledge of the BRAC innovations in agricultural work, as the book's editors, we remain responsible for any errors and omissions.

Mushtaque Chowdhury, AM Muazzam Husain
Md. A. Saleque and Hugh Brammer

Abbreviations

ABC	Agriculture Business Centre
ADB	Asian Development Bank
AEZ	Agro-Ecological Zone
AFSLP	Agriculture Food Security and Livelihood Programme
AFSP	Agriculture and Food Security Programme
AI	Artificial Insemination
AI	Avian Influenza
AISP	Artificial Insemination Service Provider
AMCU	Automated Milk Collection Unit
ARST	Agriculture Research and Seed Testing
ASC	Area Sales Centre
ATDP	Agricultural Technology Development Project
AVRDC	Asian Vegetable Research and Development Center
AYT	Advance Yield Trial
BADC	Bangladesh Agriculture Development Corporation
BAIF	Bharatiya Agro Industries Foundation
BARC	Bangladesh Agriculture Research Council
BARDC	BRAC Agricultural Research and Development Centre
BARI	Bangladesh Agricultural Research Institute
BAU	Bangladesh Agricultural University
BBP	BRAC-Baor Programme
BBS	Bangladesh Bureau of Statistics
BDFP	BRAC Dairy and Food Project
BER	Bangladesh Economic Review
BFRI	Bangladesh Fisheries Research Institute
BINA	Bangladesh Institute of Nuclear Agriculture
BLRI	Bangladesh Livestock Research Institute

BRRI	Bangladesh Rice Research Institute
CAP	Community Agriculture Promoter
CARE	Cooperative for American Relief Everywhere
CARI	Central Agriculture Research Institute
CBFM	Community Based Fisheries Management
CBO	Community Based Organization
CC	Community Connector
CCA	Central Container Area
CCBS	Central Cattle Breeding Station
CFPR-TUP	Challenging the Frontiers of Poverty Reduction- Targeting the Ultra Poor
CGIAR	Consultative Group on International Agricultural Research
CIAT	International Center for Tropical Agriculture
CIMMYT	International Maize and Wheat Improvement Center
CIP	International Potato Center
CLP	Community Livestock Promoter
CLPP	Community Livestock and Poultry Promoter
CP	Commercial Poultry
CPP	Community Poultry Promoter
CPWF	Partner of Challenge Programme on Water and Food
CRMA	Climate Resilience Maize in Asia
CSISA	Cereal System Initiative for South Asia
DAE	Department of Agricultural Extension
DANIDA	Danish International Development Agency
DEC	Disaster Emergency Committee
DEGITA	Dissemination and Evaluation of Genetically Improved Tilapia in Asia
DFID	Department for International Development
DLS	Department of Livestock Services
DOC	Day Old Chicks
DoF	Department of Fisheries
DRR	Directorate of Relief and Rehabilitation
DWR	Deep Water Rice
EVD	Ebola Virus Disease

F1	First Generation
FAO	Food and Agriculture Organization
FGD	Focus Group Discussion
FIVDB	Friends in Village Development Bangladesh
FMC	Fisheries Management Committee
FP	Family Poultry
FPG	Farmer Producer Group
FSC	Fisheries Sub-committee
FY	Fiscal Year
GDP	Gross Domestic Product
GED	General Economics Division of the Bangladesh Planning Commission
GF	General Farmers
GIFT	Genetically Improved Farmed Tilapia
GO	Government Organization
GoB	Government of Bangladesh
GP	Grand Parent
GPAF	Global Poverty Action Fund
GSR	Green Super Rice
HRDC	Hybrid Rice Development Consortium
HTMA	Heat Tolerant Maize in Asia
HYV	High Yielding Varieties
IFAD	International Fund for Agricultural Development
IFC	International Finance Corporation (World Bank)
IFPRI	International Food Policy Research Institute
IGVGD	Income Generation for Vulnerable Group Development
IMPP	Integrated Maize Promotion Project
INFPD	International Network for Family Poultry Development
IPM	Integrated Pest Management Practices
IRRI	International Rice Research Institute
IVS	Inland Valley Swamp
JICA	Japan International Cooperation Agency
JSDF	Japan Social Development Fund
LAIW	Livestock Artificial Insemination Worker

LEAD	Livelihood Enhancement through Agricultural Development
M4P	Making Markets Work for the Poor
MAP	Management Activity Plan
MCC	Mennonite Central Committee
MF	Model Farmers
MFI	Microfinance Institution
Mha	Million Hectare
MMT	Million Metric Ton
MoFL	Ministry of Fisheries and Livestock
MRR	Ministry of Relief and Rehabilitation
MSY	Maximum Sustainable Yield
MT	Metric Ton
MV	Modern Varieties
NCDP	North West Crop Diversification Project
NDDB	National Dairy Development Board (India)
NGO	Non-Governmental Organization
NSB	National Seed Board
OFSP	Orange Fleshed Sweet Potato
OLP	Oxbow Lake Small Scale Fisheries Management Project
OSPP	Organised Seed Production Programme
OYT	Observation Yield Trial
PA	Programme Assistant
PFN	Poultry for Nutrition
PICS	Purdue University Improved Crop Storage
PKSF	Palli Karma Sahayak Foundation
PL	Post Larvae
PLDP	Participatory Livestock Development Project
PS	Parent Stock
PSE	Programme Support Enterprise
QPM	Quality Protein Maize
RAKUB	Rajshahi Krishi Unnayan Bank
RCTP	Rural Credit and Training Programme
RDP	Rural Development Programme
REP	Rural Enterprise Project

RIR	Rhode Island Red
RMC	Rapid Milk Chiller
RMG	Ready-made Garment
SA PPLPP	South Asia Pro Poor Livestock Policy programme
SARCCAB	Support for Agricultural Research for Adaptation to Climate Change in Bangladesh
SAU	Sylhet Agricultural University
SCA	Seed Certifying Agency
SCDP	Second Crop Diversification Project
SDG	Sustainable Development Goal
SEDF	Soros Economic Development Fund
SEDF	South Asia Enterprise Development Facility
SFG	Small Farmers Groups
SFYP	Sixth Five Year Plan
SLARI	Sierra Leone Agriculture Research Institute
SLDP	Smallholder Livestock Development Project
SME	Small Medium Enterprise
SRI	System of Rice Intensification
SRTI	Sugarcane Research and Training Institute
STRASA	Stress Tolerant Rice for Poor Farmers in Africa and South Asia
TAMNET	Tropical Asian Maize Network
TC	Tissue Culture
TWC	Three Way Cross
UN	United Nations
UNAP	Uganda Nutrition Action Plan
UNICEF	United Nations Children's Fund
USAID	United States Agency for International Development
USD	United States Dollar
VDC	Village Development Committee
VGD	Vulnerable Group Development
VGF	Vulnerable Group Feeding
VO	Village Organization

WB	World Bank
WEDP	Women Entrepreneur Development Programme
WFC	World Fish Center
WFP	World Food Programme
WHO	World Health Organization
WPSA-BB	World Poultry Science Association, Bangladesh Branch
WSSV	White Spot Syndrome Virus
WTO	World Trade Organization
ZYT	Zone Yield Trial

Contributors

Dr. A.K. Fazlul Haque Bhuiyan is a Professor of Animal Breeding and Genetics, Faculty of Animal Husbandry, Bangladesh Agricultural University (BAU), Mymensingh. In addition, he is active in national and international research projects, policy formulation and professional programme implementation at various levels of government, international, private sector, and NGOs. He received University Prizes, International Young Scientist Awards, Commonwealth Scholarship (UK) for PhD studies (University of London, UK) and Post-doctoral Fellowships through AvH (Germany), JSPS (Japan), Norman Borlaug (USA), and Cochran (USA). Professor Bhuiyan accomplished an impressive number of research projects of which UNEP-GEF-ILRI-FAnGR Asia (GEF), Red Chittagong Cattle (USDA and WVB), Seed Bull Production (World Bank), and Strengthening Animal Husbandry Education (HEQEP, World Bank) are notable. He has published 154 scientific articles (76 internationally) and four e-books. He also worked as consultant for FAO, UNEP-GEF, ILRI, GoB (MoFL, MoEF), CARE, SAARC, World Bank, and BRAC.

Dr. Jiban Krishna Biswas is a Plant Physiologist and is former Director General of the Bangladesh Rice Research Institute. A graduate of the Sher-e-Bangla Agricultural University, he completed his MS in Crop Botany from Bangladesh Agricultural University and PhD in Crop Science from Central Luzon State University, the Philippines. He was a JSPS post-Doctoral Fellow at Yamagata University, Japan for two years. He is well known for his work in developing a good number of rice varieties and technologies through Plant Physiological inputs for favourable and unfavourable ecosystems. He has taught in different universities as Adjunct Faculty. He has 65 scientific papers in different national and international journals, 430 popular articles (Bangla and English) in leading national dailies, and six books to his credit. He was awarded the Bangladesh Academy of Agriculture Gold (BAAG) Medal for outstanding leadership in rice research and development, the Bangabandhu Gold Medal, and the Krishibid Institution Bangladesh (KIB) award for his dynamic leadership. He is currently working as a National Consultant for Healthier Rice Programme of IRRI, Bangladesh.

Mr. Hugh Brammer worked on reconnaissance soil surveys in the Gold Coast/Ghana 1951–61, then joined FAO to organise the reconnaissance soil survey of East Pakistan during 1961–71. After serving as Senior Soil Scientist in Zambia during 1972–74, he returned to Bangladesh in 1974 to assist the Ministry of Agriculture as land use (later agricultural development) adviser until his retirement from FAO in 1987. Mr. Brammer then worked as a consultant for FAO and the World Bank until 1995, including on Bangladesh's Flood Policy Study (1989), the Flood Action Plan (1989–95), and a Greenhouse Effects Study (1992). He subsequently wrote seven books on soils, agriculture, and land use in Bangladesh. In 2006, Mr. Brammer initiated a comprehensive study of arsenic in groundwater in the Geography Department, University of Cambridge, which culminated in joint authorship of *Arsenic Pollution: A Global Synthesis* (Wiley-Blackwell, 2009) and publication of several journal articles on the impacts of arsenic contamination on agriculture. Since 2007, he has assisted in a study to produce a guideline on the use and interpretation of pre-partition maps of Bengal held in British museums and libraries. He is currently supporting a number of studies on arsenic contamination of soils and rice in Bangladesh. Mr. Brammer is the recipient of numerous awards, in particular, the Bangladesh President's Gold Medal for Agriculture in 1979, FAO's B.R. Sen Award in 1981, the Order of the British Empire (OBE) by the British Government in 1987, and the Royal Geographical Society's Busk Medal for Scientific Discovery and Research in 2006.

Dr. Mushtaque Chowdhury is Professor of Population and Family Health at Columbia University. He previously served as the Vice Chair, Executive Director, and Director Research of BRAC. He is the founding Dean of the James P. Grant School of Public Health at BRAC University During 2009-12, Dr Chowdhury worked for the Rockefeller Foundation as Senior Adviser and acting managing Director. In 1992-93, he was a MacArthur Fellow at Harvard University. He has contributed over 200 articles in national and international journals and authored many books in the areas of education, health, nutrition, rural development, environment, poverty, and NGO studies. He serves on the boards and committees of a number of international organizations and initiatives, and has received several awards including the prestigious Medical Excellence Award from the Ronald McDonald House Charities, Innovator of the Year Award from Brigham Young University, Leadership Excellence Award from the Dhaka University Statistics Department Alumni Association, and the Best Impactful Book award from the University Press Limited. Dr. Chowdhury did his BA from the University of Dhaka, MSc from the London School of Economics, and PhD from the London School of Hygiene and Tropical Medicine. He is the current President of the Dhaka University Statistics Department Alumni Association.

Professor S.D. Chowdhury started his teaching and research career at Bangladesh Agricultural University, Mymensingh in 1978 where he served

as Professor and Head of Poultry Science and Dean of Faculty of Animal Husbandry. He received his PhD from the University of London. Professor Chowdhury has conducted research in various areas of poultry science and has published 112 research papers in national, regional, and international journals. He is also a leading member of the World's Poultry Science Association, Bangladesh Branch. He conducted postdoctoral research in the field of Nutritional Biotechnology at Chung-Ang University, Republic of Korea during 2001-2002. He also has training in poultry nutrition and egg quality from Roslin Institute, Edinburgh, UK and University of Hohenheim, Germany. He worked as consultant for ACI logistic Ltd., PKSF, DANIDA, INFPD of FAO, IFC-SEDF and USAID funded research assignments. He was honoured by the AG Agro Industries Ltd. of Bangladesh in 2015 for his outstanding contribution to the development of the Bangladesh Poultry Sector and received the "Global Research Impact Award 2019" from Bangladesh Agricultural University Research System (BAURES) in recognition of outstanding global research impacts.

Professor A.M. Muazzam Husain is an agricultural economist and pioneer in rural development and policy research. He studied at Dhaka University (BA and MA) and Texas A & M University (PhD). He was a Professor and Dean of the Faculty of Agricultural Economics at Bangladesh Agricultural University. He was the Research Director for BRAC and worked as the Chairperson of the Department of Economics and Social Sciences at BRAC University. He also worked as consultant for many national and international organizations including the Planning Commission of the Government of Bangladesh, DFID, UNDP, WFP, World Bank, FAO, Ford Foundation, ILO, GTZ, Oxfam GB, CARE, WorldFish, Concern, ICCO Cooperation, and IRRI. He has several publications to his credit. He has been awarded a gold medal by the Bangladesh Agricultural Economists Association in recognition of his outstanding contribution in the field of Agricultural Economics.

Dr. Md. A. Saleque is the Adviser for Agriculture and Livestock Programme at BRAC International (BI). He is responsible for planning, coordinating, and providing technical assistance and guidelines for implementation of agriculture, food security, and livelihood projects in eight countries in Asia and Africa. A development professional with over 35 years of experience, he has worked for BRAC Bangladesh as Programme Head, Agriculture and Programme Support Enterprise (PSE) and as a Project Coordinator at FAO. At BRAC International, he directs a wide range of projects on agricultural value chain development, Making Markets Work for the Poor (M4P), economic development, livelihoods, food aid and food security, agri-nutrition, agri-finance, asset and cash transfer, social enterprises and sustainable agriculture. His work also involves collaborating with different international and national

organizations and donors including IFAD, DFID, World Bank, ADB, WFP, EU, Master Card Foundation, JICA, USAID, Gates Foundation, and FAO. He is a member of various professional and scientific societies at national and international levels and has a number of publications to his credit. He is highly regarded for his contribution to his field and has provided numerous consultancies in Bangladesh and abroad.

Professor Md. Saifuddin Shah obtained both his BSc (Hons) in Fisheries and MSc in Fisheries Biology from the Bangladesh Agricultural University and PhD in Fish Genetics and Biotechnology from the University of Wales, UK, under a Commonwealth Scholarship. He carried out three post-doctoral research assignments at Washington State University, Tokyo University, and Nagaoka University, under JSPS and Japan Center of Excellence funding. Professor Shah has 43 years of professional experience in teaching and academic and research administration management at university level. He joined BAU as a Fellow in 1974. Later, he became Assistant Professor in BAU before moving on to become the Chief Scientific Officer at the Bangladesh Fisheries Research Institute, Mymensingh in 1986. In 1995, he switched back to teaching and joined as a Professor of Fisheries in Khulna University's Fisheries and Marine Resource Technology Discipline. He served as Head of the Department and Dean of the Life Science School, Member of the Academic Council, Member of the Syndicate, Students' Director, Provost of the Residence Halls, and Vice-Chancellor of the University. Professor Shah has wide experience in development planning in fisheries and has worked in different donor-funded fisheries projects of the government. He has published 120 research articles in national and international journals, a book on Fish Genetics, and another on Bengali poetry.

Foreword

Bangladesh has made great strides in its efforts to improve the lives of its citizens. Although much remains to be done, the country is already admired globally as a success story. The economy has improved, social development in terms of improvement in education and health has set in, and food security has been attained for everyone. This is partly due to the significant progress made in the agriculture sector. Over the past few decades, food production has trebled while the population doubled leading to increase in per capita food availability. Apart from government, the non-governmental sector has made important contribution to what is now called 'Bangladesh's agricultural revolution'. Needless to mention, the NGO BRAC has been at the forefront of all these.

In its efforts since the early days, a very high priority has been given by BRAC to the agricultural sector. The success of BRAC in the growth and development of agriculture especially the phenomenal improvement in the lives of small, marginal farmers and rural workers in improving food security, nutrition and overall well-being has been impressive. BRAC has significantly contributed in improving the productivity and technological progress. The success of the agriculture programmes of BRAC has earned due international recognition. The bestowing of the prestigious World Food Prize to BRAC's Founder and Chairperson, Sir Fazle Hasan Abed in 2015 bears a glowing testimony to this.

I am very pleased to know that BRAC's experience in the growth and development of agriculture in Bangladesh and in six countries of Asia and Africa is being captured through the publication of this book. I think this is a noble and timely effort. Unfortunately the BRAC story in the development of the agriculture sector is relatively unknown. BRAC's innovative ways of addressing issues and problems in different sub-sectors such as crops, poultry, livestock, and fisheries are path-breaking. Its success in creating different agricultural value chains such as one in the livestock is exemplary. These are part of the story that have been told so eloquently through this book. BRAC also has successfully taken the Bangladesh experience beyond its borders. We feel so proud to know how the solutions born in Bangladesh are being replicated to benefit the poor and vulnerable populations in several countries of Africa and Asia.

I am delighted to know that the different chapters of this book have been contributed by distinguished experts in their own areas of expertise. I express sincere thanks to the authors, editors, the publisher and BRAC for their initiative and efforts in the publication of this valuable book. I am sure this book will be of interest to a wide range of audience including students, the academia, researchers, practitioners, and development partners in Bangladesh and globally.

Kazi M. Badruddoza, PhD, DSc
National Emeritus Scientist
Formerly Chairman, Bangladesh Agricultural Research Council
Recipient of the *Shwadhinata Padak* award (2012)
Tir and Prothom Alo Lifelong Sammanona Patra (2018), Krishi Puruskar

Overview

Bangladesh has made substantial gains in its socioeconomic development over the past few decades in almost every sector, including poverty alleviation, education, women's empowerment, nutrition, and health. Apart from the government, many other stakeholders, including NGOs, are credited for these advances. BRAC has been deeply involved in Bangladesh's development since its inception in 1972. After its establishment, BRAC began relief and rehabilitation for the rural poor to cope with the devastation of the liberation war. Soon after, it turned to development activities for the alleviation of poverty. The range of interventions included the formation of village-level informal groups of the rural poor, social development activities in the areas of women's empowerment, education, health, and training, and micro-finance.

Agriculture was one of BRAC's early interventions. Its agriculture development programme was a direct response to the challenges of food insecurity, poverty, and unemployment at the grassroots level. BRAC implemented its programme through adaptive research, research and development, participatory demonstration, extension services, technology validation, and the creation of value chains. This book documents over four decades of BRAC's work in the agriculture subsectors of crops, poultry, livestock, and fisheries. It also presents its experiences in replicating Bangladesh's experience in selected countries of Africa and Asia.

As agriculture remained the mainstay of Bangladesh's rural economy and income earned from farming was considered more effective in reducing poverty than other income-generating activities, BRAC put special emphasis on the development of the various subsectors of agriculture. An overview of its work in different subsectors is given in the paragraphs that follow.

The Crop Subsector

Crop, the primary subsector of agriculture in Bangladesh, has made impressive gains since independence. The production in rice, the staple crop, and a few others like maize, potato, and vegetables have registered significant growth through the use of modern technologies and extension services. Agriculture sector GDP increased five to six times, maintaining an annual growth rate of 3.5 percent in the recent past. Unfortunately, climate change and other extraneous factors remain challenges that hamper growth.

BRAC has been contributing significantly in these areas, mainly through R&D, production and marketing, extension, and rehabilitation programmes. In R&D, BRAC established an agricultural research and development centre and seven substations for field-level research and trials. It provided extension services in rice, maize, sunflower, vegetables, pulses, and oilseeds. BRAC has developed its hybrid maize production to become the largest producer in the country. BRAC also adopted innovative adaptive approaches in technology dissemination, extension, and training programmes to increase production in stress-prone areas. Other agriculture-related programmes undertaken by BRAC include agroforestry, micro-finance for the agriculture value chain, the tenant farmers' development, and vegetable export.

Working closely with the government, it participated in several extension and rehabilitation programmes, including the Northwest Crop Diversification Project and post-cyclone rehabilitation programmes. BRAC's seeds and agro-entrepreneurship project produces and markets quality seeds, thereby playing a major role in enhancing agricultural production and food security in the country.

The Poultry Subsector

BRAC is a pioneer in improving family poultry and developing commercial poultry in Bangladesh. It evolved a poultry model through a process of learning-by-doing to reduce the mortality of the birds and improve productivity. The model specifically targeted poor women in rural areas and involved new cadres of volunteers, including poultry workers, key rearers, model breeders, poultry mini-hatchery operators, feed sellers, and egg collectors. To develop the poultry subsector, it established six poultry hatcheries to produce quality day-old chicks and feed mills to supply balanced feed. BRAC worked with the government in developing a new semi-scavenging crossbreed, *Sonali*, which has now become popular throughout the country.

It also collaborated with government, national, and international organisations in poultry development activities. Its innovative interventions addressed the absence of cold chains. For example, BRAC poultry workers transported vaccines received from the government livestock department to villages by putting the ampoules inside ripe bananas to keep the vaccine cool and potent. BRAC has also pioneered packaged poultry meat in the country.

The Livestock Subsector

The valuable role played by BRAC in the livestock subsector includes its contributions in artificial insemination (AI) of cows and goats, dairy and cattle development, fodder and feed production, formation of producers groups, provision of micro-finance, training, marketing, and capacity building activities. All of these significantly contributed to the growth of the subsector.

A core component of BRAC's work on livestock is the promotion of AI for both cows and goats. Under this programme, BRAC trained volunteers to collect frozen semen from its bull stations and provide the services directly at the farmer's doorstep, a unique innovation. Semen is distributed to various parts of the country from BRAC Area Sales Centres.

In furthering the value chain, BRAC established a dairy plant through which it collects milk from smallholder farmers in rural areas, processes the milk into different dairy products, and markets them in urban areas. BRAC Aarong has a 22 percent share of the milk market in Bangladesh.

Its livestock activities have helped in promoting the broader goals of securing food and nutritional security for the people of the country.

The Fisheries Subsector

BRAC started its activities in fisheries development in a modest way in the late 1970s through re-excavated pond cultivation of fish for the rural poor to increase their employment, income, and nutrition opportunities. Over more than three decades, it became a key contributor to the growth and development of fisheries in Bangladesh. It achieved this through R&D and innovative technology development in the areas of hatchery production of seed, semi-closed and open water capture fisheries, and, in general, aquaculture.

Besides seed production of prawn and pyramid breeding of carp, the establishment of hatcheries for cohort breeding of mono-sex GIFT Tilapia helped the phenomenal growth in its production nationally. BRAC played an important role in semi-closed and open water fisheries management in a collaborative manner with the government and other organisations, by mobilising fishing communities through group formation, training, and provision of microcredit. BRAC helped aquaculture production by the introduction of more species into the culture system, by the intensification of input utilisation, and provision for the conservation of different species.

Through all these activities, BRAC played a central role in helping Bangladesh to become the third-highest producer of freshwater fish in the world.

BRAC's Agriculture, Food Security, and Livelihood Programmes beyond Bangladesh

BRAC, through BRAC International (BI), has taken its experience in agriculture to six countries beyond Bangladesh: Tanzania, Uganda, South Sudan, Liberia, and Sierra Leone in Africa and Afghanistan in Asia.

The key factors and challenges faced by the agricultural sector in these countries included scarcity of cultivable land, inadequate training, weak extension services, limited technical knowledge, low use of modern inputs, lack of mechanisation, limited access to credit, underdeveloped markets, climate change, lack of post-harvest facilities, and gender inequality. Recognising the key factors and challenges in these countries, BRAC used two approaches: direct delivery and the hybrid "making markets work for the poor" (M4P).

In these countries, emphasis was given to the creation of pro-poor value chains, improved agricultural production and income, climate-smart agriculture, and the involvement of youth and women. The innovations that BRAC introduced included banana plantlets, feed calculator apps, nutrition-sensitive crops like bio-fortified cassava, orange-fleshed sweet potato, iron-rich beans, Kuroiler chickens, and maize and vegetable varieties. As in Bangladesh, BRAC trained thousands of volunteer extension agents in those countries for implementing the interventions.

The key programme participants were lead/model farmers, demonstration farmers, general farmers, community livestock promoters, community agricultural promoters, agro-vets and agro-dealers, and traders and wholesalers. BI developed extension models for agriculture, poultry, and livestock.

The specific development programmes of each of these six countries were determined by BI considering their needs, challenges, and opportunities. BI also received support and cooperation from different national and international partners and organisations in implementing its programmes. It successfully replicated some BRAC models in these countries and developed several innovative models in response to country context. It established social enterprises to support the overall system in the agriculture and livestock sectors. BI's programmes have already reached three million rural poor people in these countries.

BRAC's global impact on agriculture and rural development has been widely recognised. In 2015, the Founder of BRAC, Sir Fazle Hasan Abed, was awarded the prestigious World Food Prize, adding to the many accolades that he and the organisation that he led have received for the pathbreaking work that has spearheaded BRAC into its position as the world's largest and Number One NGO.

Chapter 1

Introduction

Mushtaque Chowdhury, Hugh Brammer
and Muazzam Husain

1.1 Bangladesh in Recent History

Bangladesh fought out its independence in 1971 through a bloody War of Liberation. With a population of over 160 million living on 144,000 square kilometres, Bangladesh is the most densely populated country on earth, and is the eighth most populous country in the world. At the time of independence, the country was desperately poor, the second poorest country in the world after Upper Volta (now called Burkina Faso). An agrarian economy, the country frequently suffered from natural disasters such as floods, droughts, and cyclones. Geographically, it is surrounded on three sides by India. On its south is the Bay of Bengal. Burma (Myanmar) lies along part of its south and south-east borders. (Map 1.1)

Henry Kissinger, the United States Secretary of State between 1973 through 1977, labelled Bangladesh as a country without hope, "an international basket case" (Chowdhury et al. 2013). Now, nearly a half century later, the country has turned around. It is a country of hope. Quoting David Lewis, Guha (2012) wrote, "Once written off as a basket case, Bangladesh is now spoken of as a basket of innovation."

In 2013, *The Lancet*, a prestigious medical journal, ran a series on Bangladesh's recent achievements and challenges. Introducing the story, the editors termed the recent gains in Bangladesh's health outcomes as "one of the great mysteries of global health" (Das and Horton 2013). The infant mortality rate declined from 250 per 1,000 live births at the time of independence to less than 50 in 2010. Maternal mortality declined from 700 to 194 per 100,000 live births during the same period. At the time of independence, Bangladesh had a total fertility rate of 6.0 per woman, which had declined to 2.3 by 2010. The national contraceptive prevalence rate increased from close to zero to over 60 percent. Similarly, the availability of potable water increased to over 90 percent, although the discovery of arsenic in water from hand pumps reduced this to some extent (Chowdhury 2004). In sanitation, Bangladesh has made great strides. The mortality rate from childhood diarrhoea, which was one of the leading causes of mortality nationwide, declined significantly thanks to the major promotion of Oral Rehydration Therapy (ORT) by BRAC. Bangladesh now has the highest use rate of ORT in the world according to a review of recent national Demographic and Health Surveys (DHS 2018).

Bangladesh's improvements in the health of its population were not due solely to health programmes; they resulted also from programmes that addressed the social determinants of health (WHO Commission on Social Determinants of Health 2008). The poverty rate, which is the proportion of people who live in poverty, reduced from over 60 percent in the 1990s to 24 percent in 2014 (Alam 2018). Bangladesh now has the highest rate of participation in microfinance programmes for the poor among developing countries.

Important gains have been made in the education sector. The net enrolment rate at the primary school level reached over 90 percent in 2010, up from about 40 percent in 1971 (Nath, Chowdhury & Ahmed 2015). The opportunity for technical and higher education has also vastly increased. Significant gains have been made in women's empowerment as a result of access to microcredit, affirmative action to promote girls' education (which has resulted in having more girls in school than boys), and employment in the readymade garments industry, which employs mostly women and is responsible for 15 percent of the country's GDP and 80 percent of exports.

Life expectancy at birth in Bangladesh has increased by about 40 percent—from about 45 years in 1971 to over 70 years at present. In addition, the gender gap in life expectancy has been "corrected." Until the 1980s, Bangladesh was one of only a very small number of countries where women lived a shorter life. Now, women's life expectancy is about two years more than that of men (Chowdhury et al. 2013). In most health indicators, Bangladesh has outperformed its powerful and economically stronger neighbours, such as India and Pakistan. In addition, the speed at which this has happened is exceptional. As mentioned by *The Economist*, this has no historical precedent except perhaps the Meiji Restoration of nineteenth century Japan (The Economist 2010).

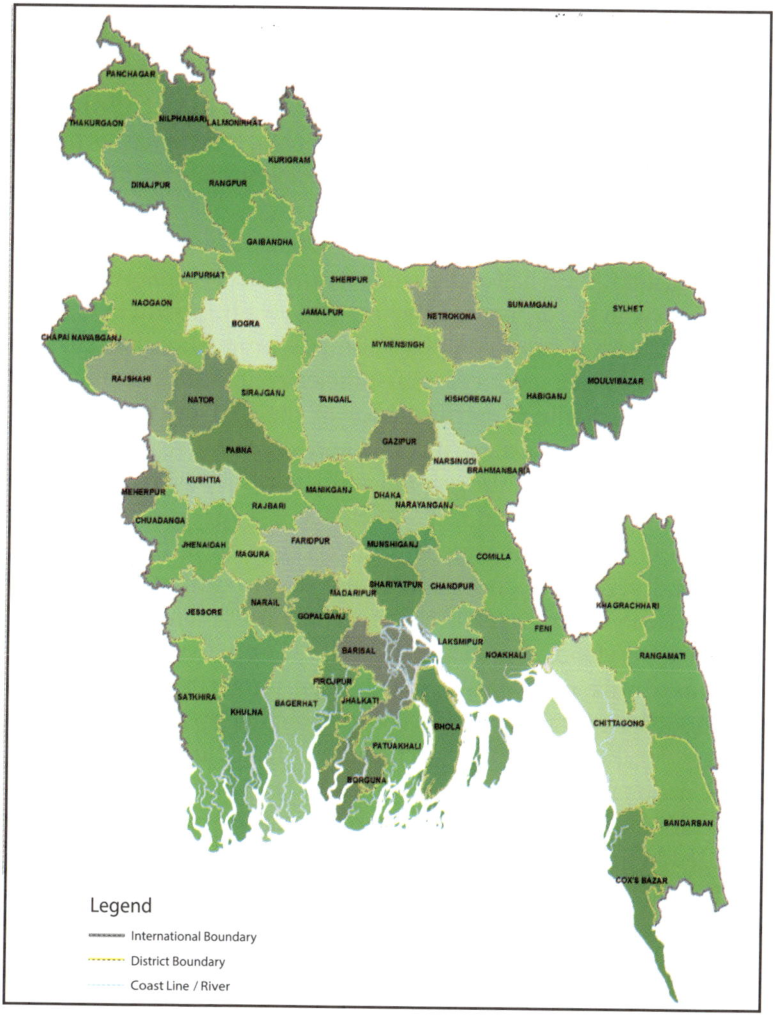

Source: Maps of Bangladesh, 2010 available at http://maps-of-bangladesh.blogspot.com/2010/12/district-map-of-bangladesh.html

Map 1.1: Bangladesh district map

Bangladesh was once considered as one of the poorest countries in the world in terms of gross domestic product (GDP) per capita. At the time of independence in 1971, Bangladesh's GDP was about USD 85. Fortunately, there has been a significant improvement since then with the GDP rising to USD 1827 currently (2019). A 44 percent reduction in the upper poverty line and a 57 percent reduction in the lower poverty line means that several million Bangladeshis have come out of poverty (Ferdousi and Dehai 2014). In fact, during the last decade or so, Bangladesh's rate of economic growth has surpassed seven percent a year, and the country is in an enviable position in the world in this respect.

Equally, the country has made important strides in agricultural development. Almost half of the national workforce is employed directly or indirectly in the agriculture sector. This steady growth in agriculture along with a strong emphasis on rice production has enabled Bangladesh to achieve near self-sufficiency in cereal production. The sound agricultural performance of the past decade has been instrumental in raising farm incomes and increasing real agricultural wages, thereby contributing significantly to rural poverty reduction. The achievement of food self-sufficiency is a major milestone for Bangladesh. Steady progress with diversification in favour of fish, meat, and vegetable production is also contributing to nutritional improvements. Over the last five years, since formulation of the National Livestock Development Policy, Bangladesh has progressed significantly in terms of milk, meat, and egg production and formed an important livelihood base for millions of resource-poor livestock keepers in this country. Total aquaculture production has increased and its contribution to the national economy is significant, as it provides about 60 percent of the animal protein intake, and more than 17.7 million people are engaged in this subsector on full- and part-time basis.

The next section briefly introduces some important aspects of the agricultural sector of Bangladesh.

1.2 Agriculture in Bangladesh

1.2.1 The outlook

According to a World Bank report, the achievements of Bangladesh agriculture are an "untold story despite being key to reducing poverty since 2000" (World Bank 2016). Indeed, the rural economy, particularly agriculture, has been a powerful driver of poverty reduction in the country. According to another World Bank report, agricultural growth accounted for 90 percent of the reduction in poverty between 2005 and 2010 (World Bank 2016a). Despite the recent acceleration in the overall growth of its agriculture sector, the share of agriculture in Bangladesh's GDP has been on a secular decline since independence. About three-quarters of the population live in rural areas and depend on agriculture, directly or indirectly, for their livelihood. Agriculture contributes about 18 percent to GDP but is responsible for 43 percent of employment which, according to Alam (2016), is a "mismatch." Growth in agriculture increased from about two percent per annum during the 1970s and 1980s to about three percent per annum during the 2000s. Such growth and increased emphasis on rice production has enabled Bangladesh to achieve near self-sufficiency in cereal production (Planning Commission 2015). Since 1974, the country has not experienced any famine conditions. As marginal farmers and landless farm labourers constitute a major part of the poor, the strategic importance of agriculture as a way for sustaining poverty reduction will remain.

Bangladesh agriculture is dominated by the crop subsector that accounts for about 60 percent of agricultural value addition. Among the other subsectors, the fisheries subsector has shown commendable growth and the livestock and poultry subsectors have also shown good growth (Alam 2016). A World Bank policy document painted the following picture of future investments in agriculture for sustainable poverty reduction:

> "Faster and more inclusive rural growth with job creation will require greater agricultural diversification together with more robust rural non-farm enterprise development. A shift in production from rice to higher-value crops will significantly reduce malnutrition, trigger more rapid growth in incomes, and create more and better on-farm and non-farm jobs, especially for women and youth. Livestock and fisheries also offer tremendous potential for reducing malnutrition and increasing incomes and jobs in a severely land constrained economy, but struggle because of inadequate government support" (World Bank 2016).

1.2.2 Environmental background of agriculture

There is a great diversity and complexity of physical environments that determine agricultural opportunities and limitations in the country (Brammer 2012; 2014; 2016). This is not only within the country and its different districts, but also within individual villages. In Bangladesh, eighteen physiographic regions are recognised, divided into many more subregions. Floodplains occupy 79 percent of the country, uplifted blocks 9 percent and hills 12 percent. Four kinds of floodplain regions are recognised: piedmont, river meander, tidal, and estuarine. There are marked differences in landscape and soils between the four uplifted blocks and within the hill region.

Farmers typically own several small fields in different parts of a village, which enables them to diversify their cropping patterns on different land types and soils and also provides them with some security against crop losses by floods or drought.

Bangladesh has a tropical monsoon climate with a summer rainy season lasting 5 to 7 months and a cool winter season lasting 2 to 3 months. The pre-monsoon season (March-May) has the highest temperatures and intermittent heavy rain showers, with some strong wind (locally called *Kal boishakhi* or deadly nor'wester); tropical cyclones accompanied by storm surges affect southern areas in some years. The monsoon season (June-September) has the highest rainfall, humidity, and cloudiness; more than 80 percent of the annual rainfall usually falls in this season. The post-monsoon season (October-November) is hot and humid with decreasing rainfall. The dry season (December-February) is relatively cool and sunny, with little or no rainfall. The mean annual rainfall ranges between ca 1,250 mm in the centre-west and over 5,000 mm in the north-east with great variations between years. The mean annual temperature is about 26^{0}C, ranging between 18^{0}C in winter and 30^{0}C in the pre-monsoon season.

A wide range of soils occur in Bangladesh, and they often occur in complex patterns. Eighteen general soil types are recognised.

Several kinds of natural disasters can affect farmers' crop production: floods, drought, cyclones, storm surges, *kal boishakhi*, soil sanitisation, riverbank erosion, and burial by new alluvium. Agriculture now faces two additional, man-made disasters: arsenic contamination of soils and crops (especially rice) irrigated with arsenic-contaminated groundwater and loss of land to the expansion of settlements due to population increase. More details on the environmental background of Bangladesh agriculture are given in the Annex to this chapter.

1.3 BRAC in Bangladesh's Development

BRAC is a Bangladeshi non-governmental organisation (NGO). Formerly known as the Bangladesh Rural Advancement Committee, it was established in 1972 to assist refugees returning to Bangladesh after the liberation war. Imbibed with the spirit of independence and nation-building commitment, the founders of the organisation transitioned it from relief efforts to development programming with a focus on the poor and on women, their children, and on other marginalised groups in the country. In 2002, BRAC established a programme in Afghanistan to test its relevance and effectiveness in another country and culture (Chowdhury, Alam, & Ahmed 2006). Since then, the organisation has expanded into 11 countries beyond Bangladesh. These countries include Afghanistan, Myanmar, Nepal, Pakistan, and the Philippines (in Asia), and Liberia, Rwanda, Sierra Leone, South Sudan, Tanzania, and Uganda (in Africa). Fundraising offices are located in the United Kingdom, the Netherlands, and the United States. With the vision of "*A world free from all forms of exploitation and discrimination where everyone has the opportunity to realise their potential*" (BRAC 2019), BRAC works for poverty elimination and women's empowerment.

By several counts (including the number of full-time staff and number of people it reaches directly), BRAC is now the largest NGO in the world. Based on the criteria of innovation, impact, and sustainability, the Swiss organisation NGO Advisor has rated BRAC consecutively for four years as #1 among 500 NGOs in the world. (NGO Advisor 2018). BRAC now touches the lives of nearly 120 million people around the world through its interventions in poverty alleviation, healthcare, education, agriculture and food security, women's empowerment, environment, microfinance, and enterprises. According to *The Economist* (2010), BRAC "has probably done more than any single body to upend the traditions of misery and poverty in Bangladesh."

There are several unique features of BRAC that distinguish it from other NGOs and governments.

1.3.1 The unique features of BRAC

Staying true to its mission

From the very beginning, BRAC's goal has been poverty alleviation and empowerment of the poor and of women. Over the years, the organisation has changed its strategy as a result of its own experience and changes in the broader society, both in Bangladesh and globally. However, the seminal goal of poverty reduction has remained unchanged, and there has been no drift in this. Adding to this is the continuous leadership that it has received from its founder and Chairperson Sir Fazle Hasan Abed, who has been at the helm of BRAC since its founding in 1972.

Taking a broad view of poverty

To BRAC, overcoming poverty is not only about increasing income or employment. BRAC believes that a person is poor because they do not have access to quality healthcare, because they do not have access to quality education, because they are not gainfully employed, because women are not sufficiently empowered, and because the environment is under threat. As such, BRAC undertakes programmes that address the underlying causes of poverty, not merely its symptoms. BRAC's current programmes span the following areas: education (primary, secondary, and tertiary), health, capacity building and human resource development, women's empowerment (including promotion of women's human rights), agriculture and food security, microfinance, disaster management, and adjustment to climate change. As shown below, BRAC undertakes interventions that address all these issues.

Learning from experience

BRAC has long been described as a "learning organisation" in the sense that it learns from its own experience and from the experiences of others (Korten 1987). It embraces failures and works with added zeal to face challenges that arise. Take the case of ORT promotion. When BRAC started teaching mothers about ORT, using salt and sugar, the ORT usage rate (i.e., the percentage of cases of childhood diarrhoea for which ORT was given) was abysmally low, less than 10 percent. It became apparent that the workers who were responsible for providing ORT education were themselves not convinced of the effectiveness of ORT. To overcome this, the workers were brought to the ICDDR,B hospital in the capital city of Dhaka to see for themselves how ORT worked in patients who were dehydrated from diarrhoea. The workers were energised by observing how children suffering from severe dehydration were rehydrated with ORT and recovered completely. In yet another example, in the early 1970s, BRAC experimented with a health insurance scheme whereby members of a family were insured by paying 30 kilograms of rice. After running this scheme for two years, BRAC abandoned it because, even though it was financially sustainable, it reached only the well-to-do sections of the community, and the poor households did not find enough incentive to obtain the insurance.

Giving priority to evidence

BRAC's programmes have benefited enormously from its adherence to evidence-based practices and the generation of its own evidence of programme effectiveness as well as from the experiences of other NGOs. Unlike most other NGOs, BRAC has invested significantly in developing its capacity for research, evaluation, and monitoring. Over the years, BRAC's Research and Evaluation Division in Bangladesh and its Independent Evaluation and Research Cell (IERC) based in Uganda have undertaken hundreds of studies that have helped BRAC programmes monitor their progress and improve their effectiveness. For more than four decades, BRAC has been a pioneer in what is now called implementation research (Chowdhury et al. 2014), an area of rapidly growing discourse in global development. BRAC's Research and Evaluation Division is one of the largest, if not the largest, of such units of any NGO globally.

Embracing innovation

One of the features that distinguishes NGOs from other development actors such as governments is their ability to innovate. BRAC is no different. Most of the programmes that BRAC runs have some innovations built into them. Many of these innovations have been widely recognised and replicated. The incentive system that it developed for the TB/DOTS programme has led to remarkable improvements in detection and treatment completion (El Arifeen et al. 2013). Another example is the livelihood improvement programme for the "ultra-poor." The "ultra- poor" are the poorest of the poor who are in the bottom 10 to 15th percentile on the income scale. Most poverty alleviation programmes, including microfinance, are unable to effectively reach this group and thereby ignore them. BRAC developed a "graduation" approach by which ultra-poor women are given a package of inputs, including productive assets, for two years. Examples of assets that are provided include cows, goats, chickens, or a small grocery store. Women are trained on how to take care of the assets they have received. They also receive a small stipend and access to any healthcare that might be needed. At the end of the two-year period, most of the participating women are able to move on and access traditional market-based poverty-alleviation programmes such as microfinance. This programme was tested in Bangladesh; it has now been replicated in over 30 countries across the world by the World Bank, the Ford Foundation, and other organisations.

Studies done in Bangladesh and in other countries by BRAC and by academic institutions such as the London School of Economics, the Massachusetts Institute of Technology, the World Bank and Yale University have documented a 95 percent success rate in "graduating" participants out of their "ultra-poor" status. The participants improved their incomes and livelihoods. The nutritional status of children improved significantly and these gains were sustained long after women completed their direct involvement with the programme (Banerjee et al. 2015; Raza & Poel 2017). BRAC has introduced many innovations in its agriculture and food security programmes which are the main focus of this book. Innovations in crop agriculture, poultry, livestock, and fisheries are narrated in different chapters.

Prioritising sustainability

BRAC is unique among NGOs in terms of sustainability. Ever since its inception, BRAC has endeavoured to become self-financed as much as possible. BRAC's first income-generating enterprise, a modern printing press, was established in 1978. As of now, there are 17 enterprises run by BRAC which, on the one hand, are contributing to the broader society by creating employment and producing profits and, on the other hand, are using these profits to support the ongoing expenses of BRAC's development programmes. In addition to these enterprises, BRAC has also invested in commercial ventures. The BRAC Bank, a fully commercial financial institution, is one such investment. Of BRAC's total expenditures of US$ 990 million in 2016 for its programmes in Bangladesh, about 85 percent were self-generated. For the remaining 15 percent, BRAC is dependent on its development partners including the governments of the United Kingdom, Australia, and the Netherlands, the Global Fund for AIDS, Tuberculosis, and Malaria, the Bill and Melinda Gates Foundation, and others.

Collaborating with government

BRAC works very closely with the government. BRAC believes that the government has the responsibility to its citizens to ensure that they have the means for obtaining a basic livelihood, education, and essential healthcare, but due to multiple constraints it cannot fulfil that responsibility. The early governments in Bangladesh recognised this limitation, as have subsequent ones, and they have welcomed the participation of NGOs to help fulfil these obligations. In a unique gesture, the government created spaces for NGOs to work and flourish in the country. BRAC works with the government in many sectors. The TB/DOTS programme, mentioned earlier, is an interesting example of how the collaboration works. In this case, the entire programme is implemented by NGOs while the government provides regulatory, supervisory, and monitoring oversight. The government also provides drugs for free distribution to TB patients via NGOs. In yet another example, BRAC University offers graduate-level courses specifically tailored for government officials. This includes a master's degree programme in governance and development and in education for mid-level functionaries of the Ministry of Education. In agriculture and food security, BRAC has worked closely with the government in implementing selected programmes, many of them nationally. These include the Income Generation for Vulnerable Group Development (IGVGD), Smallholder Livestock Development Project (SLDP), Northwest Crop Diversification Project (NCDP), Fourth Fisheries Project, and Oxbow Lake Project. All of these and others are discussed in different chapters of this book.

Scaling up

BRAC is known for its scale. As BRAC's founder Sir Fazle Hasan Abed once wrote in 1989:

> When BRAC was started in 1972 we thought that it would probably be needed for two to three years, by which time the national government would consolidate and take control of the situation and the people would start benefitting from independence. But as time passed, such a contention appeared to be premature. After 16 years, we feel that we have not outlived our utility and need to do more and more (Abed & Chowdhury 1989).

A byword often heard at BRAC is that "small is beautiful but large is necessary." Over the years, BRAC has grown to become the world's largest NGO. In Bangladesh itself, BRAC is the largest NGO as also in several other countries, including Liberia, Sierra Leone, Tanzania, and Uganda. BRAC's programmes touch the lives of 120 million people around the world, of which 110 million are in Bangladesh. Its programmes in other countries are growing rapidly.

More on BRAC are available in Smillie (2009) and via BRAC's website: www.brac.net.

1.4 Why this Book?

Ever since its inception, agriculture has been an important component of BRAC's development efforts. Agriculture is seen as a major conduit for poverty reduction, food and nutrition security, and women's empowerment. Taking advantage of the government's liberal policy towards NGO involvement in development, BRAC gradually got involved in various agriculture subsectors including crops, poultry and livestock, and fisheries. BRAC saw opportunities in research and development (R&D), and extension and creation of value chains. Over the years, it became a major player in the agriculture sector of Bangladesh. It played an important role in what is now called the "agriculture revolution" that took place in the country, which includes poultry and livestock improvement through artificial insemination and introduction of new crops such as maize. BRAC's work in agriculture and rural development has been widely recognised.

In 2015, Sir Fazle Hasan Abed was awarded the prestigious World Food Prize with the following citation: "... Under Fazle's leadership of more than 40 years, BRAC's agricultural and development innovations have improved food security for millions and contributed to a significant decline in poverty levels through direct impacts to farmers and small communities across the globe" (World Food Prize website, accessed November 9, 2019).

For various reasons, including more responsive government actions and increased engagement of the private sector, BRAC has withdrawn from many of its earlier involvements. Many of the innovations that BRAC did are now being implemented by others. The role that BRAC played in the growth of the agricultural sector is unfortunately not well documented and this book attempts to fill this gap. In a commentary, *The Economist* magazine had described BRAC as "one of the world's best kept secrets." This volume tries to reveal some of these secrets.

The authors, most of whom belonged to different agriculture universities and institutes in Bangladesh, contributed to the book (Chapters 2-5) based on their research carried out during 2017-18. In addition to secondary material, their sources of information included field visits and interviews with relevant individuals who were connected and/or knew about the BRAC interventions. A list of the people interviewed is given in the annex. The author of Chapter 6 worked for BRAC who oversaw the replication of Bangladesh experience overseas.

1.5 Organisation of the Book

The book has seven chapters. Chapter 1 introduces the book with some detailed discussions on the history and recent progress of Bangladesh, the agriculture sector in the country, and the role of BRAC. Chapter 2 presents issues in the crops subsector and how BRAC has tried to address them over the years. Following a similar structure, Chapter 3 presents the poultry work of BRAC. Chapters 4 and 5 present the livestock and fisheries subsectors respectively. Chapter 6 describes how BRAC replicated the Bangladesh agricultural models in six other countries of Africa and Asia through a unique South-South paradigm of collaboration. The last chapter, Chapter 7, discusses the salient lessons learned from BRAC and their implications for broader agricultural development in Bangladesh and globally.

References

Abed F.H. and Chowdhury AMR (1989). Role of NGOs in international development. In: M Reich & Maruio E (eds.): International cooperation for health, Dover, Massachusetts, Aubern House.

Alam S (2016). Transforming the agricultural economy towards an industrial economy. In: QK Ahmad and S Ahmed (eds): Bangladesh's Development: some issues and perspectives. Dhaka, Palok Publishers.

Banerjee, A., Duflo, E., Goldberg, N., Karlan, D., Osei, R., Pariente, W., . . . Udry, C. (2015). A multifaceted program causes lasting progress for the very poor: evidence from six countries. *Science, 348*, 6236-6242.

BRAC (2019). Annual Report 2018, Dhaka.

Brammer H (2012). The physical geography of Bangladesh. UPL, Dhaka

Brammer H (2014). Climate change, sea-level rise and development in Bangladesh. UPL, Dhaka

Brammer H (2016). Bangladesh: landscapes, soil fertility and climate change. UPL, Dhaka

Chowdhury A. M. R. (2004). The arsenic problem in Bangladesh. Scientific American, July.

Chowdhury, A. M. R. (2014). The mantra of delivery. Retrieved from https://ssir.org/articles/entry/the_mantra_of_delivery

Chowdhury A. M. R., Alam A, & Ahmed J. (2006). Translating development knowledge and experiences: From Bangladesh to Afghanistan and beyond. *Bull World Health Organization, 84*, 677-681.

Chowdhury A. M. R. et al. (2013). The Bangladesh paradox: exceptional heath achievement despite economic poverty. The Lancet. DOI:https://doi.org/10.1016/S0140-6736(13)62148-0

Das P and Horton R (2013). Bangladesh: innovating for health. The Lancet, 382 (9906):1681-1682

DHS. (2018). The DHS Program: Demographic and Health Surveys. Retrieved from https://www.dhsprogram.com/publications/index.cfm

El Arifeen, S., Christou, A., Reichenbach, L., Osman, F. A., Azad, K., Islam, K. S., . . . Peters, D. H. (2013). Community-based approaches and partnerships: innovations in health-service delivery in Bangladesh. *Lancet, 382*(9909), 2012-2026. Retrieved from http://www.ncbi.nlm.nih.gov/pubmed/24268607. doi:10.1016/S0140-6736(13)62149-2

Ferdousi S and Dehai W (2014). Economic growth, poverty and inequality trend in Bangladesh. Asian Journal of Social sciences and Humanities: 3(1).

Guha R (2012). The two Bengals. The Daily Telegraph (India), 23 April.

Korten, D. C. (1987). Third generation NGO strategies: a key to people-centered development. *World Development, 15*(supplement), 145-159.

Lewis D (2011). Bangladesh: politics, economy and civil society. Cambridge University Press, Cambridge, UK.

Nath, S. R., Chowdhury, A. M. R., & Ahmed, K. S. (2015). *Moving from MDG to SDG: Accelerate progress for quality primary education.* Dhaka, Campaign for Popular Education.

Planning Commission (2015). The Seventh Five Year Plan, Dhaka, Government of Bangladesh.

Raza, W., & Poel, A. (2017). Reducing malnutrition through the graduation approach. Retrieved from http://www.cgap.org/blog/reducing-malnutrition-through-graduation-approach.

Smillie I (2009). Freedom from Want. Dhaka, University Press Limited.

The Economist. (2010). BRAC in business. *The Economist.* Retrieved from http://www.economist.com/node/15546464

World Bank (2016). Bangladesh: Growing the economy through advances in agriculture. https://www.worldbank.org/en/results/2016/10/07/bangladesh-growing-economy-through-advances-in-agriculture (accessed November 9, 2019).

World Bank (2016). Dynamics of rural growth in Bangladesh: sustaining poverty reduction.http://documents.worldbank.org/curated/en/951091468198235153/Dynamics-of-rural-growth-in-Bangladesh-sustaining-poverty-reduction (accessed November 9, 2019).

Annex

The environmental background to agriculture in Bangladesh

Hugh Brammer

This brief annex is written for the benefit of non-Bangladeshi readers to help them understand the great diversity and complexity of physical environments which determine agricultural opportunities and limitations not only within the country and its different districts, but also within individual villages. More detailed information is given in Brammer 2012, 2014a and 2016a.

Physiographic regions

Eighteen physiographic regions are recognised (Figure 1.1), divided into 66 subregions (Brammer 2012). Floodplains occupy 79 percent of the country, uplifted blocks 9 percent, and hills 12 percent. Four kinds of floodplain are recognised (piedmont; river meander; tidal; and estuarine), and there are big differences between the four uplifted blocks and within the hill region.

Local complexity

Figures 1.2 and 1.3 illustrate the local complexity of floodplain landscapes. Figure 1.2 is a satellite image showing parts of the active Jamuna river floodplain and the adjoining Jamuna meander floodplain. It shows the close pattern of settlements (the linear, dark green areas) on the higher ground of former levees of small rivers, and *beels* (the black and blue areas) in former backstamp's and meander loops. Figure 1.3 shows a part of the Old Ganges River floodplain in south-western Bangladesh with settlements on the former levees and *jaors* in cut-off meander loops. Note the scales given in the bottom right corner of each image.

Figure 1.4 illustrates a typical cross-section of depth-of-flooding land types and soils in a river floodplain village. Note the differences in seasonal depths of flooding, soil texture, and reaction (pH) between the highest and lowest parts which can occur with distances of 0.5 km or less. Farmers typically own several small fields in different parts of a village. This enables them to diversify their cropping patterns on different land types and soils; it also provides them with some security against crop losses by floods or drought.

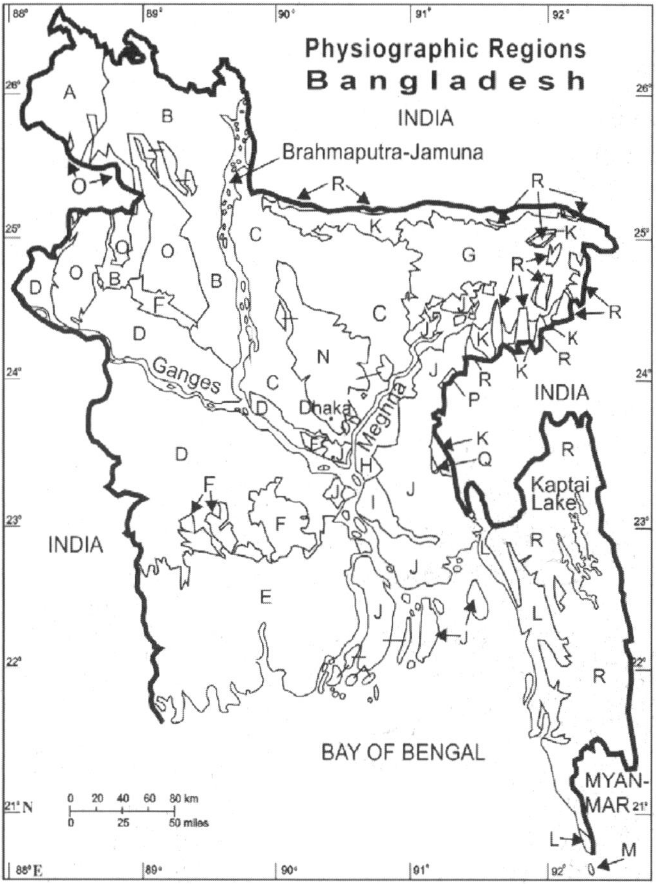

LEGEND

Floodplains
A. Old Himalayan Piedmont Plain
B. Tista Alluvial Fan
C. Brahmaputra-Jamuna Floodplains
D. Ganges River Floodplain
E. Ganges Tidal Floodplain
F. Old Floodplain Basins
G. Surma-Kusiyara Floodplain
H. Middle Meghna River Floodplain
I. Lower Meghna River Floodplain
J. Meghna Estuarine Floodplains
K. Northern and Eastern Piedmont Plains
L. Chittagong Coastal Plains
M. St Martin's Island

Uplifted blocks
N. Madhupur Tract
O. Barind Tract
P. Akhaura Terrace
Q. Lalmai Hills

Hills
R. Northern and Eastern Hills

Figure 1.1: The physiographic regions of Bangladesh

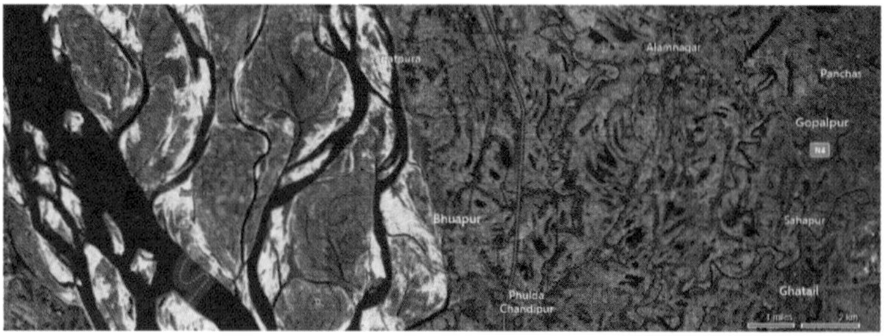

Figure 1.2: Satellite image of Jamuna river floodplain and adjoining meander

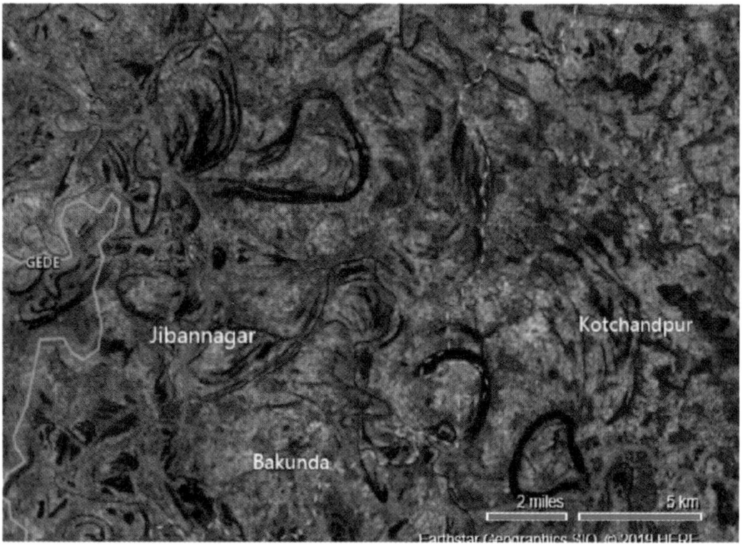

Figure 1.3: Parts of old Ganges floodplain with settlements

Climate (See also Climate change below)

Seasons

Bangladesh has a tropical monsoon climate with a summer rainy season lasting 5-7 months and a cool winter season lasting 2-3 months. The *pre-monsoon season* (March-May) has the highest temperatures and intermittent heavy rain showers, some with strong wind; tropical cyclones (aka hurricanes, typhoons) accompanied by storm surges affect southern areas in some years. The *monsoon*

LAND TYPE (Depth of flooding)	SOIL SERIES								
HIGHLAND (Not flooded)	Home-steads, tanks								
MEDIUM HIGHLAND (MH) (0-90 cm)		Sara	Gopalpur						
MEDIUM LOWLAND (ML) (90-180 cm)				Ishurdi	Pakuria	Garuri			
LOWLAND (L) (180-300 cm)							Santhia		
VERY LOWLAND (VL) (>300 cm)								Ghior	Arial
Approx. % of unit	10	5	5	5	5	10	30	25	5
SELECTED SOIL DESCRIPTIONS									
Drainage class		swpd	pd	pd	pd	pd	pd	vpd	vpd
Topsoil texture		sil	sicl	sic-c	c	c	c	c	c
Subsoil texture		sil	sicl	sic	c	c	c	c	c
Subsoil colour		lob	lob	ol	dgb	dgb	dg+ob	dg+ob	dg
SELECTED LABORATORY DATA									
Topsoil OM %		0.4	1.2	1.4	1.0	1.8	1.4	3.1	1.8
Topsoil pH		8.1	7.9	8.1	7.6	7.0	6.4	6.4	5.4
Topsoil clay %		9	34	30	42	50	51	76	79
Topsoil $CaCO_3$ %		4.4	3	8.1	3.6	0	0	0	0
Subsoil OM%		0.4	0.4	0.4	0.6	0.8	0.8	0.8	0.5
Subsoil pH		8.0	7.9	8.0	7.6	7.4	7.7	7.5	6.8
Subsoil clay %		10	29	41	55	59	64	86	62
Subsoil $CaCO_3$ %		6.2	7.5	9.2	9.2	0	0	0	0

Figure 1.4: Cross-section of depth of flooding land types and soils in a flood-plain village

season (June-September) has the highest rainfall, humidity, and cloudiness; more than 80 percent of the annual rainfall usually falls in this season. The *post-monsoon season* (October–November) is hot and humid with decreasing rainfall; tropical cyclones affect southern Districts in some years. The *dry season* (December-February) is relatively cool and sunny, with little or no rainfall.

Rainfall

Mean annual rainfall ranges between ca 1,250 mm in the centre-west and >5,000 mm in the north-east, but there is great variation between areas (e.g., 843-2,062 mm at Rajshahi and 3,334-5,620 mm at Sylhet). About 85-90 percent of the annual total rainfall generally occurs between April and September (*the rainy season*), but there can be great variation between years in the begin and end dates as well as in total rainfall received, creating problems for farmers dependent on rain-fed farming.

Temperatures

The mean annual temperature is about 26°C throughout the country. Mean monthly temperatures range between about 18°C in winter and 30°C in the pre-monsoon season. Extreme temperatures range between about 5°C (minimum) in winter and 40°C (maximum) in the pre-monsoon season. The highest and lowest temperatures occur in western districts; seasonal differences are lower near the coast.

Soils

A wide range of soils occurs in Bangladesh, and they often occur in complex patterns. Eighteen *General Soil Types* are recognised: 14 in floodplain areas; six on the uplifted blocks; and one in the hill areas. Two important characteristics need to be recognised.

- Most floodplain soils are not flooded by river water, as is popularly believed; they are flooded by rainwater ponded on floodplains when adjoining rivers are flowing at high levels with water entering the country from upstream. Typical floodplain soils therefore have top soils and subsoils with different properties from the original alluvium. They have developed colours, structure, and porosity that are not present in stratified alluvium; and top soils have more organic matter and are often lighter in texture and more acidic than lower horizons.
- The soils occur in complex patterns: not only between regions but also within villages (as is illustrated in Figure 1.4). They can also vary between fields and within fields due to differences in manure and fertiliser applications, land levelling, tank silt application, irrigation, etc. This variability and complexity need to be taken into account in conducting field trials and in soil sampling for fertility analyses.

Natural disasters

Several kinds of natural disasters can affect farmers' crop production in different parts of the country: floods, drought, cyclones and storm surges, line-squall (*kal baishaki*), soil salinisation (permanent as well as temporary following a storm surge), riverbank erosion, and burial by new alluvium (Brammer 1999). Figure 1.5 illustrates the main rice cropping patterns in relation to land types and shows the seasonal incidence of different natural disaster hazards. The risk of drought impacts has greatly decreased in the past 30 years with the wide expansion of irrigation.

Agriculture now faces two additional, man-made disasters: arsenic contamination of soils and crops (especially rice) irrigated with arsenic-contaminated groundwater (Brammer 2012) and loss of land to the expansion of settlements due to population increase. Arsenic contamination of soils and crops can be reduced by using rice cultivation methods that use less water (SRI;

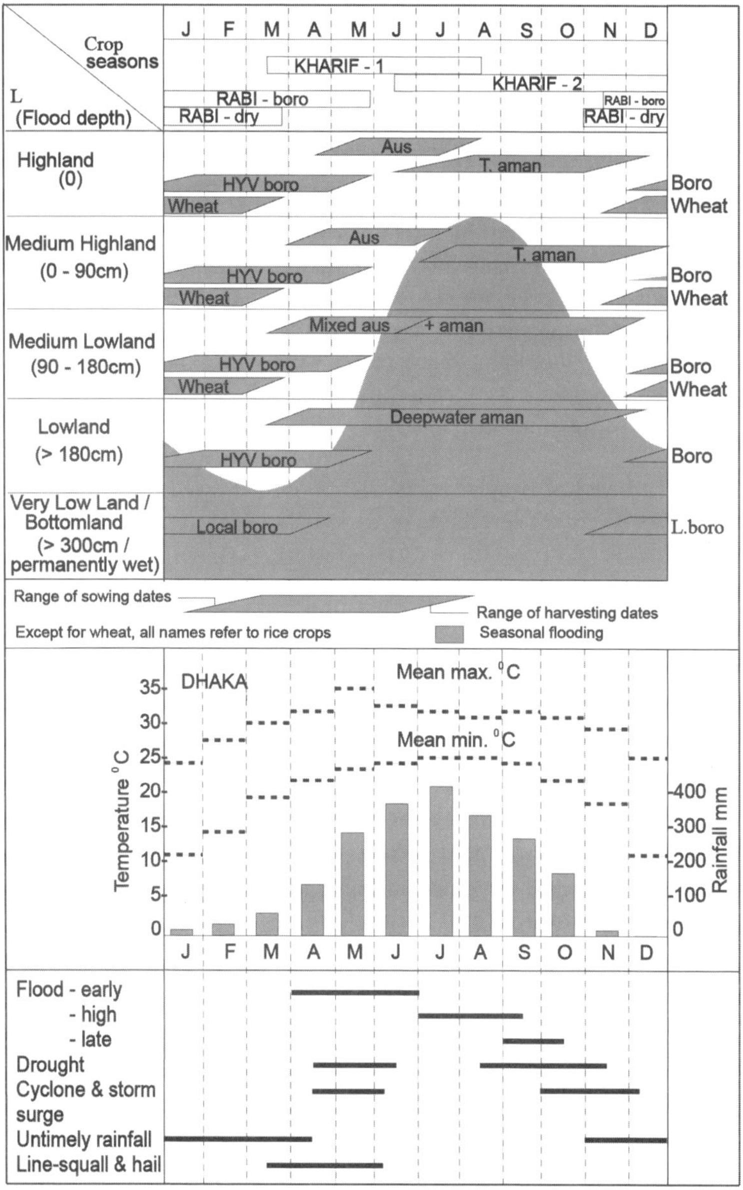

Figure 1.5: Main rice-cropping pattern in relation to land types and seasonal natural disasters

Alternate Wetting and Drying); it can be avoided by using uncontaminated deep groundwater. The loss of land to urbanisation needs to be addressed by increasing crop yields in other areas; additional yield increases are needed to increase crop production in pace with population growth.

Climate change and sea-level rise

Analysis of 50 years of Bangladesh's temperature and rainfall data showed no evidence of climate change in the country to-date, nor has the frequency or severity of floods or drought increased; there was, in fact, a great reduction in the frequency of cyclones in the past 20 years (Brammer 2014a; 2016b) compared with the previous four decades. Sea-level rise is currently occurring at three mm per annum, and the rate is expected to increase with time. However, it needs to be kept in view that Bangladesh's coastal regions have dynamic landscapes in which measures can be taken to reduce the impacts of sea-level rise (Brammer 2014b; Auerbach et al. 2019). Increasing salinity in the south-west of Bangladesh is due more to reduced river flow to the region than it is to sea-level rise.

References

Brammer, Hugh. 1999. *Agricultural Disaster Management in Bangladesh.* Dhaka: The University Press Limited (UPL).

——. 2012. *The Physical Geography of Bangladesh.* Dhaka: The University Press Limited (UPL).

——. 2014a. *Climate Change, Sea-Level Rise and Development in Bangladesh.* Dhaka: The University Press Limited (UPL).

——. 2014b. "Bangladesh's Dynamic Coastal Regions and Sea-Level Rise." *Climate Risk Management* 1, no. 1: 51-62. doi: 10.1016/j.crm.2013.10.001

——. 2016a. *Bangladesh: Landscapes, Soil Fertility and Climate Change.* Dhaka: The University Press Limited (UPL).

——. 2016b. "Floods, Cyclones, Drought and Climate Change in Bangladesh: A Reality Check." *International Journal of Environmental Studies* 73, no. 6: 865-886. doi: 10.1080/00207233.2016.1220713

Chapter 2

Role of BRAC in Growth and Development of Agriculture (Crops)

Jiban Krishna Biswas

2.1 Introduction and Background

> Everything we did in Bangladesh we did with one focus: getting poor people out of poverty because we feel that poverty is dehumanising.
>
> —*Sir Fazle Hasan Abed, KCMG*

Poverty alleviation, employment generation, and food security are some of the daunting challenges for Bangladesh. Agriculture is one of the approaches to address these challenges. The growth in agriculture is at least twice as effective in reducing poverty compared with growth outside agriculture. Such growth reduces poverty directly by raising incomes, and indirectly through generating employment and reducing food prices. The pro-poor agriculture growth is centred on smallholder farmers whose livelihoods are made more competitive and sustainable through institutional and technological innovation and empowered through producer organisations (World Bank 2008).

Crop production plays a vital role by providing the staple food, rice, and other food items to satisfy the needs of Bangladesh's huge and growing population. Rice is the traditional synonym of food and its production dominates the whole crop sector. Rice production increased by 2.8 percent per year in the 1980s and by 3.5 percent per year since1990/91 until a few years ago. Since the late 1980s, most of this growth occurred through the development and adoption of high-yielding and stress-tolerant rice varieties supported by irrigation of *Boro* rice (dry season), supplementary irrigation of *Aman* rice, and introducing *Boro* rice in low-lying areas by replacing rain-fed traditional *Aus* varieties, jute and, other rain-fed crop varieties. However, there has been some degree of diversification over time from this mono-crop rice agriculture with the introduction of non-cereal and high value crops (SFYP 2015). The production of maize has increased by around 1000 percent since independence. The major challenges in the crop sector are to increase productivity and profitability, reduce production costs and market volatility, increase resource-use efficiency, improve quality seed production and distribution, expand efficient irrigation facilities and farm mechanisation, link farm products with markets, and provide credit support to farmers.

The Government of Bangladesh has created the space for NGOs to contribute to national development. BRAC is an NGO that took up this challenge, and it has been implementing different interventions since its inception in 1972. The activities in and around agriculture include crop agriculture, horticulture, agro forestry, poultry, livestock, and fisheries. This chapter looks at BRAC's work in crop agriculture, its Research and Development (R&D) and extension activities, and potential future roles.

2.2 Growth and Development of Crop Agriculture in Bangladesh

2.2.1 Crop agriculture in the national economy

Bangladesh has made great strides in eliminating poverty and hunger. Outlining the reasons, Professor Glenn Denning of Columbia University remarked, "These kinds of success have demonstrated that if you bring certain things like economic growth, improved agricultural productivity, a focus on farmers' market accessibility and social safety-nets for the most vulnerable—you can bring hunger down" (LaFrinchi 2015).

The elimination of hunger was achieved through the development of agriculture in which the integrated efforts of farmers, scientists, extension agents, and policymakers played a central role. The agriculture sector has recorded substantial growth. The GDP (2016) is 20.8 times greater than that of 1971. Agricultural GDP has increased by 5.6 times. The average rate of growth in GDP in agriculture reached 3.5 percent during the Sixth Five Year Plan 2011-2015 (SFYP). However, despite the remarkable impact of the agriculture sector on economic growth, its share is progressively declining with the expansion of non-agricultural sectors. The share of agriculture declined from 58.4 percent in 1973/74 to 15.6 percent in 2014/15. This change, however, is in alignment with the national economic goals (Deb 2016). Nonetheless, agriculture is the highest employer in the country. The numbers of persons engaged in this sector were16.4 million in 1983-84, increasing to 25.7 million in 2010; but the share of employment in agriculture reduced from 51.7 percent in 2002-03 to 47.3 percent in 2010. The crop subsector is following a similar trend: it accounted for almost 12 percent of the GDP and 56 percent of the agriculture value added (Hossain 2012; Hossain et al. 2016). It is expected that during the Seventh Five Year Plan (FY 2016 to FY 2020, the sector as a whole will play an important role in achieving the overall goal of "accelerating growth, and empowering citizens" (Deb 2016).

The country has achieved moderate success in agriculture diversification despite the crop sector's decline in its share in the agricultural value added from 67 percent in the 1970s to 58 percent in 2012. Nonetheless, crops still remain the most important subsector of the entire agriculture sector. The staple food and other important food items associated with rural livelihood improvement are directly related to the crop subsector (SFYP 2016). Overall, a significant growth has occurred in the production of rice, maize, potatoes, and vegetables. The current status of different crops is summarised in the next section.

2.2.2 Crop improvement and diversification

Rice: The staple crop, rice, occupies more than 75 percent of the total cropped area in Bangladesh. Bangladesh has three major rice seasons: *Aus* (April-August), *Aman* (July-December and *Boro* (November-June). *Boro* rice has increased its coverage with the increase of irrigation facilities. The other two rice crops are either rain-fed or partially irrigated. Groundwater provides about 70 percent of the irrigation water for rice. Many *Aman* and *Aus* High Yielding Varieties (HYV) became popular under rain-fed conditions. Rice growth rate attained 2.8 percent in the 1980s and 3.5 percent since 1990/91 (Hossain et al. 2016a).

The total rice coverage is about 11.42 million hectares (ha) over the three rice growing seasons. Most of the modern rice varieties are not photosensitive, so they can be cultivated almost throughout the year. In some specific ecosystems, farmers may harvest three rice crops a year from the same parcel of land, but this practice is not economic. The *Aus*, *Aman*, and *Boro* areas were respectively 9.2, 48.4 and 42.6 percent. In 2014, *Boro* and *Aman* contributed 55.6 and 37.9percent respectively of the total rice production, but *Aus* only 6.4 percent (Table 2.1).

Although the total rice area did not change much during the last four and a half decades, there was a major shift in the proportions of the area and production of the three rice crops. The area under HYVs of *Boro* rice increased from 0.32 million hectares (Mha) in 1971/72 to 4.11 Mha in 2007/08 and 4.86 Mha in 2014/15. HYVs have replaced most of the traditional *Aus* varieties. In 1971/72, traditional *Aus* coverage was 2.95 Mha, but more than two thirds of the *Aus* area was given up to *Boro* by 2014/15. Around 50 percent of the traditional Deep Water Rice (DWR) area was transformed into irrigated *Boro* land. *Aman* coverage experienced little change since 1971 (Figure 2.1). Around 50 percent of the total native rice varieties (12,487) are stored in the Bangladesh Rice Research Institute (BRRI) gene bank (Hamid et al. 1982). Only around eight percent of the recorded landrace varieties are still available with farmers in some fragile pocket areas like saline, drought-prone, deep water, and hilly areas of Bangladesh (Hossain et al. 2013).

Table 2.1: Rice statistics in 2013/14

Season	Coverage (Mha)	Total production (MMT)	Yield (clean rice metric tonne per hectare)	Yield (paddy* metric tonne per hectare)	% of total area	% of total production
Aus	1.04	2.23	2.38	3.37	9.17	6.41
Aman	5.53	13.19	2.23	3.17	48.46	37.94
Boro	4.84	19.34	3.99	5.66	42.68	55.63
Total	11.41	34.76	2.86	4.06	100**	100**

Note: *Unhusked rice; **Figures as rounded up.

Source: Data is compiled by Bangladesh Rice Research Institute (BRRI) and collected from Department of Agricultural Extension (DAE) and Bangladesh Bureau of Statistics (BBS).

It took a long time to develop a variety exclusively for the *Aus* season, so the *Aus* area under MVs remained more or less static at

0.41 Mha. The coverage of HYVs of transplanted *Aman* (T. *Aman*) reached 3.34 Mha. Over the four decades, the area under local *Aus* declined from 2.95 Mha to 0.43 Mha, while local T. *Aman* decreased from 3.38 Mha to 1.60 Mha and deepwater *Aman* from 1.77 Mha to 0.48 Mha. The local *Boro* area decreased from 0.54 Mha in 1971 to 0.14 Mha in 2014. However, the recent trend for all of the eco-types is more or less static.

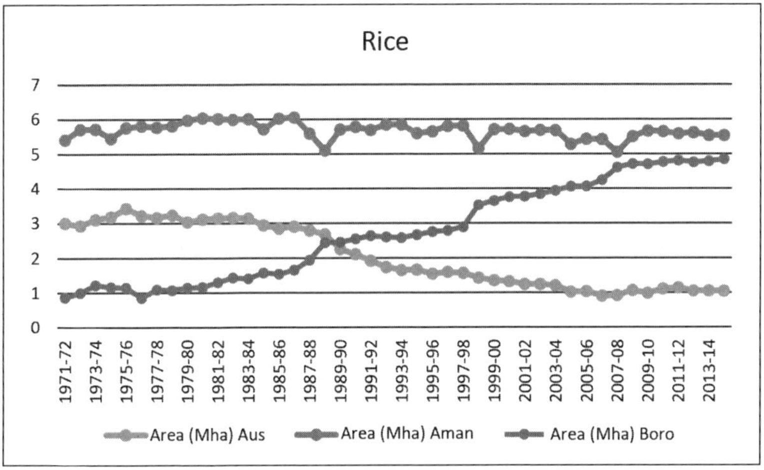

Source: BBS, 2017.

Figure 2.1: The rice coverage (Mha) trend from 1971-72 to 2013-14

Although the *Aus* area reduced to one-third of that in 1971, the total production changed little overtime due to the introduction of high-yielding varieties. The *Aman* area was 5.41 Mha in 1971 and has changed little till today, but yields increased by 2.31 times compared to those in 1971, also because of the introduction of HYVs. The *Boro* area is now around 4.84 Mha, almost six times greater than in 1971. *Boro* now provides 55 percent of total rice production up from 42 percent of the area coverage, sizable increases from 1971 when there were less than 1 million hectares yielding about two million metric tons (MMT) (Figure 2.2).

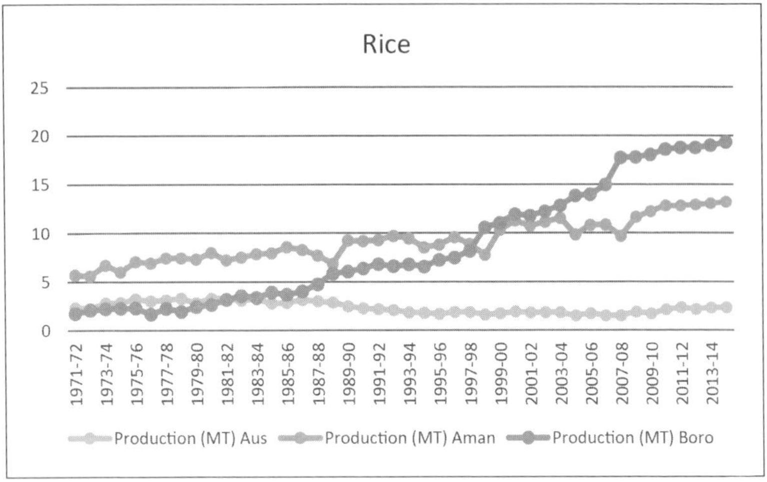

Source: BBS, 2017.

Figure 2.2: The total rice production (MMT) trend from 1971-72 to 2013-14

Wheat: In 1971/72, wheat coverage was 0.13 Mha and total production was 0.113million metric tons (MMT). The area went up to 0.88 Mha in 1998/99 almost seven times in 27 years. However, the area came down to 0.39 Mha in 2006/07 and maintained more or less the same level up to 2013/14. The total production followed the same trend as that of the area until 2006/07 with the highest peak (1.90MMT) in 1998/99. However, despite minimal increase of the area in recent times, production has increased (Figure 2.3) due to recent innovative approaches in wheat research and development.

Maize: Maize was an insignificant crop in Bangladesh up to 2000/01. The area then increased progressively; in comparison, total production increased quite significantly (Figure 2.4). In 1971/72, the coverage and total productions were 0.0028 Mha and 0.002 MMT, respectively. In 2014, the area increased to 0.30 Mha to produce 2.124 MMT (Figure 2.4). The corresponding increments in percentage terms were 110 and 1062 respectively. The substantial increase in area and production was mainly due to increased demand by the expanding commercial poultry sector. However, the phenomenal rise in output was possible mainly because of the use of high yielding hybrid seeds by BRAC and some private sector organisations.

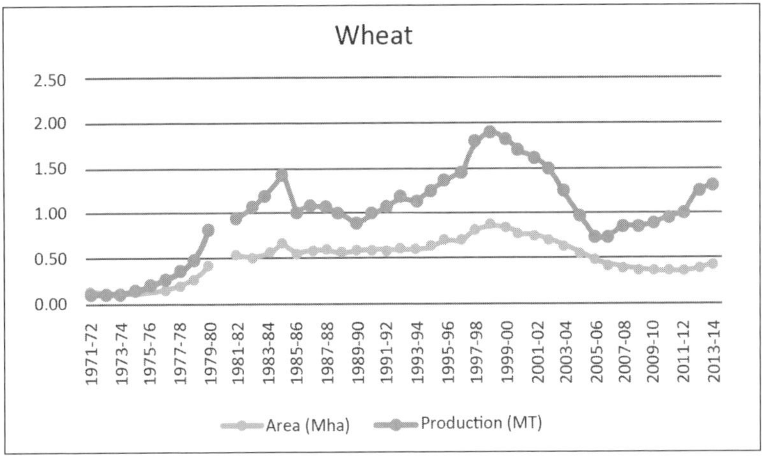

Source: FAOSTAT Database.

Figure 2.3: The wheat coverage (Mha) and total production (MMT) trend from 1991/92 to 2013/14

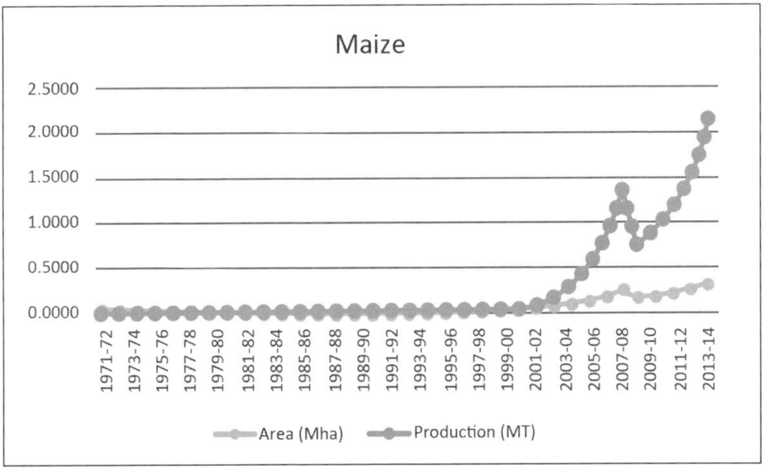

Source: FAOSTAT Database.

Figure 2.4: Trends in maize coverage and total production, 1971-72 to 2013-14

Oilseeds: The area under oilseeds cultivation between 1971/72 and 1987/88 was around 0.30 Mha. Then the coverage showed a sharp increase to around 0.55 Mha and maintained more or less the same level up to 1997-98. There was then another decrease from 1997/98 to 2004/05 followed by a modest increasing trend again up to 0.43 Mha in 2013/14. The total production followed a broadly similar trend to that of the area. (Figure 2.5). It is evident that the yield per unit area was more important than the area coverage in increasing total production in recent years.

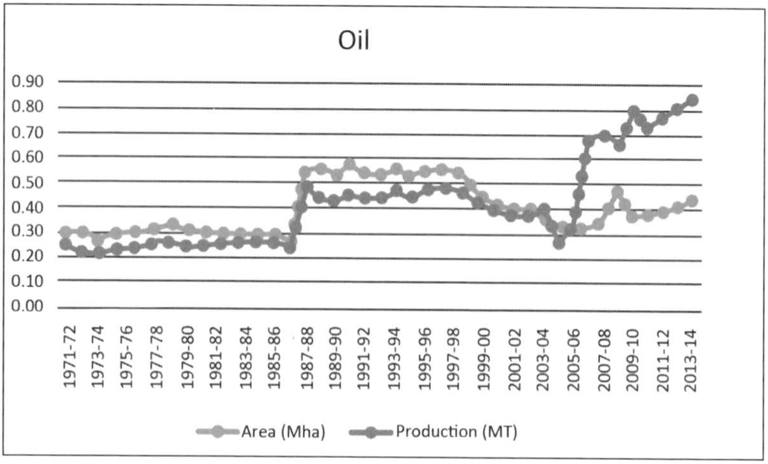

Source: FAOSTAT Database.

Figure 2.5: Oil seeds coverage (Mha) and total production (MMT) trend from 1971/72 to 2013/14

Pulses: The area under pulses cultivation was around 0.30 Mha during 1971/72 to 1982/83. There were two leaps: one from 0.30 Mha in 1982/83 to 0.53 Mha in 1983/84 and the other from 0.48 Mha in 1989/90 to 0.73 Mha in 1990/91.A broadly similar pattern was observed in total production also. The total production during the first decade since 1971/72 was around 0.25 MMT which jumped to more than half a million metric tons and maintained the level up to 1997/98. The production experienced a significant decrease again from 1997/98 to 2008/09 followed by a modest increasing trend (Figure 2.6).

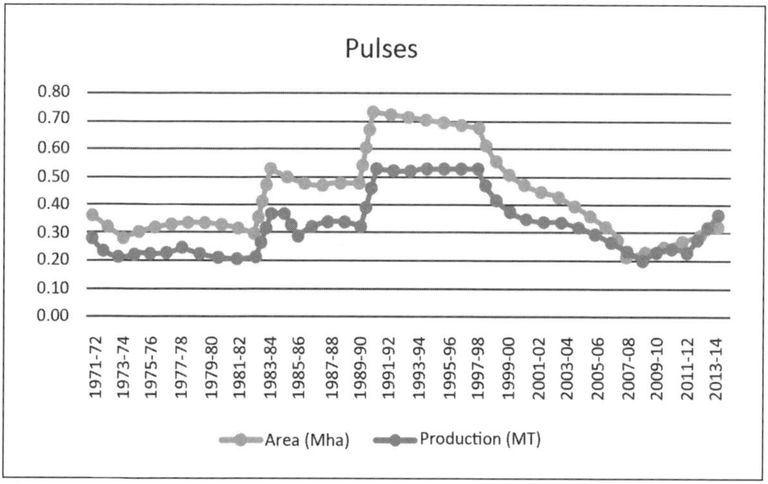

Source: FAOSTAT Database.

Figure 2.6: Pulses coverage (Mha) and total production (MT) trend from 1971/72 to 2013/14

Potato: The potato coverage of 0.46 Mha in 1971 increased 5.75 times up to 2013/14, and production increased 19.45 times compared to 0.74 MT in 1971. The sharp growth of production since 1997/98 was enough to make the country self-sufficient in potatoes (Figure 2.7). This increased productivity was possible mainly due to the introduction of improved varieties by Bangladesh Agricultural Research Institute (BARI) and the use of tissue-culture-generated quality potato seed. These potato seeds are mainly produced and sold by the Bangladesh Agriculture Development Corporation (BADC) and BRAC.

Vegetables: In 1990/91, the area under vegetables cultivation was only 0.07 Mha which increased more or less in a linear pattern up to 2013/14 to 0.18 Mha. The increase in production up to 2005/06 was slow but linear, followed by a sharp increase from 2005/06 to 2007/08. It then reached a plateau and declined to some extent in 2008/09 (Figure 2.8). BRAC's vegetable sector has played a significant role by developing and supplying improved, customer-preferred vegetable varieties to the growers.

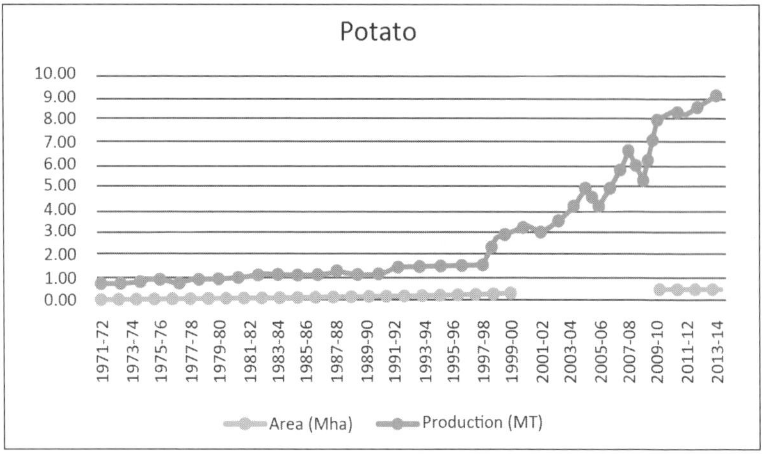

Source: FAOSTAT Database.

Figure 2.7: Potato coverage (Mha) and total production (MT) trend from 1971/72 to 2013/14

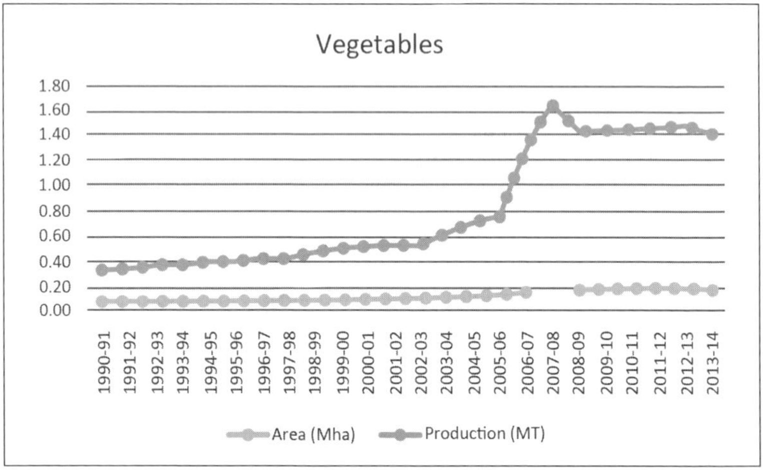

Source: FAOSTAT Database.

Figure 2.8: Vegetable coverage (Mha) and total production (MT) trend from 1991/92 to 2013/14

2.3 BRAC Interventions in Crop Agriculture

Since its inception, BRAC has incorporated agriculture as part of a systems approach to addressing poverty in partnership with relevant government agencies, multinational corporations, and many international research centres. Crop-agriculture (agronomic and horticultural) is one of the most important components of the system. In the early 1970s, BRAC initiated preliminary extension work through homestead gardening with landless and marginal farmers to improve their livelihoods and nutritional status. Encouraged by the enthusiastic participation of the stakeholders, BRAC extended its service to the mainstream crops. BRAC has invested in the development of improved crop varieties and production technologies and has conducted applied and adaptive research across the country. The extension and microfinance services provided by BRAC facilitate food security and poverty alleviation.

As an NGO, BRAC pioneered R&D activities in agriculture. In 2000, it established the BRAC Agricultural Research and Development Centre (BARDC) at Gazipur. The maintenance of active liaison and collaborations with different institutions across the world is one of its hallmark strategies. It collaborated with the International Rice Research Institute (IRRI) to develop hybrid rice varieties and with International Maize and Wheat Improvement Center (CIMMYT) to develop hybrid maize varieties. The IRRI-China research project on Green Super Rice, partially funded by the Bill and Melinda Gates Foundation, is another collaborative project to develop low-input inbred rice varieties.

At present, BRAC runs not only a research and development unit but also some innovative service-oriented establishments like plant biotechnology and soil testing laboratories, and well equipped seed production farms and seed processing plants. The varietal development programme of hybrid rice, hybrid maize, and vegetables together with premium quality, short-duration rice varieties through introduction and adaptive trials with farmers' participation is one of the prime approaches of BRAC. Recently, BRAC extended its activities to focus on fragile environments by introducing inbred rice varieties, pulse, and oil crops. A BRAC-IRRI collaboration was launched to develop low-input and stress-tolerant (drought, submergence, and salinity) rice varieties. The chronology of BRAC agriculture development is presented in Table 2.2.

Table 2.2: Chronology of BRAC seed and agro enterprise development

Year	Programme (Activities)
1972	Inception of agricultural development activities within a limited framework for farmer training and homestead gardening.
1984	BRAC brought all of its agricultural development activities under the Manikganj Integrated Programme and the Rural Credit and Training Programme (RCTP),
1987	BRAC expanded the Income Generation for Vulnerable Group Development (IGVGD) Programme and the Rural Development Programme (RDP) and also initiated commercial vegetable cultivation under BDP.
1994	Started promotion of hybrid maize production seed in collaboration with the Integrated Maize Promotion Project (IMPP) funded by CIMMYT.
1996	Started organised vegetables seed production with technical support from BADC.
1997	BRAC started hybrid maize seed production with technical support from Pacific Seed Co. Ltd. as a business model and set up a tissue culture laboratory at Uttara.
1998	Initiated tissue culture activity at Uttara in a rented house and established maize research centre was established in at Sherpur, and Bogura, and started maize research activity.
1999	Signed Memorandum of Understanding (MOU) with BRRI and started HYV seed production with their support.
2000	Established Agricultural Research Development Centre (BARDC) at Gazipur and shifted the tissue culture laboratory to Gazipur from Uttara. BRAC installed a modern seed processing plant at Sreepur, Gazipur and started seed sales through dealers to the farmers. Started hybrid rice and vegetable research activities. Besides this, hybrid rice seed production was started with technical collaboration from Hi-Tech Seed Co. Ltd, China.
2003	BRAC released first hybrid vegetable variety named "Bulbuli."
2005	Developed hybrid maize variety released with the brand name "Uttaran."
2006	Developed hybrid rice variety released with the brand name "Shakti."
2011	All agricultural activities of BRAC were organised under the Agriculture and Food Security Programme.
2014	Seed research, seed production, processing and marketing were reorganised and reformed as "BRAC Seed and Agro Enterprise."
2016	Initiated micronutrient business.
2017	Second tissue culture laboratory established at Birol, Dinajpur.

Source: Md. A Saleque and Md. Azizul Haque, 2018 (personal communication).

2.3.1 Research and development activities[1]

BRAC's approach to research is problem-oriented, adaptive, and participatory in nature. As mentioned already, BRAC has its own research establishment at Gazipur through the BARDC. In addition, it has field research stations in Dasuria (Pabna), Trisal (Mymensingh), Sherpur (Bogura), Bittipara (Kushtia), Meherpur Sader (Meherpur), Dinajpur Sader (Dinajpur), and Birol (Dinajpur), equipped with modern laboratory facilities and competent scientists. With a small group of 12 scientists and 20 scientific assistants (plant breeders, agronomists and horticulturists), BARDC conducts laboratory and field trials related to problems which are relatively less addressed by the government organisations. BRAC generally uses contact farmers and their fields to conduct location-specific adaptive research activities.

Elite germplasms of widely cultivated crops with specific traits of interest are collected from relevant research organisations across the world for screening and observation tests at BARDC. Promising lines go through a series of tests over the years, like Observation Yield Trial (OYT), Advance Yield Trial (AYT), and Regional Yield Trial (RYT) before being recognised as a recommended variety. Some of the prospective lines are used as parents to develop a better variety. For rice, early maturing and tolerance to stresses like salinity, drought, and submergence are on the priority list.

BRAC disseminates its discoveries in different steps. Any technology or innovation to be popularised among the farmers is first verified in the contact farmers' fields. Generally, a group of enthusiastic farmers participate in large-scale block demonstration, where farmers are invited to express their opinions on the performance of the crop. BRAC also invests in applied biotechnological research to develop disease-free plantlets through micro-propagation of various crops following different tissue culture techniques. The tissue culture laboratory is associated with six greenhouses for hardening the in-vitro plantlets as well as for the off-season seedling production. Currently, this laboratory is producing plantlets of banana, potato, medicinal plants, and some ornamental plants like cacti and flowers.

BRAC is active in agronomic and adaptive research. A considerable number of studies are in progress in different agro-ecological zones

---

1 www.brac.net/agricultural

of the country to evaluate the performance of the prospective lines. Research on cultural management practices is done to validate and scale up varieties and technologies.

Agricultural extension services are provided by the Agriculture and Food Security Programme (AFSP) through large-scale block demonstrations. Farmers are provided with partial grants to practice improved agriculture, i.e., increasing cropping intensity and adopting climate-smart crop varieties with an emphasis on high-value non-rice crops. BRAC's extension programmes operate in fragile environments like saline and drought-prone areas.

The following subsections briefly describe some of BRAC's research activities on rice, maize, potato, vegetables, pulses, and oilseed crops.

Rice

Hybrid rice: The Government of Bangladesh encouraged the private sector to carry out trials with hybrid rice seeds directly imported from abroad. The government authorised the National Seed Board (NSB) to release varieties after limited trials by the Seed Certifying Agency (SCA). Accordingly, a few seed companies undertook on-farm trials at several locations in the 1997-98 *Boro* season. The government permitted four companies (Mallika Seed Company, Ganges Development Corporation, ACI, and McDonald) to import 2,200 metric tonnes of hybrid seeds for the 1998-99 *Boro* season after the devastating floods of 1998 (Husain et al. 2001). Four varieties were imported which were *Allok-6021, Loknath-505, Amorsree-1, CNSGC-6* (*Sonar Bangla-1*). BRAC procured the hybrid rice seed varieties *Alok 6201* and CNSGC-6 imported by ACI and Mallika, and sold them to farmers to gain first hand experience. Hybrid rice research was initiated by BRRI in 1983 but only for academic purposes. In 1993, a few female parent lines (CMS-Lines) and experimental rice hybrids from IRRI were evaluated at BRRI research farms. Their programmes are ongoing and six varieties have been released. At the non-governmental level, BRAC has been engaged in rice hybrid research and development activities since 2000 with parental line support from IRRI. Over the period, BRAC developed potential male and female parental lines and released six hybrid rice varieties. Its first hybrid is named "*Shakti* (BW001)," Besides, BRAC registered 13 exotic hybrid rice varieties in collaboration with different private seed companies of China and India.

With assistance from IRRI, BRAC conducted a socioeconomic assessment in 2001 that examined farm-level adoption patterns, differential performances, relative profitability, and constraints to adoption of two new varieties. The study concluded that the hybrid rice had the potential to increase yields by 15-20 percent over inbred HYVs (Hossain et al. 2003).

BRAC has been collecting new hybrid rice combinations for variety screening. It imports parent lines (R-Male line and A-Female line) from China in collaboration with Chinese seed companies (Yuan's Hi-tech Seed, Hejia Hi-tech Seed) to produce hybrid rice seed locally. A number of BRAC scientists were trained in China and IRRI to produce seeds in Bangladesh. The father of hybrid rice, Dr. Yuang Long Ping, also visited BRAC projects. BRAC developed two hybrid rice varieties named *Shathi* and *Shakti*. These two varieties performed well in farmers' fields with attributes such as a vigorous root system, earlier and increased tillering, and a large panicle with more grain and less unfilled grain. The yield increased by 25-35 percent compared with conventional or modern varieties; thus the farmers were quite encouraged to take up hybrid rice cultivation.

Inbred rice: BRAC was interested in developing short-duration, high-yielding varieties for the transplanted *Aman* (T. *Aman*) season. A breeding programme was undertaken to develop short-growth duration, low-input and stress-tolerant modern varieties. Accordingly, 82 new crosses were made including 24 multiple crosses. Forty-two F1s were confirmed as true crosses, with desirable grain characteristics recorded in the BRAC cross-list from BARDC343 – BARDC384. A total of 484 progenies were selected from breeding populations (F2, F3, F4, F5, and F6 generations) and observational trials (OT) on the basis of earliness and good grain traits. Nine fixed lines were isolated from the segregating population for the evaluation of homogeneity and grain yield advantage over the standard *Aman* varieties. Furthermore, four genotypes were selected from OT based on homogeneity, earliness, diseases tolerance, and good grain traits. Two promising genotypes, BARDC21-162 and IR09A235, were selected for T. *Aman* having higher yield potential with growth duration of 121-123 days.

Adaptive trials on rice (BRAC 2015): BRAC procured some Green Super Rice (GSR) breeding lines from IRRI for trial as short-duration *Boro* and drought-tolerant T. *Aman* varieties. To find out farmers' response to the promising GSR variety CNI 9012 in *Boro* season 2014-15, seeds were distributed among farmers in different locations in the north of the country. The growth duration of the variety ranged from 140 to150 days. As drought-tolerant *Boro*, a GSR line IR1-12-D10-S3 (HHZ12-DT10-SAL3) with a growth duration of 137-143 days performed the best and appeared to have good potential. In T. *Aman* 2015, some GSR lines and a line from Vietnam (OM576) were compared with BRRI dhan62.

System of Rice Intensification (SRI): SRI was introduced in Bangladesh in 1999 by the Department of Agricultural Extension (DAE) and CARE in farmers' fields in the districts of Kishoreganj. Thereafter, BRRI and BRAC initiated their own trials. In 2002, BRAC hosted an event bringing the public sector, NGO, and private sector institutions together. It resulted in the formation of a national SRI working group and steering committee with BRRI, DAE, BRAC, CARE, and Syngenta-Bangladesh. Under this committee, several trials of the SRI method were initiated in various regions with many positive outcomes, particularly for seed multiplication (SRI NNB, 2010). During 2006-2007, various government institutions, NGOs, and their partner organisations conducted SRI trials with poor and marginalised farmers across Bangladesh. This method was found to increase the yield. Promoted by the BRAC Agricultural and Food Security Programme (AFSP), the method gained popularity among the farmers in the study area. BRAC initiated demonstrations of SRI in farmers' fields in 12 districts from the dry season of 2012, following the block approach. Each block of 8-14 hectares accommodated 50-80 farmers. A benchmark survey was carried out in each location, based on rice cultivation and the feedback from farmers. Focus group discussions (FGD) identified the problems faced by the farmers and their interest in the SRI method. Small and marginalised farmers showed less interest in adopting new agronomic practices, but BRAC motivated them to accept the new technology by providing counselling, training, and demonstrations. The farmers then implemented the new methods and continued the practice on their own. Initially, the coverage was 179 hectares in 2012-13 dry season which increased to 540 and 613 hectares in 2013-14 and 2014-15 respectively.

From the 2013 to 2015 dry seasons, a total of 6,693 farmers were brought under an SRI validation and dissemination study under AFSP. BRRI dhan28, two BRAC-released hybrid varieties (*Sakti 2* and *Sathi*) were cultivated. Through the SRI method, BRRI dhan28 produced a 16 percent higher yield than non-SRI, and 52 percent higher yield than the farmers' practice. Hybrid *dhan Sakti 2* showed a five percent higher yield in SRI than non-SRI, and 17 percent higher than the farmers' practice. Similarly, hybrid *Sathi* also yielded five percent higher than the non-SRI practice and 41 percent higher than the farmers' practice. In the 2014 dry season, 2,830 farmers cultivated BRRI *dhan28* and BRAC hybrid *dhan Sathi* across the country. In 2015, 2,758 farmers cultivated BRRI dhan28, BRAC hybrid *dhan Sakti 2* and BRAC hybrid *dhan Sathi*. The results were very encouraging compared to those of non-SRI farmers. In addition to the yield difference between the SRI and non-SRI methods, the benefit cost ratio (BCR) was significantly favourable because of the lower seed rate requirement in the SRI method (BRAC-AFSP 2016).

Rice (landrace): BRAC is concerned about the biodiversity issue of rice and rice ecology. To create awareness among the stakeholders, it published a report titled "Rice Biodiversity in Bangladesh: Adoption, Diffusion and Disappearance of Varieties - A Statistical Report from Farm Survey in 2005" by Hossain et al. (2013). Harvest Plus of CGIAR under the leadership of CIAT and IFPRI commissioned this work to IRRI. IRRI, with assistance from Bangladesh Agricultural University (BAU) and the Department of Agricultural Extension (DAE), accomplished the survey work for the Bangladesh component.

Table 2.3 gives information on the relative popularity of *Aman*, *Boro*, and *Aus* rice varieties based on surveys carried out in 600 randomly selected blocks (usually three villages per block) representing the whole country. The top three *Aman* varieties in 2004 were BR11 (26.5% of the area), Swarna, an Indian variety(11.6%), and Paijam (7.5%).In a similar survey in 2005, the most popular *Boro* varieties were BRRI dhan28 and BRRI dhan29 which occupied 36.2 percent and 23 percent respectively of the total cultivated area. In 2005, most of the *Aus* varieties were found to be of landrace origin. The top eleven *Aus* varieties grown were BRRI *dhan28* (9.0% of *Aus* area), Haitta (8.3%), BR2 (6.9%), BR1 (5.1%), BR3 (4.8%), IR50 (3.1%), Porangi (2.7%), Parijat (2.7%), Kalo *boro* (2.6%), BR27 (2.4%), and BR21 (2.3%).

The most important aspect of these surveys was to generate information about landrace varieties on the verge of extinction. The greatest biodiversity was in the *Aus* season. A few farmers in some isolated areas were found to be cultivating landrace varieties adapted to specific problematic environments. The contribution of these farmers is very important for the conservation of biodiversity (Hossain 2013).

Table 2.3: Rice diversity in Bangladesh (based on Hossain et al. 2013)

Coverage (%)	Category-wise total coverage (%)	No. of varieties	Category
Aman			
more or less 50	49.79	4	Popular
3-0.04	41.73	104	Unpopular
<0.04	08.48	406	Endangered
Total		515	
Boro			
more or less 50	50.38	2	Popular
3-0.04	36.84	68	Unpopular
<0.04	03.78	191	Endangered
Total		261	
Aus			
more or less 50	49.76	11	Popular
3-0.04	47.82	73	Unpopular
<0.04	02.42	222	Endangered
Total		295	

Source: Hossain et al. 2013.

BRAC collected and conserved on-farm landrace rice germplasm material. In January-December 2015, 181 rice germplasms were in a trial undertaken to observe their potentialities. Of these, 117 aromatic and 77 non-aromatic genotypes were considered for pure line selection.

Maize

Prior to the development of the poultry-industry, maize was not a crop of economic importance in Bangladesh. Recognising its prospects, some companies like Kushtia Seed Store and ICI Seed International came forward to import small amounts of different hybrid maize seed varieties for trial. BRAC was the main buyer of this seed. Of the varieties introduced, Pacific 11 produced a much higher yield than the varieties developed by BARI. Thereafter, BRAC started importing hybrid maize seed from Pacific Seed Company (an Australian company), Thailand. It imported one metric ton of seed in 1993, five metric tonnes in 1994 and 135 metric tonnes in 1995. It started its own seed production in 1997 by importing parent lines from Thailand. BRAC not only distributed the seeds, it also provided loans and signed a contract to buy the grains back at a fixed price to minimise the farmers' risk. To develop its own hybrid maize, BRAC strengthened its maize R&D activities in 1996. The objectives was to increase farmers' profitability through higher-yielding hybrid maize and to create employment opportunities throughout the year. Since 1997, BRAC is engaged in the production of hybrid maize seed using the parent materials of Pacific Seed Company. The maize research and development activities were strengthened in 2000 and collaboration was established with CIMMYT for maize germplasm and technical training. BRAC commercialised its first hybrid seed in the winter of 2005-06.

The R&D activities on maize were carried out at four locations. The activities acquired new momentum through the strengthening of relationships with CIMMYT in 2000 when it received 58 CIMMYT tropical-yellow early and late inbred lines. Since maize was previously only a minor crop in Bangladesh, the availability of local germplasm was very limited. The R&D activities continued with the collection of inbred lines from CIMMYT, the maintenance and crossing of collected inbred lines, and evaluation of hybrid combinations as well as the new hybrids of Pacific Seed Company (now Advanta) and other popular hybrids available in the market. BRAC developed three yellow hybrids: Uttaran in 2005, Uttaran 2 in 2007, and Uttaran Super in 2013, plus one Quality Protein Maize (QPM) white hybrid named Uttaran 3 in 2013. BRAC also became a part of the Tropical Asian Maize Network (TAMNET) hybrid trials, through which it identified a few promising tropical late hybrids. BRAC works closely with CIMMYT to establish climate resilient maize for heat, water logging, and salinity tolerance.

Adaptive trials on maize (BRAC 2015): BRAC has developed one double-cross and one three-way cross hybrid with parent lines from Pacific Seed Company. A trial was conducted with 96 three-way cross (TWC) hybrids. Out of these materials, 11 hybrids performed better than the check (*Uttaran 2*). These lines were evaluated further in *kharif-2014*. Three hybrids (two single-cross and one three-way cross) were identified as the best performers considering their better yield, growth duration, and acceptable plant and cob height. These three hybrids were demonstrated at seven locations in Chuadanga, Manikgong, Bogura, Lalmonirhat, and Dinajpur regions. Out of 62 single-cross hybrids in another trial, seven were found better in the *rabi* season (October-March) 2015.

Vegetables

The main objective of vegetable research is to develop demand-led hybrid varieties. The other objective is to develop improved management practices to increase yield and quality. BRAC's vegetable research activities have been carried out in BARDC, Gazipur, and three regional research farms since 1996. The BRAC vegetable sector has five types of activities, which are variety development, variety screening, generation of new technologies, development of uncommon varieties, and seed production.

Variety development[2]: The vegetable sector deals with research and seed production on some common vegetable crops such as: fruiting vegetables (okra, pumpkin, cucumber, bitter gourd, ridge gourd, and hot pepper), leafy and salad vegetables (spinach, red amaranth, kang kong, broad leaf mustard, and jute mallow), podded vegetables (yard-long bean, country bean, mung bean, and cowpea), stem and bulb vegetables (onion and stem amaranth), Western brassica (cauliflower, cabbage, and kohlrabi), root and tuber vegetables (radish), and indigenous vegetables including jute mallow (*Corchorus olitorious*), lafa shak (Malva verticillata), athua shak (*Chenopodium sp*), rahmi shak (*Bacopa monierii*), and gandhavadali (*Pterida foetida*).

Variety screening programme: The vegetable crops imported from overseas are screened under this programme to identify the best adapted

---

2 Sitesh C Biswas: http://www.slideshare.net/DrSiteshBiswas/brac-its- vegetable-sector-bangladesh

one(s). As the cole-crops (such as cauliflower, cabbage, broccoli, turnip, and carrot) do not flower in Bangladesh, farmers have to rely on seeds imported from countries like Japan, China, Taiwan, Thailand, USA, and India. Seed of the best varieties are selected and imported. Only quality seeds obtained from the companies are finally sold to the growers through the seed marketing network. The vegetable sector is also engaged in developing improved varieties (both OP, i.e., open-pollinated and F1 hybrids) of diverse genotypes. The vegetable sector is producing seeds of economically feasible crops such as bitter gourd, bottle gourd, pumpkin, okra, cucumber, and hot pepper suitable for Bangladesh's agro-climatic conditions. BRAC's recommended varieties up to 2016 are shown in Table 2.4.

Table 2.4: List of hybrid and OP varieties recommended by BRAC

Sl No	Name of the Crop	No. of Varieties	Variety Name
	Hybrid		
1	Bitter Gourd	01	Bulbuli
2	Ridge Gourd	01	Green Star
3	Bottle Gourd	01	Green Super
4	Pumpkin	01	Beauty
5	Okra	01	Ever Green
6	Tomato	02	Tripti-1, Tripti-2
7	Brinjal	03	Surovi, Giant Green, Super Singnath
	Open Pollinated		
1	Radish	01	Suphola40
2	Cucumber	01	Suphola-1

Source: Md. Azizul Haque, personal communication, 2018.

Recently, BRAC has also identified some other promising hybrids of bottle gourd, ridge gourd, sponge gourd, tomato, and ash gourd which are under multi-location trials for the verification of their performance in different agro-ecological locations. Many other lines are in the pipeline.

Generation of new technologies: Along with the development of new varieties, the vegetable sector is also developing new technologies. Technologies like cut-and-come-again for harvesting spinach, growing vegetables under polythene tunnels, and cloning the F1 kang kong hybrids were standardised and transferred to vegetable seed farms and contract growers.

Development of uncommon varieties: Along with the development of F1 hybrid and OP varieties, the vegetable sector also works with some uncommon vegetable crops like red okra, red spinach, white pumpkin, purplish red yard-long bean, purple hot pepper, red chenopodium, yellow-seeded mung bean, heat-tolerant country bean, and some other beans. Most of these coloured vegetables are rich in anthocyanin, beta-carotene, and iron, and yellow-seeded mung bean has 33 percent reduced level of fat. The heat-tolerant country bean is a boon to vegetable growers as it can be grown in the monsoon season when there are few vegetables on the market. These beans are sold at high prices during that off-season, ensuring the growers a worthwhile profit.

Ongoing research activities in vegetable production: BRAC's ongoing research activities include the production of breeder, foundation, and commercial seeds of different field crops, including vegetable crops.

Pulses and oilseeds

Mungbean: BRAC started its research activities in pulse crops in 2000-2001. It developed an improved mungbean variety through selection from elite germplasms. A yellow seed coat line was selected from the different mungbean accessions.

The selected yellow seed coat (YS-I) line was tested against a control variety (BARI *moog-5*) at BARDC, Gazipur. The yield and yield-contributing attributes of YS-I were found to be much higher than those of BARI moog-5. Programmes were undertaken to produce certified seeds and foundation seeds of mung bean in 2001/2002 (Islam et al. 2012).

Groundnut: Groundnut is an important oilseed crop grown under rainfed conditions, particularly in the *char* areas of Bangladesh. Although several varieties have been released by BARI and BINA, the yields of those varieties are not considered to be satisfactory. With a view to developing an improved variety, germplasm from local and exotic accessions were collected and evaluated at BARDC, Gazipur. One variant from BRC-003 (white testa coloured) and BRC-005 (China-1) were selected for adaptive trial (Islam et al. 2012). The line accession BRC-005 is expected to be good for confectionery purposes (Biswas et al. 2017).

Sunflower: Sunflower is an important oilseed crop grown all over the world as a source of good quality edible oil. This crop is characterised by its large showy flowers that have a huge number of seeds containing 44-45 percent of edible oil. Linolenic acid is an important constituent of sunflower oil, unlike rapeseed oil which has erucic acid. The linolenic acid is beneficial for human health and the popularity of sunflower has gradually increased in recent years. Moreover, since it is a photo-insensitive crop, sunflower can be grown throughout the year in Bangladesh. Furthermore, sunflower requires less irrigation and it can also be cultivated in coastal areas since it has some tolerance to salinity. BRAC started a variety screening programme in 2001-2002 with some reputed companies. In an adaptive trial in the coastal areas in 2010-11 with Agura-4 and Hysun-33 received from Advanta, Hysun-33 performed better in terms of yield and growth duration with short plant stature that was tolerant against gusty wind. BRAC recommended Hysun-33 for commercial cultivation (Islam et al. 2012).

2.3.2 BRAC seed and agro-enterprise

The shortage of high-quality seed is one of the major constraints in increasing the productivity of agricultural crops in Bangladesh. A major portion of these seeds is produced without using any modern technology to ensure high yield and disease-free varieties. BRAC used to purchase seeds from different private companies at home and abroad and supplied them to the farmers in the rural areas. But problems like poor packaging, low quality, high price, and distribution issues started to show up. In response, BRAC decided to start its own seed production in 1996. So far, the programme has produced a wide variety of certified high-quality seeds. In this process, BRAC's first production was hybrid vegetable seed in 1996, followed by hybrid maize seeds in 1997,rice and onion seeds in 1998, pulse and oil crop seeds in 1999, hybrid rice seeds in 2000, and potato seeds in 2001 (Saleque 2007). The seed subsector was not considered to be an industry and was treated as a risky business. BRAC used to procure foundation seeds of improved varieties of different vegetable from BADC and would have contract growers in Meherpur, Dinajpur and Thakurgaon districts multiply them. As the quantity of seed from BADC was not enough to satisfy BRAC's expanding needs, it set up its own production centres and temporary production processing centres in 1995-96.

BRAC has 9 seed production facilities, 20 production centres and about 7,500 contract farmers all over the country. It is the country's largest producer of hybrid maize seed and second largest producer of potato seed. It has the largest market share for the seeds of rice (hybrid and high-yielding varieties), maize, potatoes, and vegetables. It has established 5 seed processing centres with a processing capacity of 12,000 metric tons per year, along with 11 modern storage systems with a capacity of 4,400 metric tons. To ensure high-quality seeds, the enterprise uses an automatic polymer seed-coating treatment (fungicide) and an automatic packaging system. BRAC is the pioneer in promoting the production of seed as a business enterprise.

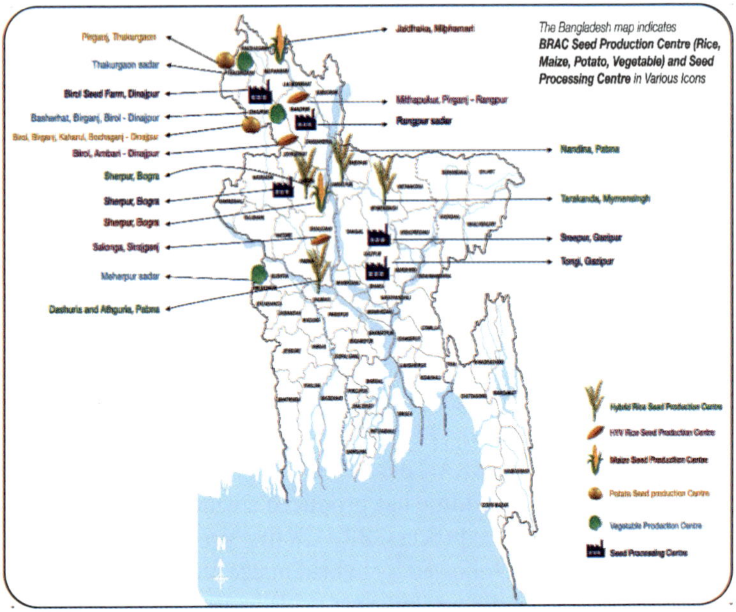

Source: BRAC Seed and Agro Enterprise 2017.

Figure 2.9: BRAC seed network across the country

BRAC's seed and agro-enterprise have built the value chain system of production and distribution through a wide network of 650 dealers and more than 7,000 sub-dealers (Figure 2.9). BRAC Seed and Agro Enterprise is now marketing seeds of 30 hybrid varieties and 27 OP varieties of vegetables, 13 hybrid varieties and 21 high-yielding varieties of rice, 12 hybrid varieties of maize, and 5 varieties of potato. During the 2016-2017 production season, the enterprise marketed 1,500 metric tons of hybrid rice seed, 1,300 metric tons of high-yielding varieties of rice seed, 760 metric tons of hybrid maize seed, 98 metric tons of vegetable seeds, and 14,600 metric tons of potato seeds (BRAC Seed and Agro Enterprise 2017).

Hybrid maize seed production

BRAC imported hybrid seed parents from the Pacific Seed Company to develop Pacific 11 and Pacific 60 varieties, which are well accepted by farmers. Another prominent variety is 900M introduced by Krishi Banijya Bitan. These varieties cover about 80-90 percent of the maize area. BARI hybrid maize-5 and hybrid maize-7 occupy about 5-6 percent, and there are a few other improved varieties, for example, from Syngenta (NK 40) and Monsanto. Initially, BRAC had some composite lines, but with the increasing demand for hybrid seed, they are now producing only hybrid seed. BRAC produces seed through contract growers who receive inputs (parent seed, fertilizers, pesticides) and training provided by BRAC (Lynamm et al. 2010). BRAC's production of hybrid maize seed since 1997 is shown in Figure 2.10.

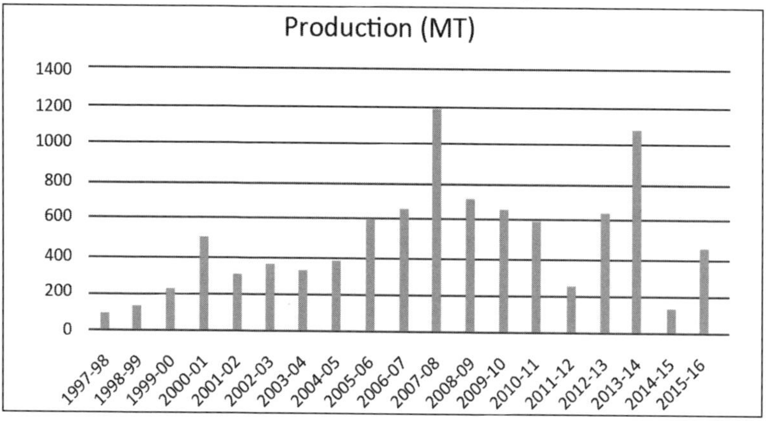

Source: BRAC Seed and Agro Enterprise, 2017.

Figure 2.10: Yearly seed production from 1997/98 to 2015/16

Potato seed production programme[3]

BRAC began its tissue culture (TC) activities, an initiative to produce disease-free potato seed, in 1997 in a rented house at Uttara, Dhaka. Based on previous challenges that BRAC encountered on the performance of some of their potato varieties, it decided to produce quality seeds through tissue culture. This decision led to the production of micro tuber in 1998 and plantlets of high-yielding exotic varieties in 1999. Afterward, BRAC shifted the laboratory to its newly established facilities at Gazipur. Potato seed production consists of the following components.

a. In vitro potato plantlet production;
b. Mini tuber multiplication;
c. Breeder seed production;
d. Foundation seed production; and
e. Certified seed production.

In vitro potato plantlet production: The growth of invitro plantlet production from 2000-2016 is presented in Table 2.5. Initially, the production of the planting unit was quite significant (200,000), but production fell to one-third of the initial production within a few years. However, it has picked up again significantly in the recent past.

Mini tuber and breeder seed production: Strict hygienic culture is maintained in every step of the production process of in vitro potato plantlets (G0), mini tuber nucleus seed potato (G1), and breeder seed potato (G2). All possible measures are taken to get the cultural area vector-free.

Foundation and certified seed production: Production of foundation seed potatoes (G3) started in 2001-2002 under open field conditions with trained professionals taking care of all the intercultural operations in the field. In subsequent years, BRAC grew certified seeds (G4) through contract growers. BRAC representatives provided training, breeder seeds, and other relevant inputs to the farmers. All certified seed potatoes are distributed to the commercial growers through registered dealers. At present, BRAC has around 3,000 trained contract farmers.

3 Personal communication: Md. Azizul Haque, Deputy General Manager, Production and Research, BRAC Centre, Dhaka.

Table 2.5: In vitro potato plantlet production (2000-2017)

Production Year	Planting Unit
2000-2001	200,000
2001-2002	92,000
2002-2003	78,000
2003-2004	143,000
2004-2005	92,000
2005-2006	32,000
2006-2007	51,000
2007-2008	57,000
2008-2009	62,000
2009-2010	67,000
2010-2011	90,000
2011-2012	69,000
2012-2013	69,000
2013-2014	75,000
2014-2015	190,000
2015-2016	221,000
2016-2017	354000

Source: BRAC Seed and Agro Enterprise, 2017.

The multiplication procedure is monitored at every stage by a group of experts (internal and external). The year-wise trend of seed potato production is shown in Table 2.6.

Rice (hybrid) seed

BRAC is the pioneer of hybrid rice variety development, seed production, and marketing in Bangladesh. During *Boro* 1998-99, BRAC marketed 204 metric tonnes of hybrid rice seeds procured from two private companies, enough to plant 14,500 ha. BRAC provided training to 100,000 farmers in hybrid rice cultivation techniques, but the overall performance of hybrids was not satisfactory as the farmers and extension workers lacked experience with the techniques of hybrid rice cultivation. To overcome these problems, BRAC made arrangements with multinational seed companies, and collected exotic hybrid rice varieties from China and India for adaptation trials under Bangladesh conditions. The Chinese varieties performed better than the Indian ones. Accordingly, BRAC was able to release a variety called *Jagoron* (GB4) during the *Boro* season 2000-01.

Table 2.6: Year-wise seed potato production in metric tonnes (MT) (2000-2017)

Production year	Mini tuber	Breeder Seed	Foundation Seed	Certified Seed	Total
2001-2002	19.260	167	0	0	186.260
2002-2003	13.260	296	1566	0	1875.260
2003-2004	4.750	143	1686	1600	3433.750
2004-2005	6.539	124	1540	3170	4840.539
2005-2006	7.690	85	1163	2310	3565.690
2006-2007	3.955	129	983	2716	3831.955
2007-2008	5.405	108	957	3067	4137.405
2008-2009	7.569	106	1058	4690	5861.569
2009-2010	8.466	149	1072	4418	5647.466
2010-2011	6.910	151	1277	5185	6619.910
2011-2012	6.630	170	1442	5440	7058.630
2012-2013	17.480	155	1589	6543	8304.480
2013-2014	19.190	158	1490	8349	10016.190
2014-2015	19.010	194	1774	9298	11285.010
2015-2016	19.725	185	1913	11596	13713.725
2016-2017	31.933	278	2853	14890	18052.933

Source: BRAC Seed and Agro Enterprise, 2017.

BRAC's hybrid and inbred rice seed production: Following the amendment to the 1993 seed policy in 1998, some provisions were incorporated for hybrid rice variety registration and seed import. At the beginning, most seeds were imported from China in exchange for a huge amount of foreign exchange. BRAC decided to acquire the knowledge of hybrid rice seed production technologies and build up its capacity to produce seed within the country. BRAC started hybrid rice seed production in 2000-01 with the technical support of Chinese experts. Initially, hybrid rice seeds were produced in leased and BRAC's own land. Later, to generate rural employment and increase incomes, BRAC started engaging contract growers: eventually, more than 1,300 farmers were directly engaged. The growth of hybrid and inbred rice seed production is shown in Table 2.7.

Table 2.7: Year-wise hybrid and inbred rice seed production (2000-2017)

Production Year	Hybrid Rice Seed		Inbred Rice Seed		
	Cultivated Area (ac)	Produced Seed (Metric tonnes)	Cultivated Area (ac)	Produced Seed (Metric Tonnes)	Remarks
2000-2001	44	19	1498	777	
2001-2002	284	142	1557	848	
2002-2003	371	191	1338	1176	
2003-2004	352	129	1440	722	
2004-2005	385	184	640	391	Only produced in Aman season
2005-2006	674	408	288	111	
2006-2007	1250	1357	180	67	
2007-2008	949	1028	276	114	
2008-2009	1133	1161	809	528	
2009-2010	633	756	736	545	
2010-2011	607	613	765	769	
2011-2012	854	1032	768	801	
2012-2013	1140	1612	1453	1114	
2013-1014	977	1445	1361	1387	
2014-2015	1094	1288	2703	2302	
2015-2016	814	674	1288	986	
2016-2017	647	673	1823	1292	

Source: BRAC Seed and Agro Enterprise, 2017.

Vegetable seed[4]

The annual vegetable seed requirement in Bangladesh is around 4,500 metric tonnes, of which only 38-39 percent are quality seeds produced and imported by the government, NGOs, and other private companies. The shortfall is supplied by the farmers, but this is not considered quality seed.

To reduce dependency on foreign seeds, BRAC's vegetable sector is developing new demand-led varieties and supplying improved vegetable varieties to growers. In this way, the BRAC vegetable sector is playing an important role in contributing to national food and nutritional security. Figure 2.11 shows the trends of production in BRAC's vegetable seed production programmes.

4 Personal communication: Md. Azizul Haque; Deputy General Manager, Production & Research, BRAC Centre, Dhaka-1212.

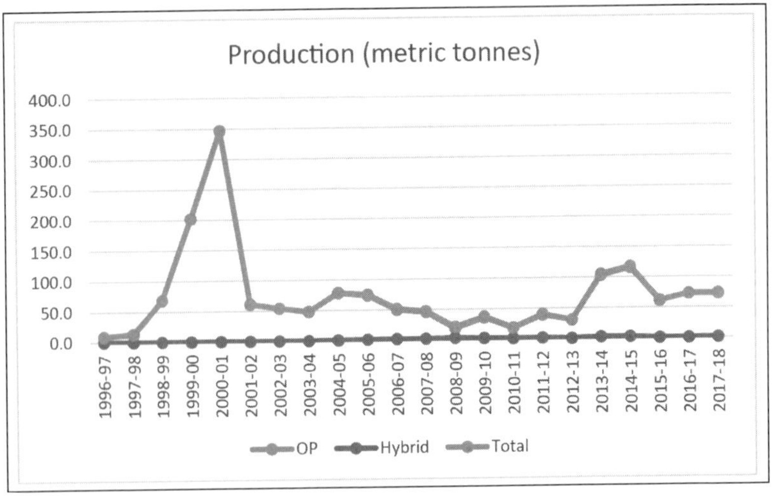

Source: BRAC Seed and Agro Enterprise, 2017.

Figure 2.11: Growth of vegetable seed production under the BRAC vegetable seed production programme

2.4 Agricultural Extension Programmes

As mentioned earlier, BRAC started its agricultural activities in the early seventies and gradually expanded its activities across the country through its different programmes and projects. In addition to vegetable cultivation through kitchen gardening, a pilot experiment on rice, wheat, and maize was initiated in 1986. A year later, the BRAC agriculture extension programme was incorporated with BRAC's mainstream Rural Development Programme (RDP)) and IGVGD (Income generation for Vulnerable Development Programme). The programme continued up to 2000 and provided training, technology transfer, input supply, credit support, and different extension services to a large number of smallholder farmers. The activities also included vegetable cultivation, social forestry and agroforestry, crop diversification (maize, rice, sunflower, potato, etc.), soil testing and fertilizer recommendation, and strengthening the supply system of HYV and hybrid seeds of vegetable, rice, maize, and potato. The programme reached more than 850,000 farmers in 437 upazilas across Bangladesh (Saleque 2007).

The agriculture extension programme was implemented under the Employment and Income Generation programme up to 2000, after which it was operated as a programme support enterprise (PSE) which coordinated agricultural research and development and production of rice, maize, and vegetable seed. The Asian Development Bank (ADB) came forward to assist BRAC in formulating the Northwest Crop Diversification Project (NCDP). Gradually, a new programme, the Agriculture and Food Security Programme (AFSP), was launched to coordinate all the agricultural activities (research and development, extension, seed production, credit and marketing) in 2009 (Hossain 2016). Some of the BRAC's extension programmes are described below.

2.4.1 Strengthening the agriculture and food security programme

The Agriculture and Food Security Programme (AFSP) aimed to contribute to achieving sustainable food security through climate-resilient and sustainable agricultural technologies. Problem-oriented, controlled and action (applied and adaptive) research was conducted to develop improved crop varieties (inbred and hybrid) and appropriate cultural practices by 2015 for better productivity through laboratory and farmers' participatory approaches. The crops in the priority list were rice, maize, vegetables, pulses, and oilseed crops. Two ecologically contrasting regions (southern and northern: 56 upazilas of 15 districts) were included for adaptive trials and fast-track dissemination of appropriate technologies. The primary goal was to alleviate the poverty of small and marginal farmers through increased cropping intensity and the introduction of other kinds of profitable and appropriate agro-entrepreneurship.

Direct cash inflow was necessary to achieve these goals because many farmers could not afford to buy the inputs in time. Therefore, the programme provided cash grants to buy critical inputs and apply them within the time necessary for higher productivity to ensure food security in vulnerable communities. Farmers of different blocks were trained to cultivate rice in the *Aus*, *Aman*, and *Boro* seasons of 2015. Farmers who had experience on the benefits of hybrid rice cultivation during the Cyclone Sidr rehabilitation project, were advised to cultivate hybrid rice during both the *Boro* and *Aus* seasons to achieve even better productivity than was obtained from HYVs. It was estimated that farmers provided about 55 percent of rice production cost, mainly in terms of labour, fertilisers, and irrigation, and the project paid 45 percent to purchase inputs that required cash. In addition to the cash infusion, farmers were provided with technical knowledge of rice cultivation. Farmers' activities were monitored as and when necessary to harness more benefits.

2.4.2 Northwest Crop Diversification Project (NCDP)

In line with government priorities, the NCDP was initiated to accelerate economic growth in the country's northwest region through the production of improved/high-yielding varieties of vegetables, fruits, spices, and other high-value crops (HVCs) by small- and medium-scale farmers. The NCDP was an ADB-funded project whose objectives were to:

a. promote high-value crop (HVC) production and more efficient marketing of HVCs;
b. establish a sustainable partnership between the public-sector service agencies and NGOs to provide extension services, need-based training, and credit support to the targeted small farmers.

The project components were farmer training and extension, farmer mobilisation and credit support, adaptive research, marketing support, pilot agribusiness credit line, and support for project management.

The project area comprised 60 upazilas in 16 districts, all under the then Rajshahi Division. It covered about 28.5 percent of the privately-owned land area of Bangladesh and 5.7 percent of total farm holdings of the region. Small farmers interested in growing HVCs have limited access to credit institutions. Ensuring credit on time to the right person through the right procedure is a huge task. BRAC, with other NGOs like Proshika, RDRS, and Grameen Krishi Foundation (GKF), played a significant role in mobilising credit for HVC farmers.

In close partnership with DAE, BRAC and the other NGOs formed 12,415 Small Farmers Groups (SFG) with 16-20 members per group. Half of the 340,430 members were women. Awareness building, a weekly group meeting, and technical training on HVCs were mandatory tasks for SFG members. The Bangladesh Bank made the Rajshahi Krishi Unnayan Bank (RAKUB) the executing agency to distribute credit through the NGO partners. According to the ADB completion report in November 2011, the project distributed 514,182 loans amounting to BDT 2,514.45 million to 258,577 project farmers. The recovery rate was 100 percent.

The monitoring and evaluation survey reported that the amount of credit utilisation increased successively due to increasing effective demand. The higher demand for credit forced the NGOs to approach RAKUB to increase the revolving credit fund from BDT100 million to BDT 150 million. More credit was given for crops like potato, maize, and eggplant. Moderate credit support was extended for the cultivation of banana, tomato, green chili, onion, garlic, aromatic rice, ginger, and country bean.

A revolving credit fund was created to sustain economic returns after project completion, supported by the NGOs. The average amount of credit increased by 54 percent in the second year. The subsequent increases were 31 percent, 23 percent, and 15 percent in the 3rd, 4th, and 5th years respectively (ADB 2011).

2.4.3 Crop intensification in the coastal region of Bangladesh

The farmers of the areas affected by Cyclone Sidr and Cyclone Aila were under the intensive care of the government, BRAC, and some other organisations in the aftermath of the catastrophes. But that was a temporary solution. For the longer term, BRAC came up with another project totally based on agriculture called "Crop Intensification for Achieving Food Self-Sufficiency in the Coastal Regions of Bangladesh." It was implemented in 26 upazilas of 7 coastal districts with a grant of Euro 5.0 million from the European Union, together with Euro 0.56 million contributed by BRAC. Farmers in the project area cultivated hybrid rice in the *Aus*, *Aman*, and *Boro* seasons and inbred rice (HYVs) in the *Aman* and *Boro* seasons under instructions from the experts. Maize, pulses, and sesame were cultivated as oil crops in the *rabi* season. Each farmer was given a grant for cultivating hybrid rice of BDT 23,939, BDT 19,550, and BDT 23,859 per hectare in the *Aus*, *Aman*, and *Boro* seasons respectively. For the cultivation of inbred (HYV) rice, the allocation was BDT 21,966 in the *Aman* season. Similarly, the allocations per hectare per farmer for other crops were BDT 17,900 for maize, BDT 18,031 for sunflower (a new crop), and BDT 12,194 for sesame. The allocations for mung, watermelon, and grass pea were BDT 12,350, BDT 12,350, and BDT 6,175, respectively.

Hybrid rice and maize were new crops for the coastal belt. Therefore, training modules highlighting these two newly introduced crops were prepared. The modules were restricted to the practical aspects of crop selection and cropping patterns for the relevant Agro-Ecological Zones (AEZ), and cultural practices like fertiliser, water, and pest management. BRAC arranged frequent field visits for farmers (male and female) around the blocks, as well as for government and NGO officials, local leaders, social workers, and mass media people for appropriate dissemination of the introduced technologies. Most of the BRAC staff and the beneficiaries were trained by experts. In total, 219,143 neighbouring farmers availed the opportunity to attend field days.

Most of the farmers in the coastal region traditionally cultivated one rice crop a year. BRAC recognised the opportunity to improve the cropping pattern in those areas. They relied on their own expertise, experience, and discussions with BRRI, BARC, and DAE experts to design location-specific new cropping patterns (Table 2.8). Insufficient grant money was a concern for many of the interested farmers (within and outside the block area), but they made the plan successful by using their savings or borrowing money from BRAC or from relatives (ADB 2011).

Table 2.8: Cropping patterns developed by BRAC in the coastal region

Project Districts	Before BRAC Project Implementation	Patterns Followed by BRAC Project in previous Block	New Patterns Developed by BRAC
Barguna	Fallow- Aman- Boro/Rabi Aus - Aman- Fallow	Aus- Aman – Boro/Rabi	Aus- Aman –Boro/Rabi (45%) Aus- Aman – Boro (22%) Aus- Aman – Rabi (22%) Fallow- Aman- Rabi (11%) Total 100%
Jhalakhathi	Fallow Aman - Boro	Aus- Aman – Boro/Rabi	
Patuakhali	Aus - Aman – Rabi (Khesari)	Aus- Aman – Boro/Rabi	
Pirojpur	Aus- Aman- Fallow Aus - Aman – Rabi (Khesari)	Aus -Aman - Rabi	
Bagerhat	Aus - Aman - Rabi (Khesari)	Aus- Aman – Boro/Rabi	
Khulna	Fallow -Aman – Sesame Fallow - Aman – Boro	Fallow-Aman- Rabi Aus-Aman – Boro	

Source: Eusuf and Associates, 2012.

2.4.4 Second Crop Diversification Project (SCDP)[5, 6]

The ADB-funded NCDP for 2001-2009 was one of the most successful crop-diversification projects; thus, a similar follow-up project called the "Second Crop Diversification Project" (SCDP) was organised for execution in 52 upazilas of 27 districts of the Southwest and Northwest regions and implemented during 2010-2016. This project was supported by the ADB. SCDP focused on those areas where NCDP did not have any support. The SCDP directly supplemented government policies for food security and agriculture sector growth. The project assisted other activities like the Agribusiness Development Project, particularly by promoting value addition to HVCs and strengthening value-chain integration by developing backward and forward linkages between farmers and consumers, including service provision by private sector agribusinesses, technically and financially qualified microfinance institutions (MFIs), and wholesale banks.

BRAC, as a partner NGO, was engaged to form and endorse farmers' groups and to extend credit to the interested groups. Targeted farmers' groups were formed through validation and new selection. DAE and BRAC collaborated closely to organise training for HVC farmers on production and value addition—one of the criteria required to make them eligible for credit support. By 30 June 2016, a total of 12,000 farmers' groups were formed (5,620 male), enrolling a total of 251,927 members (138,852 male).

Agreements between BRAC and wholesale banks, Eastern Bank Limited (EBL) and Bangladesh Small Industries and Commerce Bank Limited (BASIC Bank) were signed. The Bangladesh Bank was in charge of monitoring. Funds were advanced to BRAC to extend credit support to the beneficiaries. Wives and husbands were co-signees of the loan agreements. Approximately 65 percent of women co-signees managed the credit. The credit availed by 201,647 members (120,898 female) amounted to BDT 5,943.9 million (BDT 3,831.8 million to females). BRAC deployed qualified field staff for group mobilisation, awareness-raising, helping to arrange technical training, and extending credit support. DAE field staff, in collaboration with BRAC, organised

---

5 www.adp.org/project/40534-013/main

6 http://bangladeshmoves.com.bd/news/second-crop-diversification-project-scdp-clinched-adbs-best-title-of-2013/

demonstration trials in the selected farmers' fields to show the potentials of the readymade technologies. The Project Monitoring Unit (PMU) organised capacity development training for field staff to serve the farmers better. Community facilitators were recruited and deployed in the field.

The direct beneficiaries of the SCDP were marginal, small, and medium farmers with landholdings up to three hectares. Landless people obtained spill over benefits through employment opportunities. The project had the following impacts:

- increased HVC production and commercialisation;
- reduced HVC post-harvest losses, improved product quality and value addition, and enhanced market efficiency;
- enhanced capacity of public sector institutions and participating partners in supporting farmers to increase their incomes; and
- increased participation of women in commercial agricultural activities.

The Second Crop Diversification Project by Bangladesh Bank and the Agricultural Extension Department clinched the best project title of ADB in 2013 out of 67 projects; BRAC played a significant role as the microcredit provider (Hossain 2016).

2.4.5 Tenant farmers development project

The large community of tenant sharecroppers formerly had little access to credit programmes. Hence, BRAC formulated an innovative approach entitled the *Borga Chashi Unnayan Prakalpa* (BCUP)—Tenant Farmers' Development Project—to offer credit as well as extension services to tenant farmers, with support from the Bangladesh Bank. Under an agreement signed by Bangladesh Bank and BRAC in October 2009, the bank provided a soft loan (with 5% annual interest) of BDT 500 crore (US$ 75 million) to BRAC (Hossain et al. 2016). The funding was initially given for three years to provide credit to 300,000 tenant farmers with a farm size of two acres (0.80 ha). The farms were either fully (pure tenant) or partially (tenant-owner) rented under different tenancy arrangements. The project was extended for an additional three years from 2012. The project provided customised credit services to the tenant farmers at the minimum rate of interest (10% per year) at a flat rate. The effective rate was 15-20 percent, based on the declining-balance method, depending on the mode of repayment of the principal and interest (Bayes and Hossain 2011; Hossain et al. 2014).

2.4.6 Post-cyclone rehabilitation programmes

Post-Sidr

BRAC extended its emergency rehabilitation programme to Cyclone Sidr victims with some innovative approaches in the crop subsectors. With funding from the European Union (EU), hybrid rice and maize were introduced. However, inbred rice was not excluded from the programme. Vegetables, fruits, betel leaves, and homestead nursery plantations were also included, with special reference to small and marginal farmers. Women were preferred. Cumulative totals of 28,380 and 6,938 hectares were brought under rice and maize cultivation respectively. Maize was a new introduction to the area. Vegetable and betel leaf farmers were the worst victims of the cyclone. The cumulative coverage under vegetables/fruits was 13,074 hectares, and 405 hectares of land were brought under betel leaf cultivation. Under the programme, farmers were offered grants to cover the cost of cultivation (land preparation, irrigation, and inputs). The Benefit Cost Ratio (BCR) was the highest at 73.5:1 for vegetables. The BCR for rice and maize were 6.6:1 and 6.3:1 respectively. The farmers assigned to nurseries and homestead plantation made a significant contribution too. Around 2,000 nursery beneficiaries received grants, and they supported 200,023 beneficiaries. The programme had significant cognitive and economic impacts on the participants. In some cases, the per capita income surpassed that of the pre-Sidr stage. The newly introduced crops Hybrid rice and maize were accepted by the farmers (Bayes 2010).

Post-Aila

The prime objective of this programme was to rehabilitate the cyclone Aila-affected population by creating income generation activities. With the assistance of the EU, BRAC extended its emergency interventions to the Aila-affected area along with the government of Bangladesh. The beneficiaries were selected from families having limited access to the mainstream development programmes. Ethnic minorities and families headed by women were prioritised in the beneficiary list. The most important direct intervention in crop agriculture sector was vegetable cultivation. The Aila evaluation report stated that the number of beneficiaries in different fields was more than 100,000, amongst which vegetable and social forestry numbered more than 60,000 (Ahmed et al. 2012).

2.4.7 Some innovative adaptive approaches

Some additional technology dissemination, extension, and training activities of BRAC are reviewed below.

Zinc-enriched rice variety validated in farmer's field: AFSP took an initiative in *Aman* season 2015 to alleviate zinc deficiency in 30 different locations of the northern part of Bangladesh through the dissemination of zinc-enriched BRRI *dhan62*.

Climate adaptive research activities-summer tomato cultivation: Although tomatoes are in high demand throughout the year, the crop is usually grown only from November to March (cool season). Along with other research institutes like BARI, BRAC carried out adaptation trials of specific tomato varieties in summer all over the country. The net income from summer tomato production was 4-5 times higher than that of winter tomatoes.

Rice and rice farming system for fragile environments: BRAC-AFSP conducted some adaptive trials with 300 Green Super Rice genotypes in 10 different locations. Most of the genotypes were developed to survive in fragile environments (drought, salinity, submergence, and cold). The varieties were evaluated to explore their growth under different stress conditions. One of the objectives of BRAC agriculture research and AFSP is to convert single-cropped areas to double or triple cropping to enhance food security. It also invested in developing short maturing and high yielding varieties.

Dissemination of stress tolerant rice variety: Several dissemination trials were conducted in the *Aman* season in different stress-prone areas. Submergence-tolerant rice variety BRRI dhan51 and BRRI dhan52 were taken to 65 locations. Drought-tolerant BRRI dhan56 and BRRI dhan57, and salinity-tolerant BRRI dhan41 were also introduced in relevant areas. BINA dhan8 and BINA dhan10 were introduced in the

Boro season 2014-15 at different saline locations of Khulna, Bagerhat, and Satkhira regions.

Cultivation of maize in fallow char areas in the North: Around 617 hectares of 2,945 farmers' fallow land on Jamuna, Brahmaputra, Dharala and Tista river *chars* in Rangpur and Bogra regions were brought under maize cultivation in *rabi* season 2014. The average yield was 10.86 t/ha.

Introducing sunflower as an edible oil crop in coastal areas: BRAC successfully introduced sunflower as a new crop to more than 25,000 farmers covering 6,500 hectares of land in coastal areas. The average yield was 2.80 t/ha. Sunflower shows moderate resistance to soil salinity and requires little irrigation.

Integrated aquaculture-agriculture in gher: BRAC has worked on the process of integrated aquaculture-agriculture technologies which ensures the maximum production of fish, crops, and vegetables in different seasons of the year at the same place. It reduces the space requirement and also improves the livelihoods of marginal communities (BRAC 2015).

2.5 Other Agriculture-related Programmes

2.5.1 BRAC agro-forestry programme[7]

BRAC's social forestry programme, launched in 1988, increase awareness about afforestation. It also created a sustainable supply of high-quality seedlings, while creating additional income and employment opportunities for rural women. BRAC aims to bring all available land in the rural areas (homestead, roadside, embankments, and marginal fallow land) under tree cover with the active participation of the rural poor. The key components of the social forestry programme are horticulture nursery, grafting nursery, agroforestry, etc. BRAC started the nursery programme to supply good quality seedlings locally. Nursery workers are given training by BRAC. Each nursery is on 7-10 decimals of land and produces 10,000 seedlings annually. A grafting nursery has been set up to meet the increasing demand for HYV seedlings. The grafting project is based on the asexual propagation of fruit trees. BRAC is the pioneer in promoting *Amropali* and some other varieties

7 Saleque (2007), Effective way to integrate small farmers in the value chain: Experience of BRAC.

of mangos in Bangladesh. BRAC launched an agroforestry project on degraded private and government *Khas* land in 1991. The purpose of the project was to produce wood, fuel, fodder, fruits, and vegetables from the same plot (Naher 2007).

2.5.2 Vegetable export programme[8]

BRAC started exporting vegetables to different countries of Europe and Asia in 1997-98. With technical support from the Hortex Foundation, the main objective of the export programme was to link poor farmers to the international market. The vegetables used in European dishes such as potatoes, French beans and broccoli were exported. In addition, green chili, long bean, bitter gourd, okra, and parval were exported on a demand basis. French bean is an exotic vegetable but it grows well in Bangladesh. BRAC provided training and technical assistance to the contract farmers. Necessary packaging arrangements were established in Tongi within a short distance of the airport.

BRAC followed Good Agriculture Practice (GAP) for the exported vegetables and they were produced organically. Women from the poorest families were employed for cleaning, washing, sorting, and grading. In the first year, French bean was introduced and exported successfully to England, France, Belgium, and Holland. BRAC exported 472 tons of fresh vegetables and 800 tons of potatoes in 2003 to wholesalers and supermarkets of England, France, Germany, Belgium, and Italy in Europe, to UAE and Bahrain in the Middle East, and to Singapore, Malaysia, and Hong Kong in Southeast Asia. Initially, there was an increasing demand and BRAC constructed a sophisticated vegetable packaging house at Tongi to ensure proper cold chain. Unfortunately, BRAC had to stop vegetable export due to issues mostly beyond BRAC's control: BRAC had to use the Bangladesh Biman cargo, but the cargo service was irregular and uncertain. There were frequent cancellations of flights without any prior information and delays which adversely affected the perishable vegetables.

2.6 Conclusion

The Agriculture (Crop) sector has experienced a dynamic change on its way to sustainable food security. The average growth rate in agricultural

8 Personal communication, A. Saleque: Advisor, Agriculture and Livestock.

GDP reached 3.5 percent during the Sixth Five Year Plan (GoB 2015). The achievement of food self-sufficiency is a major milestone for the country The factors behind these advances included "rapid technological change and more options for farmers created through agricultural research, increased market opportunity, the higher level of profit and income, policies, public investment in agriculture, and delivery of essential inputs." (Deb 2016). Food availability by itself does not ensure adequate access to food, although it is a necessary precondition. If people have access to livelihoods, they would have access to food and nutrition. Better livelihood access also leads to improved living standards, better education, and better knowledge of health (Begum et al. 2013).

BRAC implemented extensive programmes in the agriculture sector in order to improve the livelihood of poor and marginalised farmers through extension and rehabilitation programmes like the Northwest Crop Diversification Project and the post-Sidr and post-Aila cyclone rehabilitation programmes. BRAC has implement edits agricultural programme in collaboration with several national and international research organisations and donor agencies. It has developed market linkages and provided services to small and marginal farmers through microfinance activities. BRAC seed and agro-enterprises play a major role in quality seed production and supply to stimulate overall food production and it has also encouraged others to invest in this sector.

> When the world is free from hunger and poverty and social discrimination, BRAC's work will be done. Until then, BRAC will strive to find practical and scalable approach to eradicate poverty in whatever form it exists.
>
> — *Mahabub Hossain*

References

ADB. 2011. *Northwest Crop Diversification Project Completion Report*. Manila: Author.

Ahmed S., Akteruzzaman Huq, M. N. Gazi, M. S., Khan, N. I. and N. Mahmud. 2012. *Evaluation of the "Restoring Socio-economic Stability and Strengthening Community Resilience in Areas Affected by the Cyclone AILA" Project. Final report* (unpublished). Dhaka: The Foundation for Research on Educational Planning and Development (FREPD).

Bayes, A. 2010. *Impact Assessment of EU Funded Post-Sidr Livelihoods Rehabilitation* (unpublished). Dhaka: Socioconsult Ltd.

Bayes, A. and M. Hossain. 2011. "Change in Tenancy and Labour Markets and Impact on Livelihoods in the Rural Bangladesh: Findings from a Longitudinal Survey 1988-2007." Paper presented in the conference of the Asian Society of Agricultural Economics (ASEA), Hanoi, Vietnam, 13-15 October, 2011.

BBS (Bangladesh Bureau of Statistics). 2017. *Statistical Pocket Book of Bangladesh.* Dhaka: Bureau of Statistics, Ministry of Planning, GoB.

Begum, M.E.A., M. I. Hossain, and L. D'Haese. 2014. "Food Security in Bangladesh: Present Status and Trend." *Progressive Agriculture* 24, no. 1 & 2: 263-271. doi: 10.3329/pa.v24i1-2.19178

Biswas, S.C., S.C. Nath, and M. Hasan. 2017. "Development of Large Seedc ' Confectionery Type Peanut Line through Reselection." *Plant Environmc Development* 6, no.1: 5-13.

BRAC. 2015. *Strengthening Agriculture Food Security Programme: Progress Report (January-December 2015).* Dhaka: Agriculture and Food Security Programme, BRAC.

BRAC. 2017. *BRAC Seed and Agro Enterprise.* http://www.brac.net/brac-enterprises/item/899-brac-seed-and-agro-enterprise

BRAC-AFSP. 2016. *BRAC Agricultural and Food Security Programme. System of Rice Intensification (SRI): BRAC Experiences.* Dhaka: BRAC.

Deb, U. 2016. "Agriculture Transformation in Bangladesh: Extent, Drivers and Implications." Keynote speech. Bangladesh Agricultural Economics Association 15th Annual conference (22-23 January 2016). BARC Auditorium, Dhaka.

Eusuf and Associates. 2012. "Crop Intensification for Achieving Food Self-Sufficiency in the Coastal Region of Bangladesh (7 District) Programme." Evaluation Report (unpublished).

FAO (Food and Agriculture Organization of the United Nations). 2017. *FAOSTAT Database.* Rome. Italy: Author.

Hamid, A., M. Nasiruddin, M. Haque, and E. Haque. 1982. *Deshi Dhaner Jat* (Local rice varieties). Gazipur, Bangladesh: Bangladesh Rice Research Institute. https://pdfs.semanticscholar.org/c245/372952f27998f6101141184d93955c3938cc.pdf

Hossain, M. 2012. "Four decades of Agriculture Development in Bangladesh". In *Bangladesh at Forty: Changes and Challenges*, edited by A. Bayes. Dhaka: A. H. Development Publishing House.

Hossain, M. 2016. "Introduction". In *Driving Development: A Story of BRAC's Evolution and Effectiveness*, edited by M. Hossain, S. N. Kairy, and A. Bayes, 1-14. Dhaka: UPL and BRAC.

Hossain, M., M.S. Islam, S.C. Nath, M.A. Saleque, and M. Hossain. 2016. "Agriculture for Food Security." In *Driving Development: A Story of BRACs Evolution and Effectiveness*, edited by M. Hossain, S. N. Kairy, and A. Bayes, 141-160. Dhaka: UPL and BRAC.

Hossain, M., W.M.H. Jaim, S. Alam and A.N.M. Rahman. 2013, February. *Rice Biodiversity in Bangladesh: Adoption, Diffusion and Disappearance of Varieties, a Statistical Report from Farm Survey in 2005*. Dhaka: Research and Evaluation Division, BRAC.

Hossain, M., A. Janaiah, and A.M.M. Husain. 2003. "Hybrid Rice in Bangladesh: Farm-Level Performance." *Economic and Political Weekly*, 2517-2522.

Hossain, M., M.A. Malek, and N.C. Das. 2014. "Tenant Famers' Access to Credit and Extension Service: BRAC Tenant Farmer Development Project in Bangladesh." Dhaka: Research and Evaluation Division, BRAC.

Husain, A. M. M., M. Hossain, and A. Janaiah. 2001. *Hybrid Rice Adoption in Bangladesh: A Socioeconomic Assessment of Farmers' Experience*. Research Monograph No. 18. Dhaka: RED, BRAC and Los Banos, The Philippines: Social Science Division, IRRI.

Islam, S. M., S.C. Biswas, M.S. Rahman, and S.C. Nath. 2012. "Research-Development and Dissemination Activities for Pulses and Oil Seed Crops in BRAC." In the *Proceedings of the National Workshop - Research Achievement of Past Ten Years of Pulses and Oilseeds and Future Research strategies for Sustainable Crop Production at Bangladesh Agricultural Research Council*, Dhaka, Bangladesh.

LaFranchi, H. 2015. *From famine to food basket: how Bangladesh became a model for reducing hunger*. https://www.csmonitor.com/USA/Foreign-Policy/2015/0617/From-famine-to-food-basket-how-Bangladesh-became-a-model-for-reducing-hunger

Lynamm, J., M. Chowdhury, M. Sattar, and A. Habib. 2010. *Plant Breeding and Seed Systems for Rice, Vegetables, Maize and Pulses in Bangladesh*. FAO Plant Production and Protection Paper 207.

Naher, S. 2007. *Impact of BRAC Social Forestry Programme as perceived by the women beneficiaries*. http://archive.saulibrary.edu.bd:8080/xmlui/handle/123456789/1597

Saleque, M.A. 2007. "An Effective Way to Integrate Small Farmers in the Value Chain: The Experience of BRAC." In *Southeast Asian Regional Conference on Agricultural Value Chain Financing, Conference Proceedings December 12-14, 2007 Kuala Lumpur, Malaysia*, 51-66. Asian Productivity Organization and FAO.

SFYP (Sixth Five Year Plan). 2015. Dhaka: Ministry of Planning, GoB.

——. 2016. *Bangladesh Seventh Five Year Plan FY 2016-2020, Part 2*. Dhaka: Ministry of Planning, GoB.

SRI and BRRI. 2010. *System of Rice Intensification (SRI)*. Gazipur: Bangladesh Rice Research Institute (BRRI). http://sri.ciifad.cornell.edu/countries/bangladesh/BD_Natl_SRI_Workshop_2010.pdf

World Bank. 2008. *World Development Report - Agriculture for Development*. https://siteresources.worldbank.org/INTWDR2008/Resources/WDR_00_book.pdf

Photo 2.1: BRAC worker showing 'porgacha' (parasitic) plant to a farmer for ensuring optimum hybrid rice seed production

Photo 2.2: The smile after a good harvest says it all

Photo 2.3: Women farmers heading back to work

Photo 2.4: BRAC staff doing hands-on training for women programme participants

Chapter 3

Role of BRAC in Growth and Development of Poultry Sector

S. D. Chowdhury

3.1 Introduction

BRAC played a significant part in Bangladesh's poultry sector development. Although initial efforts for rural poultry development aimed to generate income for poor women, BRAC essentially became a pioneer in the commercial poultry sector by establishing breeder farms, hatcheries, feed mills, and a chicken processing plant in the country, also encouraging others into this business. In this chapter, the activities of BRAC relating to the growth and development of the poultry sector in Bangladesh are presented.

Approximately 20 percent of the protein consumed in developing countries comes from poultry meat and eggs (Alders and Pym 2009). In Bangladesh, the majority of the demand for meat is met by poultry. Such poultry includes mostly indigenous or native birds reared by farmers in small numbers in their households following traditional management systems. Chickens are the principal poultry species (90%), followed by ducks and small numbers of pigeons, geese, and quail (Das et al. 2008; Chowdhury 2013). Farmers in rural households maintain a small flock of chickens or ducks within their homesteads. Female members of the family usually take care of the birds by feeding household waste and crop residue (Saleque 2001; Rahman 1989), in addition to natural feed (green grasses, weeds, insects, small snails, earthworms, etc.) that the birds obtain through scavenging. The main feature of this production system is low input and low output. Nevertheless, it is important for the rural economy.

Poultry rearing in Bangladesh is broadly categorised into three systems: (1) traditional rural backyard scavenging system, (2) semi-scavenging system, and (3) commercial farming, which also includes contract farming. The first two categories fall under family poultry (FP), and the third one is commercial poultry (CP).

Family poultry (FP) production in Bangladesh comprises of the rearing of free-range scavenging chickens and ducks of indigenous origin, with or without feed supplementation; various cross-breeds, particularly a cross-breed of Egyptian Fayoumi hens and American Rhode Island Red (RIR) cocks known locally as *Sonali*; small-scale commercial broilers; cockerels from layer strains; and commercial layers reared in confinement and provided with commercial feeds (Chowdhury 2013). Most of the inputs for FP production, including labour, are supplied from the homestead, and the poultry is either consumed at home or sold locally for cash income. FP is not location-bound, and it includes small flocks of poultry (usually less than 100) raised in semi-urban and urban areas, as indicated by the International Network for Family Poultry Development (INFPD) in 1997. FP is said to be an indispensable vehicle for promoting a rural economy (Das et al. 2008).

Commercial poultry (CP), on the other hand, are broiler and layer birds. Their parents and grandparents are produced commercially by commercial producers and industrialists in confinement and fed commercial feed. Commercial broilers are meant for meat production; commercial layers are for table egg production, while parents and grandparents are reared for hatching egg production for the multiplication of future generations. All such commercial birds belong to high yielding modern strains of chicken. The ratio of FP and CP is not definitely known, but a recent report stated that the national share of eggs from commercial and family poultry was almost equal, and that of meat production was 60:40 (Bhuiyan 2011).

3.2 Growth and Development of Poultry Sector in Bangladesh

Soon after the partition of British India in 1947, six poultry farms were set up by the Government of the then East Pakistan in different locations of the province. The introduction of improved breeds and varieties from abroad, like White Leghorn, Rhode Island Red (RIR), etc., made their multiplication in farms and distribution to rural raisers possible on a small scale. In 1964, a commercial poultry farm named Eggs and Hens Ltd. was established near Dhaka city. After the liberation of Bangladesh in 1971, Biman Bangladesh Airlines set up a commercial poultry farm named Biman Poultry Complex at Savar, Dhaka, to cater to their flying services and transfer commercial farming technology to farmers (Saleque 2009). During the 1980s, the Department of Poultry Science of Bangladesh Agricultural University started an initiative that procured day-old chicks (DOCs) from the Biman Poultry Complex and sold dressed broilers to city hotels in Dhaka and live broilers at local markets in Mymensingh. During the 1980s and the 1990s, NGOs got involved in promoting FP for poor smallholder farmers to develop the poultry sector. BRAC developed a rural poultry model for poor farmers in the early 1980s that stimulated poultry rearing activities in the country. In the early nineties, some newly established private farms started operations to produce commercial broiler and layer DOCs (Saleque 2009). The government also liberalised its policies to encourage the growth of the commercial poultry sector by introducing an easier loan procedure, lower interest rate, and tax holiday for poultry inputs (vaccines, medicines, and feed additives).

A poultry sector study conducted by Chad et al., (2009) showed that there were 110,000 small flock (up to 3000 birds per flock) and medium flock (above 3000 to 20,000 birds per flock) commercial farms across the country. In March 2011, this figure fell to 75,000 following a second outbreak of avian influenza. Small and medium enterprise (SMEs) farms, which are spread all over the country, produce the bulk of commercial broilers and layers. In recent times, industrial producers with established breeder farms (parent stock/grandparent stock farms) are also moving into the commercial sector. Farmers in the SME category are mostly involved in commercial broiler production (90%) with credit support either from middlemen (dealers and agents) or from other organisations (including NGOs). Unfortunately, credit from commercial banks became very limited, particularly during the post-avian influenza outbreak period. It was reported by BRAC (2005) that about 50 percent of the commercial farms had flock sizes of between 100-500 birds. Today, farms of such flock sizes are seldom found among commercial farmers due to economies of scale and modernisation of the poultry enterprise.

According to an estimate by the Department of Livestock Services (DLS), the poultry population in Bangladesh rose to 320.06 million during FY 2015-16, of which 268.4 million were chicken and 52.2 million were ducks (BER 2016). At the end of June 2016, 18,638 layer farms, 53,894 broiler farms, 7,682 duck farms, 207 hatcheries, and 15 grandparent stock farms were registered with the government. The annual average growth rate of the poultry industry (commercial sector) over the past two decades was more than 20 percent in volume terms, and it continues to grow and playa dominant role. Currently, there are about 100,000 small (up to 3000 birds per flock), medium (above 3000 to 20,000 birds per flock),and large poultry farms (more than 20,000 birds per flock) comprising high yielding broiler, layer, and cross-bred *Sonali* birds. According to Huque et al. (2011), the population of *Sonali* birds had been increasing at a rate of 14 million a year and stood at about 150.9 million in 2010, which was about 30 percent of total production. The number of feed mills increased significantly with an increase in the commercial farms in the country. In the poultry industry, the major players are the conglomerates, which are leading business firms. Global leaders in the poultry and feed industry have also entered into the Bangladesh poultry sector. These include CP Foods from Thailand and New Hope from China. Table 3.1 summarises information on the commercial poultry sector.

Data obtained from the Bangladesh Economic Review, Ministry of Finance, 2013-2014 and the 7th Five Year Plan 2016-2020 indicate that production of total meat was 103 g/person/day and that of eggs was 70 per person per year during 2014-2015. It was found that more than 50percent of the demand for meat in the country is supplied from poultry, and per capita broiler meat consumption in Bangladesh appeared to be 3.74kg (Table 3.1). BER (2015) stated that the projected meat supply would be 110 g/person/day, and the projection for eggs would be 95per person per year during 2020-2021. About 8 to 10 million people are dependent on the poultry sector for their livelihood, either directly or indirectly (Mandal and Khan 2017),of whom 40 percent are assumed to be women. The investors are now preparing to explore the export potential for their produce.

Despite variations in the data from different sources like BBS, BER, WPSA-BB, and DLS regarding demand, production, and availability of poultry products (meat and eggs), there is a general agreement that the country needs to increase output not only to meet increased domestic consumption but also to explore export possibilities in the near future.

Table 3.1: Commercial poultry sector in Bangladesh: Facts and figures

Item	Figures
No. of GP farms in operation	6
Production of parent, stock /week	60,000-70,000
No. of breeder farms	140
Production of broiler DOCs, million/week	11
No. of feed mills	120
Proportion of major suppliers of poultry feed, % of total feed mills	10
Production of industrial feed, million tons	3.05
No. of commercial farms	100,000-120,000
Production of commercial layer eggs, million/day	20
Per capita broiler meat consumption, kg	3.74
Share of broiler meat out of total meat consumption, %	54
Expected per capita poultry meat consumption in 2020, kg	8.42
Expected contribution of poultry meat in 2020, %	78

Source: www.wpsa-bb.com/poultry-at-a-glance

In the commercial poultry sector, some of the industrial producers have been vertically integrated. They operate hatchery, broiler, and layer units, and a few of them are also involved in poultry processing, feed production, nutrition, and disease diagnostic laboratories. The commercial sector is facing continuous challenges such as price fluctuation of DOCs, high feed cost, prevalence of wet market (*market* selling fresh meat, *fish*, and other produce), unplanned growth of poultry farms, involvement of middlemen in marketing, weak bio-security, and the threat of epidemic diseases. Because of these challenges, the small-scale and medium-scale commercial broiler and layer farms that were meant for poverty reduction and rural employment generation are now decreasing gradually. Instead, the industrial sector is gradually picking up to run commercial broiler and layer farms in addition to maintaining breeder farms, hatcheries, and feed mills. Because SME production costs are always higher, farmers belonging to SMEs often fail to compete with large-scale producers and incur losses. As a result, SME farmers are dropping out of the market. Considering the importance of livelihood opportunities for SME farmers and those employed by them, this problem needs to be addressed by the government and by private sector actors.

3.2.1 Key factors, constraints, and issues in the poultry sector

A number of key factors, constraints, and issues in the poultry rearing sector have prevailed since 1971, many of which are still of concern to producers and policymakers. Some of these are described in the following paragraphs.

Traditional poultry rearing and management system

Rearing and management of poultry by rural households traditionally followed the low input-low output system. Scientific rearing and management of rural poultry was lacking.

Low productivity of the local hens

Local poultry are reared by rural people following a scavenging system supplemented by household waste and crop residues. Local hens produce 40 to 60 eggs per year and local ducks produce 60 to 80 eggs per year. Thus, productivity of local poultry is low enough for the commercial sector to venture in and meet the growing demand for meat and eggs in the country.

Unavailability of own breed/variety/strain of chicken and duck at rural level

High yielding exotic breeds/varieties/strains of poultry are not adaptable to the rural scavenging and semi-scavenging system of rearing because they need improved feeding and management and a well-planned bio-secured environment (Chowdhury 2013). On the other hand, indigenous poultry, although adapted to local conditions and resistant to many diseases, are low producers of eggs and meat. Improved breed/

variety/strains of birds are unavailable at the rural level. This situation demanded a type of bird well adapted to harsh conditions and able to produce well under scavenging or semi-scavenging systems, but the fact was that the country had not yet developed such a breed/variety/strain of chicken or duck (Fattah 2005).

Unavailability of some feed ingredients and problems of feeding

For optimal productivity, high yielding poultry need improved feeding. The government poultry farms were not in a position to support feeding in rural areas either quantitatively or qualitatively. This was because of a shortage of major feed ingredients in the country, particularly corn, which constituted approximately 50 percent of the poultry diet. In addition, the country is still dependent on the import of other ingredients for feed formulation like soybean meal, protein concentrate, vitamin-mineral premix, feed-grade amino acids, and various feed additives.

High mortality of scavenging birds and inaccessibility of village women's flocks to health and veterinary care

The diseases that affected scavenging poultry during the 1980s and 1990s were Newcastle Disease, Fowl Pox, Fowl Cholera, Fowl Typhoid, Coccidiosis, nutritional deficiency diseases, and worm infestation. Mortality was high (35-80%), particularly for baby chicks, due to diseases and predators. Although Bangladesh produced four types of vaccines, the village women who reared poultry were had limited access due to the lack of an effective service delivery system and improper transportation, preservation, and use of vaccines. Thus, shortage of vaccines and inadequate healthcare services for rural poultry were the constraints to survivability (Fattah 2005).

Inadequate and inefficient delivery system of Government Live-stock Services

Government institutions are generally responsible for the delivery of support services in rural areas, but these were neither adequate nor efficient to assist poor landless farmers. Fattah (2005) opined that the lack of infrastructure beyond upazila headquarters, weak extension services, and lack of quality-control facilities for essential inputs were constraints on sustainable rural poultry development.

Inaccessibility of formal credit to women

One of the major ways to improve the economic condition of a rural household is to ensure access to credit (Rahman 1989; Saleque 1996). Rural households, in general, and the landless poor, in particular, had very little access to credit. Rahman (1989) stated that only 7 percent of the landless and 14 percent of the rural households had access to institutional credit in the late 1980s. Fortunately, the situation has changed since the 1990swith many microfinance organisations (including BRAC) increasing their services to women in rural areas.

Lack of an organised marketing system

The marketing mechanisms for both FP and CP are not well organised. The traditional marketing system allows the flow of live birds and eggs from farmers to consumers through middlemen. The middlemen in the marketing channel are brokers/agents, wholesalers, and retailers. Farmers usually sell their products to the broker/agent at the farm gate. They have little or no alternatives. In this traditional system, the farmers are normally deprived of fair prices; often, they incur losses. A value chain analysis conducted by Chad et al. (2009) showed that when the farmers purchased broiler chicks from dealers at BDT 38, the production cost of per kg live broiler rose to BDT 94, but because of frequent price fluctuations, the farmers sold their finished broiler in the range of only BDT 80-100 per kg.

3.3 Evolution of the BRAC Poultry Development Programme: An Overview

BRAC was the pioneer of both family poultry (FP) and commercial poultry (CP) production in Bangladesh. In this section, BRAC's initiatives in the growth and development of the poultry sector in Bangladesh are presented. BRAC moved into poultry development as a conduit for employment and income generation for the rural poor. It targetedlandlessdestitutewomen,evolvedapoultrydevelopmentmodel for them, and successfully implemented it through the involvement of the government, other NGOs, and donor agencies in five large poultry projects. These were: Income Generation for Vulnerable Group Development (IGVGD), the Smallholder Livestock Development Project-I (SLDP-I), the Participatory Livestock Development Project (PLDP), the Smallholder Livestock Development Project-II (SLDP-II), and the Poultry for Nutrition (PFN).Between 1978 and 1982, BRAC's poultry programme had no specific model. Based on field experience, a comprehensive model was initiated and developed by poultry and livestock specialists in 1983 (Hossain et al. 2016). BRAC and DLS decided to work together in Manikganj subdistrict (located west of Dhaka), an area with an unusually high concentration of poor landless people. BRAC established mini poultry farms with about 300 Rhode Island Red (RIR) birds at Savar and 100 birds at Manikganj during 1979-1981. The objective was to produce HYV hatching eggs for distribution to farmers. However, the transportation of hatching eggs over long distances was a challenge.

To encourage cross-breeding with local hens and improve the genetic stock, a "cockerel exchange programme" was initiated by the government in the 1980s through which local indigenous cockerels were replaced by high yielding varieties (HYV). The government supplied HYV cockerels to the people in exchange for local ones. These pure cockerels failed to survive under village conditions. It was then felt that HYV DOCs supplied from government hatcheries might be reared in rural conditions during their early period of growth. In 1984, BRAC opened a few "Chick Rearing Units". DOCs of Fayoumi and RIR were reared for two months in these units after collection from government hatcheries and then distributed to villagers. Soon, the government supply of DOCs became inadequate to meet the growing demand.

In 1985, BRAC introduced the Income Generation for Vulnerable Group Development (IGVGD) programme on a pilot basis, mainly for poultry and livestock development, in Manikganj and gradually expanded it to other areas. BRAC also included the poultry model in their Rural Credit and Training Programme (RCTP) branches and the Jamalpur women project during 1983-1986, and later on in the Rural Development Programme (RDP) during 1987-2000. Since the government supply of DOCs was inadequate, BRAC decided to meet the demand by producing chicks themselves utilising the "Rice Husk Incubation" technique (simple and appropriate technique for the production of day-old chicks) in 1988. Poultry Key Rearers were selected and given proper training.

To support poultry farming, BRAC procured selected feed ingredients particularly oyster shell, vitamin-mineral premix, dry fish, and *til* oil-cake, none of which were locally available at that time (the late 1980s). BRAC crushed the oyster shells, dry fish, and oilcakes in its small plant and supplied the product to feed sellers in different project areas.

To lessen the high mortality of birds at the rural level, BRAC got involved in strengthening the vaccination system. BRAC discovered that vaccine failure was mostly due to improper handling, transportation, storage, and application. These problems were addressed by recruiting and training educated young village people in vaccination in Manikganj, covering 125 villages (Saleque 2017; personal communication). The mortality of birds was halved from 50 percent to 25 percent. However, frequent dropping-out of the trained youth brought about a change in the policy. Illiterate women in the villages, instead of educated young ones, were recruited to provide vaccination. To overcome the cold chain problem in rural areas, BRAC developed a method of handling and transporting vaccines to remote villages. Ampoules of vaccines supplied by government offices were inserted in ripe bananas, and the bananas were stored in jars containing cold water until distribution for application. This BRAC model of women as vaccinators (poultry workers or PW) was accepted by the government, leading to a change in their policy for the supply of vaccines and vaccination. The government field staff usually did the vaccinations, but due to the non-availability of trained persons, BRAC poultry workers provided the vaccination services.

In 1997, BRAC, in collaboration with Bangladesh Livestock Research Institute (BLRI), studied the potency of vaccines delivered from the central laboratory of the then Directorate of Livestock Services (DLS) to remote villages for application by PWs. The rate of success was 75 to 80 percent. The government issued a circular for all concerned to cooperate with BRAC in its programme for poultry development. The four smallholder livestock development projects, IGVGD, SLDP-I, PLDP, and SLDP-II, were formulated based on this poultry model with some changes in its original structure to make the model more dynamic and effective under rural conditions.

Recognising the demand for DOCs, BRAC decided to set up a commercial poultry farm and feed mill. It also established six hatcheries. In addition to its own production, BRAC also purchased DOCs from four private hatcheries in the early 1990s. Over time, BRAC's poultry operations included all poultry-related value chains and services, namely, poultry farm and hatchery operations to produce high yielding DOCs, feed mills to supply balanced feed, a broiler processing plant to produce ready-to-cook chicken and processed meat, and a poultry disease diagnostics laboratory to facilitate diagnosis of diseases. By doing so, BRAC supported rural poultry farmers in their production and drove the growth of the poultry sector by increasing the supply of high yielding varieties of chicks and processed broiler meat.

To ensure quality feed at affordable prices for the farmers involved in poultry production, BRAC opened its first poultry feed mill in Manikganj in 1996, and then in Nilphamari in 1997, and started to supply mash feed. The mash feed targeted commercial poultry farmers and the breeders who reared chickens for an extended period (usually between 80-90 weeks). BRAC established its third feed mill in Sreepur, Gazipur, in 2000, which produced pellet feed for chicken, fish, and cattle farmers. BRAC established a small processing plant in 2001 and then, based on the increased demand for quality meat, it set up a modernised plant in 2004 to meet the growing demand for dressed chicken in large metropolitan areas.

According to a report updated on 30 June 2015[1], BRAC poultry farms had a capacity of 1.75 million birds per year in 14 sheds in which there were 80 employees, of which 60 were female. BRAC chicken had a daily processing capacity of 16 MT dressed chicken (raw) and 17 types of two metric ton ready-to-cook frozen chicken. BRAC's yearly production of poultry feed was 40,000 MT in two production plants (Manikganj and Sreepur), where 116 employees were employed, of which 70 were female.

The BRAC poultry farms, feed mills, and chicken processing plants were established as programme-support enterprises and were renamed social enterprises in 2007. Previously, BRAC usually sold the DOCs

---

1 See www.brac.net/visitors

and feed directly to its targeted rural farmers. However, in 2005, BRAC delivered chicks and feed to 250 dealers around the country who, in turn, sold to the farmers.

3.4 The BRAC Poultry Development Model

In 1983, BRAC designed a specific model for poultry development based on its practical experience. The Bangladesh poultry model developed jointly by BRAC and DLS (also known as BRAC-DLS model) got recognition from the Bangladesh Government and eventually became a major development innovation. The belief that the relief-dependent rural poor could be engaged to undertake income-earning activities, starting only with a few chickens, was the basic foundation of the poultry model (Islam and Jabbar 2005). The model comprised of integrated package support to rural women. It was based on semi-scavenging poultry flocks reared under partly controlled management, where the scavenged feed accounted for a significant part of the total feed consumption. The integrated system provided supplies, services, and production components to establish and maintain a semi-scavenging poultry sector. The supply line consisted of DOC, feed, vaccines/medicines, and marketing assistance, and the service line was comprised of group formation, training, credit facilities, and extension services. Poultry workers, key rearers, chick rearers, feed sellers, model rearers, and poultry hatchers were the production components. The strategy behind the model was to establish an "enabling environment" at the village level, in which several small income-generating activities, operated by the model beneficiaries, constituted the production, supply, and marketing aspects (Jensen 1998). The main feature of the model was that the supply of inputs and services were turned into income-earning opportunities for poor people. The focus was on poverty reduction, rather than on increasing the supply of eggs and poultry meat (Dolberg 2003). The basic features of the model (Saleque and Mustafa 1996) are described in the following paragraphs.

3.4.1 Focus on women

Gender is a major focus in development, and poultry is a starting point to reach poor women (Islam and Jabbar 2005). The ownership of village poultry is entirely in the hands of women, and this is an asset over which they have some control. Poultry rearing could therefore play an important role in poverty alleviation and empowerment of women, which were the main goals of BRAC. BRAC's poultry development programme aimed at providing women with an entry point to diversify income-earning and employment opportunities. There were few or no job opportunities for landless and disadvantaged women. Poultry husbandry was an activity where many of them could participate. Therefore, BRAC's model for poultry development was primarily targeted at landless rural women. The women were involved in a chain of activities as vaccinators, hatchery operators, chicken rearers, feed sellers, producers of hatching eggs and producers of eggs for the market. Credit and marketing were integrated into the model. By doing so, considerable positive impacts in terms of income and household egg and meat consumption were noticeable.

3.4.2 Selection of beneficiaries

BRAC selected its beneficiaries for different categories of poultry activities. It organised poor and landless women into groups through programmes like its rural development programme.

3.4.3 Training of women

BRAC provided different types of training to selected rural women in poultry rearing and management.

- *Poultry Workers*: One female group member, selected from each village, was given five days' training in poultry rearing, management, vaccination, and treatment. The selected women had the physical capacity, enthusiasm, and reputation and acceptability within the community. Such poultry workers were given the responsibility to vaccinate and treat birds in their respective villages. The poultry workers attended one-day refresher courses once a month. They were supplied with vaccines and medicines twice a month to perform their duties.
- *Key Rearers*: Key rearers were given three days' training on the ideal methods of poultry rearing. Each key rearer had a good housing system to keep one HYV cock and ten hens (4-5 were HYVs).

- *Chick Rearers*: Chick rearers were given seven days' training. They reared 200 chicks from day-old to two months old and sold them to key rearers. The chick rearers were supplied with DOCs from government farms, BRAC farms, and the poultry hatcheries.
- *Feed Sellers*: One feed sales- centre was established in each area. Poultry feed producers received three days of practical training on feed preparation. Locally available feed ingredients were procured and utilised for feed preparation under the close supervision of BRAC. Later, some producers also became feed sellers. People were gradually accustomed to buying balanced feed, with the spread of HYV birds in the area.
- *Model Rearers (Breeders)*: They received three days' advanced training on poultry rearing and management. They maintained 22 HYV hens and 3 cocks to supply hatching eggs to the poultry hatcheries.
- *Poultry Hatchers*: Five small hatcheries with 5000 DOC capacity per month were established in each area. The rice husk method of incubation was practiced. Hatcheries purchased hatching eggs from model rearers and made a remarkable contribution in meeting the increasing demand for DOCs in the area.

BRAC also added two other categories in early 2000. These were broiler rearers and cage rearers/layer rearers.

- *Broiler Rearers*: They reared 100-200 day-old broiler chicks up to 6 weeks and sold them in the local market. The size of farms increased gradually with increased local demand.
- *Cage Rearers/Layer Rearers*: They first reared 36-100 pullets from 8 weeks until maturity and then up to 70 weeks for egg production. The size of these farms also increased gradually based on local demand.

Both broiler and layer rearers were chosen from upgraded key rearers who were interested in taking up these jobs. These attempts shifted farmers from subsistence to commercial operations and stimulated other people in the community to start poultry businesses.

3.4.4 Input supply

BRAC implemented the poultry development model by strengthening the supply of inputs to the different categories of poultry activities through the following actions.

- BRAC distributed DOCs to chick rearers from the government farms of the DLS. It also assisted in the distribution of DOCs produced by the rice husk hatcheries. The breeds of chicken included were Fayoumi, White Leghorn, and Rhode Island Red.

  Two-month-old chicks were sold from rearing units to the key rearers by BRAC or union parishad offices. After 1995, in addition to government supply, DOCs were also supplied from BRAC's farms and private farms. BRAC supplied feed ingredients like fishmeal, sesame oil cake, vitamin-mineral premix, etc., to the feed sellers at cost price to mix with other locally available raw materials, thus ensuring the production of complete feed. The feed sellers sold one ton of feed per month.
- Vaccines were supplied by the government and distributed by government staff to the vaccinators (poultry worker), free of charge. But the poultry workers charged a small vaccination fee to the farmers as service charge.
- Medicines were supplied by BRAC at cost price each month to poultry workers. BRAC initially gave each poultry worker BDT25 (equivalent then to USD 1)as a revolving fund to buy and sell medicines. Eggs were collected by egg collectors and marketed in the nearby towns or market areas. The smallholders also sold their eggs and chickens in the village.

3.4.5 Credit facilities

BRAC's poultry development model was backed by credit facilities for the women. BRAC provided credit as initial investment capital to start chick-rearing, feed-selling, egg-collection, and hatcheries. The credit component of the model followed a group approach in which a group consisted of five credit beneficiaries, and a village organisation (VO) was formed with eight such groups. A BRAC Programme Assistant was the contact person responsible for providing technical poultry extension services and loan collection. The credit funds under PLDP and SLDP-II were channelled from ADB through a semiautonomous apex micro-financing organisation, the Palli Karma-Sahayak Foundation (PKSF), to the NGOs registered as partners of PKSF. The Directorate of Relief and Rehabilitation (DRR) and the World Food Programme (WFP) provided the IGVGD loan fund, and BRAC provided funds for RDP. BRAC's credit facilities helped the women to solve the constraints they faced at that time, and thus had a direct influence on income generation by increasing production.

3.4.6 Phases of the poultry development model

Available reports indicate that the early evolution of the poultry development model began in the late 1970s when BRAC identified poultry as a potential source of income for rural women. BRAC's efforts to develop a poultry programme underwent continual changes and fine tuning over the time. There were three phases of this endeavour: formative, development, and replication.

Formative phase

This was the initial phase of the model comprising

- an "action research plan" in 1970
- a "cockerel exchange programme" during the 1980s
- development of the Bangladesh Semi-scavenging Poultry Development Model in 1980
- strengthening of the vaccination programme to reduce mortality, introduction of IGVGD programme in 1985
- inclusion of the model in the Rural Credit and Training Programme (RCTP) during the years 1983-1986
- the RDP in 1987

A brief account of all these activities was given in Section 3.0.

Development phase

In this phase, further development and expansion of the model occurred. The model was accepted as viable and replicable after an extensive evaluation by the DLS. Positive results were generated in terms of increased income for women, a reduction in bird mortality, and an increase in bird population when the model was practiced in 54 area offices of 32 *thanas* (now upazilas) between 1985 and 1987. In 1987, BRAC's experience in poultry development was incorporated in the relief programme for destitute women operated by the Ministry of Relief and Rehabilitation (MRR) in collaboration with the WFP. In spite of efforts for poultry development at the grassroots level, it was found in 1988 that the income earned by the rearers was very low. Because of financial constraints, the participants could buy only one or two HYV birds, preventing the development of cross-breeds and improved productivity. This led to the introduction of a credit support system by BRAC for poultry rearing in late 1988. The credit operation was also scaled up to support this programme. Provision of training and credit allowed women to become chick rearers, key rearers, or poultry workers and offered them the prospect of an income at least equivalent to the value of their food ration when their period under the scheme drew to an end (Dolberg et al. 2002).

In 1990, a new category called model rearers was created in an effort to improve the supply of chicks. These model rearers raised parent birds in complete confinement to produce fertile eggs for hatching. Other group members were provided with additional training to establish mini-hatcheries. From its inception up to 2007, the introduction of model rearers created employment opportunities for more than 1.5 million poor and marginal farmers (Saleque 2007).

Unfortunately, BRAC realised that the chicks produced from this arrangement were inferior in quality to those produced from the larger-scale operations. At the same time, the hatcheries of DLS farms were not in a position to supply large volumes of required chicks. Although funding from SLDP-I included $ 2.93 million to improve, expand, and operate DLS farms, these farms could not perform as planned because of limitations in management capabilities (Dolberg et al. 2002). To overcome this, BRAC decided to increase its production capacity. BRAC operated six poultry farms and hatcheries around the country in which it produced about 850,000 DOCs per month. BRAC established a disease diagnosis laboratory in Gazipur with the capacity to perform germ culture to detect specific diseases, rapid serum plate agglutination tests to identify antibodies, and culture sensitivity tests to assist in selection of appropriate treatments, together with post-mortem facilities. BRAC introduced cage and broiler rearing during early 2000.

BRAC also realised that the feed prepared by the feed sellers was not always of a sufficiently high standard. Therefore, it established feed mills in Manikganj and Nilphamari to carry out large scale production. By 1999, the annual production of feed from these two mills reached 10,715 MT. Another feed mill with a capacity of 42,000 MT was opened at Gazipur in 2000. With these new arrangements, the former feed sellers (feed formulators) were converted into feed distributors. A feed analysis programme was included to assess feed quality and the presence of harmful aflatoxin.

Replication phase

When the pilot Bangladesh poultry model proved to be a success, it was widely replicated during 1985-1992. It was accepted by the government and major donors like DANIDA, IFAD, World Bank (WB) and ADB for replication through development projects over the period 1992-2003.

BRAC expanded the poultry model as an income generating activity for the poor in all IGVGD areas in partnership with the government and WFP. It was replicated through different projects like IFAD/DANIDA sponsored SLDP-I, SLDP-II, PLDP-I, PLDP-II, and Poultry for Nutrition (PFN) Projects during the 1990s. Apart from BRAC, two large NGOs, Proshika and Swanirvar Bangladesh, were involved in the implementation of SLDP-I. Under PLDP and SLDP-II, ten NGOs, including the three large ones involved in SLDP-I, participated in the implementation along with DLS. A number of other agencies found the model an innovative and attractive intervention for income generation for poor women in the rural areas (Hossain et al. 2016). In 1998, ADB/DANIDA sponsored SLDP and the model was successfully applied in 380 of 460 upazilas in Bangladesh.

BRAC undertook massive poultry activities during the period 1990-2000. A large number of poor and landless women were trained and developed through different projects. Table 3.2 shows the number of trained personnel who contributed to the growth of poultry programmes during 1990-2000.

Table 3.2: Trained personnel during 1990-2000 for the growth of poultry programme

Name of participants	1990	1995	1999/2000
Poultry Worker/Vaccinator	3,541	30,135	41,228
Chick Rearer	650	8,453	14,723
Key Rearer	56,664	502,906	1,190,490
Model Rearer		7,761	11,195
Egg Collector	2,225	2,354	2,798
Hatcherer	327	955	1,349
Feed Seller	24	2,500	2,450
Cage Rearer		50	5,000
Broiler Rearer			1,000

Note: Out of the 41,228 trained poultry workers and vaccinators, BRAC selected 19,900 and upgraded them to advanced poultry vaccinators.

Source: Saleque (1999).

The components and linkages in the poultry model at the start of the implementation of SLDP-I are shown in Figure 3.1.

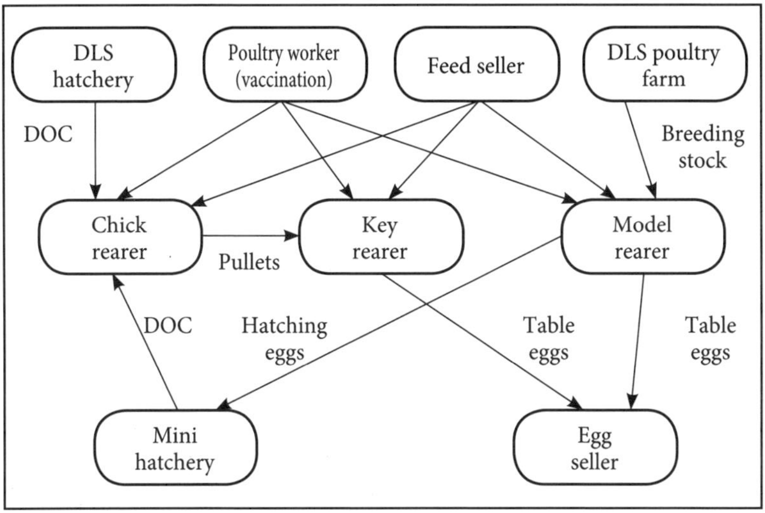

Figure 3.1: The Bangladesh Poultry Model in SLDP I (Dolberg et al. 2002)

During SLDP II and PLDP, the model was refined and further developed. The components and its changes are shown in Table 3.3.

Table 3.3: Refinement and further development of the Poultry Model in PLDP and SLDP II

Component	SLDP I	PLDP and SLDP II
Key Rearer	10 exotic hens and 1cock of different breeds	5 exotic hens of the Sonali breed, with no cock
	Local desi hens only used to generate income prior to production by exotic hens	4 desi hens used to brood and hatch fertile eggs from Model Breeders.
	No programme for rearing chicks	Chick rearing system involving feeding and "polo" shelter
	Semi-scavenging system not fully understood	Choice system to allow hens to choose own feed supplements
	Chickens only	ducks included in SLDP-II
Model Breeder	No specific exotic breed	Fayoumi hens and RIR cockerels
	20 hens plus 3 cockerels	54 hens plus 6 cockerels
	Birds kept on floor system	Macha (raised floor) system used
	Hatching eggs sold in open market or to mini-hatcheries	Hatching eggs sold to Key Rearers or to mini-hatcheries
Chick Rearer	Birds kept on floor system	Macha (raised floor) system used
	Males and females reared together	After one month, sexes separated for better feeding and management
Mini-hatchery	Used for chicken eggs	Less emphasis on mini-hatchery, and in SLDP-II, dropped entirely except for duck eggs
Poultry Worker	No provision for credit	Credit could be provided
Egg Seller	Sold both hatching and table eggs	Sold table eggs only
	No provision for credit	Credit can be provided
Feed Seller	No change	No change

An important change in the model was the focus on *Sonali* (Rhode Island Red X Fayoumi) hens which was proven to be the most appropriate breed through on-farm research in SLDP-I. BRAC was interested in another hybrid named Nera imported from Holland which supposedly performed well under the semi-scavenging system of rearing. However, Nera was not a part of the research trial in SLDP-I.

During an early assessment of poultry in Challenging the Frontiers of Poverty Reduction- Targeting the Ultra Poor (CFPR/TUP), Dada and Matin (2003) documented the evolution of the Bangladesh poultry model over different phases (Table 3.4).

Table 3.4: The evolution of the Poultry Model: Different phases

Phase	Period	Activity	Agents involved
Phase 1	1983 – 85	A first test of the model was undertaken in cooperation with the government's Directorate of Livestock Services (DLS) in Manikganj	BRAC, DLS
Phase 2	1985 – 87	Application was scaled up to 32 upazilas (formerly called Thanas) through BRAC's Rural Development Programme (RDP) and the Jamalpur Women's Project.	BRAC, DLS
Phase 3	1987 onwards	Model was applied to IGVGD programme	WFP, DLS BRAC
Phase 4	1993 – 98	In SLDP, the model was introduced on a large scale to 400,000 women with credit support as a major component.	IFAD, DANIDA, BRAC
Phase 5	1998 -2002	The PLDP, similar to the SLDP, was initiated.	ADB, DANIDA, BRAC
Phase 6	2002 -onwards	The model was applied, after some changes, to the CFPR/ TUP programme as well as poultry programme under BRAC International.	BRAC

Source: Dada and Matin, 2003; Saleque, 2017, personal communication.

3.4.7 Scaling up BRAC's innovations

A number of BRAC's R&D innovations got traction and were eventually scaled up to increase poultry productivity resulting in income generation for landless women. The framework for rural poultry development in Bangladesh was developed through a long "learning-by-doing" process (Jensen 1999). Two actors were involved in developing this process: BRAC and the government through the DLS. IGVGD, a new social-safety-net model was developed jointly by BRAC, GoB, and WFP. An innovative intervention to reach the extreme poor, it was replicated through SLDP, PLDP and PFN. The results were promising and other development programmes were built on the same concept subsequently.

The excessive mortality of chicks at the village level was reduced by developing an effective country-wide method of preservation and transportation of vaccines and by training rural women. The credit system introduced in late 1980s was effective in supporting poultry production and the recovery rate of such credit was satisfactory, indicating that the beneficiaries were able to utilise loans profitably. Since 1999, the Network for Smallholders Poultry Development has promoted agricultural sector programmes with the assistance of DANIDA, IFAD, and other agencies in adopting modified versions of the poultry model in many countries of the world, including Ethiopia, India, Swaziland, and Tanzania.

Many scholarships were awarded by the Danish Smallholder Poultry Network and SLDP to provide training at home and abroad to persons at MSc/MS levels so that these degree-holders could contribute to future training for gearing up smallholder livestock development in Bangladesh. They are now qualified to serve in different disciplines of poultry science and are contributing significantly to the country's private and public sectors.

BRAC, as a partner of South Asia Pro-Poor Livestock Policy Programme (SA PPLPP), coordinated and represented the stakeholders of Bangladesh for the facilitation of pro-poor ideas for poultry rearing. SA PPLPP was a joint initiative of two large reputed organisations namely, the National Dairy Development Board, India, and FAO. It was established in 2006 with the objective of facilitating and contributing to the development of pro-poor livestock policy and programme implementation in Bangladesh, Bhutan, and India (SA PPLPP 2017). SA PPLPP's interventions in these countries were implemented through its programme partners—BRAC in Bangladesh, DLS in Bhutan, and BAIF Development Research Foundation in India. BRAC has documented some of its success stories as GOOD Practices (GPs) on the website of SA PPLPP[2].

3.5 BRAC's Role in Addressing the Key Factors of Poultry Rearing

In the past, considerable efforts were made by BRAC to develop both FP and CP with the objective of poverty alleviation through employment

2 www.sapplpp.org

and income generation, particularly of poor landless women. BRAC considered that poultry rearing was suitable for widespread implementation as it was low cost, highly productive, required little skill, and could be incorporated into the household work schedule. The important factor that contributed to BRAC's transformation was its capacity to learn through trial and error (Saleque and Mustafa 1996).

BRAC has addressed the key factors and issues of the poultry rearing sector from time to time since independence and thus accelerated the process of commercialisation. Over the last four decades, it coordinated its activities with those of the Government of Bangladesh (GoB). The key factors and issues addressed by BRAC are described in the following paragraphs.

3.5.1 Productivity enhancement

BRAC distributed hatching eggs and DOCs/ducklings of exotic breeds to rural areas to develop local birds. Although BRAC's attempt helped in increasing production of poultry and in generating income of rural households, there were some problems of adaptation in the rural areas.

3.5.2 Birds for rural farmers: The Sonali

There was need for a type of bird which would be well adapted to harsh local conditions and could produce well under the scavenging or semi-scavenging system of rearing. Unfortunately, no such national breed/variety/strain was developed. The DLS produced *Sonali*, a cross between RIR male and Fayoumi female, which showed high performance in the semi-scavenging system. Among various breed combinations tested by DLS, *Sonali* had highest egg production and lowest mortality (Akhtar-uz-Zaman 2002). BRAC patronised it for rural development through different projects and programmes such as PLDP, SLDP, IGVGD and RDP. *Sonali's* success created an important source of cash income for poor rural families, particularly for women, and also protein for the nation. But the main challenge was that the breeding stock was not properly maintained (Saleque and Apu 2013). Furthermore, the cross-breed was localised in some northern districts of Bangladesh and the parent stock was not pure enough to be treated as a true representative of *Sonali*. These birds are mostly produced and sold for meat production as indigenous chicken since the colour of birds resembled those of local chicken. This bird is now available all over Bangladesh, and strangely, this is locally called 'Pakistani chicken'.

3.5.3 Better feed ingredients

BRAC imported essential poultry feed ingredients like dry fish, *til* oilcake, oyster shell, vitamin-mineral premix, etc., because there was no supply of appropriate chicken feed in the market (Smillie 2009).It also developed feed sellers at the rural level to increase farmers' access to feed for their poultry. Since1996, balanced feed has been manufactured by BRAC in feed mills and supplied to farmers through dealers. Maize is one of the major feed grains for poultry, constituting about 50 percent of the total commercial poultry feed. The poultry sector was wholly dependent on imported maize. BRAC pioneered maize production in the country (See Chapter 2 for details), thereby reducing dependence on imported maize.

3.5.4 Reduction of mortality of scavenging birds

BRAC developed a service delivery system and an effective transportation and preservation method to retain the potency of vaccine until its application in remote areas. BRAC also provided training to selected vaccinators who actively worked to reduce mortality of village poultry flocks significantly. It trained about 19,900 poultry vaccinators who provided vaccination services, extension services, and disease surveillance in remote areas of the country. Vaccinators were self-employed and charged market rates from poultry farmers for their services (Ciamarra and Dhawan 2010).

3.5.5 Improvement of poultry rearing and management system

The traditional rearing and management system required proper training of rural poultry rearers. BRAC trained poultry rearers (called key rearers) under various programmes and achieved success in motivating rural women to improve the rearing and management of village poultry. BRAC's involvement with IGVGD, RDP, SLDP, and PLDP projects contributed to considerably improving the housing and management of scavenging and semi-scavenging birds. However, starting from 2000,

BRAC focused more on commercial farming and provided training to farmers through its poultry programme support enterprise (PSE), which has since become known as a social enterprise.

3.5.6 Improvement in service delivery system of Government Livestock Services

BRAC collaborated with the government to extend the service delivery system through training and organisation of local human resources. This collaboration paved the way for improvement of the service delivery system, which eventually benefitted the rural farmers engaged in poultry production.

3.5.7 Access of women to formal credit

Realising that formal credit was not accessible to the vast majority of rural women, BRAC launched specialised credit programmes in the early 1980s (Rahman 1989; Hossain and Afsar 1989). As a result, significant progress occurred in the availability of credit, particularly to women in rural areas, through the expansion of commercial banks and nongovernment programmes. BRAC provided credit for the initial investment capital required to start poultry rearing, chick selling, egg collection, and other poultry-related activities (Saleque 1999), and it continues to do so through the BRAC Model Farmers (MF) programme.

3.5.8 Prevention and control of bird flu (Avian Influenza)

BRAC worked with the government, private sector, and NGOs to prevent Avian Influenza before and after its outbreak in Bangladesh through massive interventions. BRAC-trained staff raised the awareness of poultry farmers and improved the bio-security measure in their farms. BRAC handed over 1,000 PPE (Personal Protective Equipment) to DLS for use during stumping out in infected farms. In collaboration with the South Asia Enterprise Development Facility (SEDF) and DLS, it organised a one-day workshop for farmers on bio-security. It distributed disinfectant materials among 4,000 farmers in 20 districts. BRAC employees sprayed disinfectant on all vehicles carrying poultry and poultry products at three locations (Daulatdia, Tongi, and Feni) as part of bio-security measures. BRAC, SEDF, and DLS also jointly provided a one-day training for 11 groups of wet market personnel (traders/sellers) in Dhaka city and distributed hand gloves, bleaching powder, and spray machines as well as distributed more than 50,000 information leaflets to farmers (Saleque 2010).

3.5.9 Development of a marketing system

The development of an organised marketing system, as an improvement over the traditional marketing system needed logistic support from the government, NGOs, and other organisations. BRAC was able to develop egg- collector and marketing facilities for the farmers to ensure fair prices, thus accelerating the growth of layer farming. It was reported that about 2,798 egg collectors were developed (Saleque 1999).Later, it was observed that these egg collectors started to act as traders and bought eggs from the farmers to sell to urban markets.

Das et al. (2008) suggested that farmers should form a coordinating committee to lobby for better prices for their products. The responsibility of such a committee would be to collect information on the supply and demand of poultry meat and eggs in big cities, including Dhaka. A Meat and Egg Coordination Committee with representatives from different stakeholders could also develop a universal, efficient transportation system to minimise cost.

3.6 Research and Development in Poultry

BRAC carried out useful, relevant, and vital R&D activities, the outcomes of which were widely adopted by the beneficiaries. Notable R&D activities are summarised below:

- During the early stage of village poultry development, when no or very limited electricity was available, and ice making and the use of ice was very limited, the practice of preservation and transportation of vaccines to remote villages by inserting them into ripe bananas was introduced. This was a unique, path breaking technique acceptable to the villagers.
- There was a lack of trained vaccinators to support poultry rearing activities. BRAC trained village-based poultry vaccinators as a part of extension services.

- BRAC addressed the scarcity of quality hatching eggs for the multiplication of poultry flocks through the development of model breeder farms to produce hatching eggs.
- The use of sophisticated machines to produce DOCs in the villages was not only expensive but also a challenging task for the farmers. BRAC developed a modified technology for hatching chicken eggs by using the rice husk incubation system, which had previously been practiced only for hatching duck eggs by Friends in Village Development Bangladesh (FIVDB) in Khadimnagar, Sylhet. The rice husk system was an appropriate and cost-effective technology for the production of DOCs and was well accepted.
- The early growth period of HYV chicks up to eight weeks of age was very critical. BRAC's R & D established a Chick Rearing Unit to rear the HYV chicken up to eight weeks, thus preventing early chick mortality.
- BRAC promoted maize cultivation in the country, which helped the commercialisation of poultry production.
- BRAC developed local feed sellers and provided them with low-cost feed formula using locally available feed ingredients for the production of balanced feed when there was no feed mill in Bangladesh. BRAC supplied several essential ingredients (sesame oil cake, oyster shell, vitamin-mineral premixes, fish meal, etc.) to them which, until then, were unavailable locally.

3.7 Success, Challenges and Lessons Learnt

BRAC faced numerous challenges in their work in the poultry sector, learning from what went wrong and what worked, and using the learning to achieve success. With the goal of enhancing the livelihoods of poor rural women through poultry, BRAC aimed to establish a model that would be successful in not only providing chickens, but a feasible way of raising the chickens (Smillie 2009). BRAC-DLS evolved the Bangladesh Semi-Scavenging Poultry Model that became one of the world's best-known tools for reaching out to poor women. Learning based on feedback from the users of this model enabled BRAC to face challenges and succeed in its efforts for poultry development. The

Bangladesh Poultry Model is said to have benefited 3.67 million rural households involving landless, marginal, small, and poor farmers during 1984-2003 to improve their income and livelihoods. It was learned from the implementation of this model that farmers were able to respond successfully and cope with new enterprises if given the opportunity. It was also learned that the training of farmers and the establishment of linkages with inputs and service providers significantly improved the livelihoods of rural women.

An essential institutional part of the Bangladesh Poultry Model was the development of the capacity to reach a large number of beneficiaries and provide them with services at an affordable cost. BRAC took up this challenge and involved a number of international and national agencies and departments. It was successful in creating an "enabling environment" in line with its development strategy.

The intention to transform the village poultry system from a subsistence to an income-generating activity required organisation building and institutional development, particularly for input supply, marketing, group formation, awareness building, training, extension services, and microcredit schemes. It was also a challenge to put into place a system that would enable the poor women rearing chicken to become a part of a larger network. Not only were training and input important, but so also were the links to enable rural women to take part in the system commercially. BRAC accommodated all these activities in its model.

The transformation of a government institution to enable it to act through a non-governmental organisation was an essential but challenging aspect in the institutional development process (Jensen 1998). However, BRAC was able to convince the government through DLS to act in favour of their poultry development model and thereby got the necessary support needed to implement the programme across Bangladesh.

BRAC moved to the commercial poultry sector, firstly to supply broiler DOCs to its project participants and secondly, to explore a business opportunity. BRAC developed the contract-growing system through which it supplied DOCs, credit, and other inputs and bought back live broilers for its broiler processing plant at a predetermined price. The purpose of this system was not only to do business but also alleviate poverty since it targeted smallholders and the poor. It developed alternative mechanisms to promote contract farming as an income-generating activity among smallholders. However, it faced challenges since farmers violated the contracts, particularly when market prices were higher, they sold broilers in the local market instead of selling it off to BRAC. In response, BRAC changed the operational modality and solved the problem by buying the live broiler at market prices instead of a fixed price.

Another challenge arose in BRAC's initiative to improve local indigenous chickens by following the "cockerel exchange programme." Because the supply of HYV cockerels was limited, some farmers sold the high-value HYV cockerels rather than using them for breeding, especially since mortality among HYV cockerels remained high. BRAC's attempt to reduce high mortality and increase bird populations in the villages was successful when it realised that vaccination was an integral part of any intervention to promote poultry rearing and took appropriate action.

Initially, the poultry workers were not accepted by communities that did not believe in the idea illiterate or moderately literate women could do proper vaccinations, but their work was eventually appreciated highly when the poultry rearers and other community people observed positive results from the vaccinations as well as their technical advice. As a result, the poultry workers were recognised as 'poultry doctors' in the community.

The commitment of the implementation and development partners/agencies was found to be crucial for sustainability (Fattah 2005). Continued micro-finance and technical support beyond project closure was also essential for the sustainability of the programme.

3.8 Impact of the BRAC Intervention

The BRAC programme had significant positive impacts on the development of the poultry sector in Bangladesh and also in raising income and improving the livelihood of disadvantaged women who would otherwise excluded from the working sector (Saleque 1999).

3.8.1 Improvement of the poultry sector and the status of women

BRAC's contributions that improved the poultry sector are described below:

- The average number of poultry reared per farm increased to 16 in 1995 and 26 in 1997 in project areas, which was much higher than the national average of 6.8. It was found that about 47 percent of all birds were of the improved types while 53 percent were local. It was concluded that SLDP, in which BRAC played a significant role, has contributed substantially to breed improvement in the areas it covered compared with the national average of only five percent at that time (Alam 1997; Saleque 1999).
- BRAC was able to significantly reduce chicken mortality in rural areas. It developed low-cost techniques of preservation and transportation of vaccines to support poultry rearing in rural areas and thereby prevented vaccine failure. Women were trained and allowed to work as vaccinators. The outcome of this effort yielded positive results in terms of reduction of mortality of chicks from 40-50 percent to 20-25 percent and that of adult chickens to less than 3 percent at the farm level.

  Investment in SLDP activities was found profitable since beneficiaries repaid loans. The average net income per household in 1995 was BDT 427 per month. The highest income of BDT 1047 was reported for mini hatcheries, followed by BDT 761 for chick rearers, BDT 757 for feed sellers, BDT 500 for model rearers, BDT 394 for key rearers, and BDT 265 for poultry workers. The average monthly benefit/cost ratio was 1.5:1 for all farms, the highest for key rearers (3.86:1) and the lowest for feed sellers (1.06:1).It was also reported that participants in the SLDP project were able to increase their income by over 148 percent (Alam 1997). The intake of food by household members increased following the intervention of SLDP because of improvement in the economic condition of beneficiary households. There was a substantial increase in the consumption of eggs of 159 percent per week and that of chicken by 137 percent per annum. Impact surveys showed that 20-30 percent of households had moved above the poverty line within the first year of the implementation of SLDP. This was due to increased earnings of women which made it possible to buy more food and send children to school (Schleiss 1998).

- Involvement of women in poultry development activities improved their relationships with their husbands resulting in an increase of their participation in household decision-making. Sole decision-making of men sharply declined from 21percent in the pre-project period to 2 percent during the project period. The standard of living of the beneficiaries increased considerably after being in the programme with consequent improvement of the woman's position in the family. The socioeconomic status of women within the household also rose.
- Another impact of BRAC's contribution was the improvement of the nutritional status of children under five years of age. According to Khondakar and Chowdhury (1993), the figures for stunting and wasting declined from 74 percent and 22 percent respectively in 1975 to 43 percent and 13 percent in 1991.
- BRAC promoted *Sonali* birds for smallholder farmers in its project areas. This bird is now available as a meat bird in most areas in Bangladesh. According to Saleque and Apu (2013), small-scale *Sonali* bird farming was gaining popularity among the rural farmers and it made an immense change in their livelihoods. A number of hatcheries are producing the *Sonali* DOCs to supply to small and marginal farmers in rural areas. The average net profit per bird was BDT 27, creating an important source of cash income for poor rural families, particularly for women. It was also a good source of protein for the nation. However, a key challenge for the future is to properly maintain the breeding stock.
- BRAC has also stimulated the commercial production of broiler and layer birds by the private sector through setting up its farm and feed mills in the early nineties. Many private sector firms became involved in poultry production after witnessing BRAC's success in the sector. Farms were few in the early 1990s, whereas the currently commercial broiler and layer farms in the

country belonging to SMEs stood at 100,000 to 120,000.Thus, BRAC was a trailblazer.

- Similarly, BRAC started a chicken processing plant to meet the rising demands of processed meat in urban areas. It was one of the largest at that time. Several chicken processing plants were setup by the private sector after they observed that BRAC was successful in this regard.
- BRAC trained many poor and smallholder farmers in rural areas who ultimately shifted from very small operations to commercial operations resulting from increasing demand for commercial layer and broiler birds in the country.

3.8.2 Impact on national policy formulation

BRAC and DLS worked together for poultry development in Bangladesh. DLS was aware of all of BRAC's poultry development activities and extended its full cooperation as and when required. In 2001, the government formed a high powered committee to formulate a national poultry policy. BRAC was one of the committee members. The committee worked at length and formulated a national poultry development policy, which was finalised in 2005 (Das et al. 2008). The policy framework for poultry development included the aspects listed below.

1. Successful pro-poor models would be replicated for semi-scavenging poultry development.
2. Formation of poultry smallholder groups, community-based organisations (CBOs), and producers associations would be facilitated.
3. Quality control of poultry feed and feed ingredients would be ensured through the establishment of a statutory body and enforcement of regulations.
4. Production and consumption of safe meat and eggs would be ensured.
5. Production of organic meat and eggs would be promoted.
6. Criteria and guidelines would be established to ensure the supply of quality DOCs.

7. Specific guidelines would be developed and enforced for establishing environment-friendly commercial poultry farms. Small commercial farms would be converted into profit-oriented large farms following the cooperative system.
8. Poultry farms of the DLS would be utilised as breeding and multiplication farms/centres for smallholder training, technology testing, and demonstration.
9. Smallholder production and marketing of ducks and minor poultry species (e.g., quail, goose, pigeon, guinea fowl) would be promoted in selected areas.
10. The government had already declared BLRI as the National Reference Laboratory for the detection of AI virus and other emerging diseases. It would be strengthened to the international standard.
11. National Avian Flu Preparedness Plan would be implemented.
12. All commercial farms would be registered with DLS.
13. The bio-safety protocol developed by the MoFL should be followed by the concerned stakeholders.

Many items on BRAC's agenda aimed at successful poultry production and income generation were reflected in the national poultry policy.

3.9 Collaborations/Partnerships with Other Stakeholders

In formulating and implementing the BRAC poultry development programmes, some collaborations/partnerships with government, non-government, and private sectors were inevitable. BRAC maintained linkages with different partners/organisations from the onset of its development efforts. These partners/organisations are listed below and is followed by a brief account of their roles.

1. Department of Livestock Services (DLS)
2. Bangladesh Livestock Research Institute (BLRI)
3. Bangladesh Agricultural University, Mymensingh
4. SA PPLPP, a joint initiative of NDDB, India and FAO
5. IFAD, FAO, ADB, DANIDA and other donor agencies

6. Poultry related associations (e.g., WPSA, Breeder Association)
7. SEDF, IFC
8. Related ministries of the government.

BRAC's poultry programme was considered to be a case study in multi-agency action between the state, the aid community, and BRAC (Mustafa et al. 1993). From its inception, the programme was developed in close cooperation with DLS of the Ministry of Fisheries and Livestock (MoFL). Later, the aid community joined hands with DLS and BRAC, firstly the WFP and then IFAD, DANIDA, and the World Bank. The institutional arrangement for poultry development by BRAC had two aspects: (a) the providers' aspect and (b) the implementation aspect. BRAC and DLS worked with the aid community under different arrangements for the programme implementation, with the WFP and the Ministry of Relief and Rehabilitation in one set, and with IFAD and DANIDA in another set. With respect to implementation, the programme was executed by three organisations:

- BRAC implemented the programme through its RDP across the country.
- It implemented the IGVGD programme in collaboration with WFP, the local government (Union Parishad) and the Ministry of Relief and Rehabilitation, targeting specifically destitute women who received food aid from VGD of the government.
- BRAC was a partner in the implementation of the Smallholder Livestock Development Programme (SLDP) sponsored by DANIDA.

During the course of implementation of the poultry development model, there was an organisational support system component that included training in poultry rearing, group formation of target participants, and provision of credit, input, extension, and health services. Many of these required access to DLS.

As mentioned earlier, BRAC collaborated with BLRI to study the potency of poultry vaccines. During the implementation of the Bangladesh Poultry Model, BRAC's collaboration with DLS, WFP, DANIDA, IFAD, and other agencies facilitated changes and fine tuning of the original poultry model by trial and error. A major part of BRAC's collaboration and partnerships occurred during the replication phase of the Model.

There was coordination within BRAC to serve across rural and urban communities. When BRAC started production of commercial chicks and feed, it decided not to supply DOCs directly to individual farmers but through dealers, which led to a more cost-effective supply model. Also, BRAC poultry farms used feed from BRAC Feed Mills. The collaboration among the enterprises, namely BRAC Chicken, BRAC Poultry Rearing Farms, BRAC Poultry, and BRAC Feed Mills created a value-addition chain which allowed BRAC Chicken to sell high-quality processed-chicken products at a fair price.

Through linkages established during implementation of SLDP and PLDP, students were provided research scholarships leading to the award of academic degrees (mostly MS) by universities in Bangladesh and abroad (Denmark).

BRAC partnered with the private sector initially to supply DOCs for its project. It was also actively involved in different poultry-related associations globally (e.g., WPSA, INFPD) and in Bangladesh.

BRAC in partnership with SA PPLPP documented good practices in poultry development and shared the information with multiple stakeholders in Bangladesh and other countries (Saleque 2010).

3.10 BRAC's Role in the Future Development of the Sector

BRAC is positioned to make sustainable contributions to the Bangladesh poultry sector to meet future challenges for increasing poultry meat and egg production and to thus alleviate poverty.

As already mentioned, indigenous poultry, both chicken and duck, are said to be poor producers of eggs and meat. But they are well adapted to local conditions and resistant to many diseases. Today, a section of consumers prefers indigenous poultry to broilers and culled hens because they taste good, are leaner, have better pigmentation, and are suitable for preparing special dishes (Chowdhury 2013). The prices of indigenous poultry are always higher (double or nearly three times more than broiler);egg prices, in general, are slightly higher than those of commercial eggs, although the size of eggs is relatively smaller, except for duck eggs. Research conducted in recent years repeatedly proved that the productivity of indigenous poultry in terms of meat and egg could be improved significantly if scientific interventions are made in respect of nutrition and management (Das et al. 2008; Mia et al. 2016). In light of these research results, BRAC can collaborate with the government and donor agencies to develop the indigenous poultry of Bangladesh to make it more productive. The genetic diversity of Bangladesh native chickens, when compared with exotic breeds/strains, was found to be greater, and such a phenomenon provides an opportunity for poultry breeders to develop a relatively high-producing breed of chicken adapted to the rural environment to support rural poultry programmes. The country is still dependent on exotic strains of chicken to support the industrial production of poultry meat and egg. Every year, scarce foreign exchange is spent on the import of exotic strains. BRAC should direct its efforts to develop at least one boiler and one layer strain for the Bangladesh poultry industry by involving breeders, geneticists, nutritionists, and management and health specialists. In addition, as emphasised by Chowdhury (2013), an improved breed or cross-bred chicken needs to be developed incorporating native germ-plasm suitable for FP production. This is important since government research institutes and universities are currently not in a position to support such efforts in a well-planned and coordinated manner, mainly because of funding constraints. Experts may be hired from universities and research institutes for this purpose.

BRAC recently closed down some of its operations (e.g., poultry hatchery and feed mills) as it felt that it had achieved its development objectives in the sector. The decision was taken due to the establishment of large numbers of poultry hatcheries and feed mills in the private sector. However, the chicken-processing plant and commercial broiler farm are still in operation. BRAC feels that there is still a need for hygienic and standard quality meat to address food safety issues and to meet the growing consumer demand in the current market.

BRAC could still play a significant role in the above development plans because FP, commercial poultry processed meat, and food safety issues are vital at present and are expected to remain so in the coming decades. The need is not only to produce nutritious food in the country but also to explore export potential.

3.11 Conclusion

BRAC has made an extensive contribution to rural poultry development in Bangladesh by bringing landless women into mainstream employment. Its history of engagement in the development of the country's poultry sector spans the last four decades. During this journey from backyard poultry production to commercial hybrid production, it was successful in obtaining cooperation from government, non-government, and international organisations. Lessons learned and experience gathered while implementing poultry development programmes helped it to make the right decisions at the right time, thus promoting rural poultry production and income generation through self-employment and empowerment of women. Although there are success stories in increased rural poultry production, the income increase from poultry appeared to be marginal. However, the development efforts had a positive impact on livelihoods in terms of improving household diets, housing conditions, assets, and the ability to meet at least part of children's educational expenses. Government institutional weakness failed to sustain BRAC's development effort and fully harvest its fruits when donor support ended. Experience with the Bangladesh Poultry Model indicates that it is possible to reach out to rural women and their families if correct interventions are made and government support is continued. The nature of the interventions and how they should be organised will have to be decided in each situation.

A review of evidence on the impact of the smallholder poultry model for poverty alleviation stated that it was possible to reach the poor, though not always the ultra-poor(the main target of the model), and that the participants benefited positively in terms of income, consumption, nutrition, and empowerment of women (Saleque 1999). BRAC made a significant contribution to developing the commercial poultry sector during its early growth stage. Its commercial production of DOCs and feed catalysed the growth of small-scale commercial poultry farming, and consequently, self-employment and income generation of poor farmers. BRAC is continuing its processed meat production and ready-to-consume chicken food items like nuggets, roasts, chicken balls, etc., in the country.

The next logical steps for BRAC would be:

a. To involve and/or influence other national and international agencies to make significant efforts to improve the productivity of indigenous poultry under scavenging and semi-scavenging conditions, while retaining their original germplasm and keeping women in the mainstream.
b. To develop high-yielding commercial broiler and layer strains of chicken and ducks. In this process, emphasis should be given to the active participation of university and research institute scientists.

References

Akhtar-uz-Zaman, M. 2002. "Egg Production Performance of Different Breed/ Breed Combinations of Chicken in Semi-Scavenging System under PLDP." MSc Thesis. Department of Animal Science and Animal Health and Network for Smallholder Poultry Development, the Royal Veterinary and Agricultural University, Denmark and Directorate of Livestock Services, Dhaka, Bangladesh.

Alam, J. 1997. "Impact of Smallholder Livestock Development Project in Some Selected Areas of Rural Bangladesh." *Livestock Research for Rural Development* 9, no. 25. http://www.lrrd.org/lrrd9/3/bang932.htm

Alders, R.G., and R.A.E. Pym. 2009. "Village Poultry: Still Important to Millions, Eight Thousand Years after Domestication." *World's Poultry Science Journal*, 65: 181-190. doi:10.1017/S0043933909000117

Bangladesh: Micro-Finance and Technical Support Project-IFAD, Design Document, Annex-3 Livestock. (unpublished). 2002.

BBS (Bangladesh Bureau of Statistics). 2010. *Statistical Pocket Book of Bangladesh 2010*. Dhaka: Bureau of Statistics, Ministry of Planning, GoB.

——. 2015. *Statistical Pocket Book of Bangladesh 2015*. Dhaka: Bureau of Statistics, Ministry of Planning, GoB.

——. 2017. *Statistical Pocket Book of Bangladesh 2017*. Dhaka: Bureau of Statistics, Ministry of Planning, GoB.

BER (*Bangladesh Economic Review*). 2016. Dhaka: Economic Adviser Wing, Finance Division, Ministry of Finance, GoB.

Bhuiyan, A.K.F.H. 2011. "Implementation of National Livestock Development Policy (2007) and National Poultry Development Policy (2008): Impact on Smallholder Livestock Rearers." Keynote paper presented at the South Asia Pro Poor Livestock Policy Programme (SAPPLP)-BRAC workshop held on 5th April 2011at BRAC Centre Inn, Dhaka.

BRAC. 2005. *Report on Poultry Farms*. Dhaka: BRAC.

Chad, V., S.D. Chowdhury, M.K. Saha, and M.K. Hossain. 2009. *Baseline Surveys and Sector Studies in Agribusiness, Light Engineering and Textiles & Apparels in Bangladesh: Poultry, Final Report*. International Finance Corporation - South Asia Enterprise Development Facility (IFC-SEDF). Dhaka: Associates for Development Services Ltd.

Chowdhury, S.D. 2013. "Family Poultry Production in Bangladesh: Is It Meaningful or an Aimless Journey?" *World's Poultry Science Journal*, 69: 649-675.

Ciamarra, P.U., and M. Dhawan. 2010. "Small Scale Poultry Farming and Poverty Reduction in South Asia: From Good Practices to Good Policies in Bangladesh, Bhutan and India." South-Asia Pro-Poor Livestock Policy Programme (SA PPLPP). http://www.sapplpp.org/files-repository/smallscalepoultryfarmingandpovertyreductioninsa

Dada, A., and I. Matin. 2003. *Poultry against Extreme Poverty: An Early Assessment of Poultry in CFPR/TUP*. Dhaka: Research and Evaluation Division, BRAC.

Das, S.C., S.D. Chowdhury, M.A. Khatun, M. Nishibori, N. Isobe, and Y. Yoshimura. 2008. "Poultry Production Profile and Expected Future Projection in Bangladesh." *World's Poultry Science Journal*, 64: 99-118.

Dolberg, F. 2003. "A Review of Household Poultry Production as a Tool in Poverty Reduction with Focus on Bangladesh and India." Food and Agriculture Organization of the United Nations, Pro-Poor Livestock Policy Initiative, PPLPI Working paper No. 6: 1-34.

Dolberg, F., E. Mallorie, and N. Brett. 2002. "Evolution of the Poultry Model: A Pathway out of Poverty." In *Proceedings of the workshop "People Fight Poverty with Poultry. Learning from Bangladesh Experience."* Dhaka, Bangladesh.

Fattah, K.A. 2005. "Rural Poultry Development in Bangladesh: A Critical Review of Success and Failure." Paper presented at the Third Annual Scientific Conference & Graduation Ceremony, Chittagong Government Veterinary College, March 14-17, 2005.

Hossain, M., and R. Afsar. 1989. *Credit for Women Involvement in Economic Activities in Rural Bangladesh*. Research Report No. 105. Bangladesh Institute of Development Studies, Dhaka, Bangladesh.

Hossain, M., M.S. Islam, S.C. Nath, M.A. Saleque, and M. Hossain. 2016. "Agriculture for Food Security." In *Driving Development: A Story of BRACs Evolution and Effectiveness*, edited by M. Hossain, S. N. Kairy, and A. Bayes, 141-160. Dhaka: UPL and BRAC.

Huque, K.S., M.A. Saleque, and R. Khatun. 2011. "Commercial Poultry Production in Bangladesh." In the *Proceedings of the 7th International Poultry Show and Seminar, March 25-27, 2011*, organised by WPSA-BB, Dhaka, Bangladesh.

Islam, S.M.F. and M.A. Jabbar. 2005. "Smallholder Poultry Model for Poverty Alleviation in Bangladesh: A Review of Evidence on Impact." *Livestock Research for Rural Development* 17, no. 10. https://lrrd.cipav.org.co/lrrd17/10/fakh17112.htm

Jensen, H.A. 1998. "Network for Poultry Production and Health in Developing Countries." In *Women in Agriculture and Modern Communication Technology, Proceedings of a Workshop*, 48-65. Tune Landboskole, Copenhagen, Denmark.

——. 1999. "Structures for Improving Smallholder Chicken Production in Bangladesh: Breeding Strategy." ICAR Technical Series No. 3. *Workshop on Developing Breeding Strategies for Lower Input Animal Production Environments*. Bella, Italy, September 22-25, 1999.

Mandal, M.A.S. and A.L.F.R. Khan. 2017. "Poultry Industry in Bangladesh: Which Way to Sustainable Development?" Keynote presentation at the 10th International Poultry Show and Seminar of the World Poultry Science Association, BICC, Dhaka on 2-4 March 2017. http://wpsa-bb.com/wp-content/uploads/2018/07/Keeynote-paper-10th-Show-17.pdf

Mustafa, S., S. Rahman, and G. Sattar.1993. "BRAC: Backyard Poultry Development and Landless Irrigators Programmes." In *NGOs and the State in Asia: Rethinking Roles in Sustainable Agricultural Development*, edited by Farrington and Lewis. London: Routledge.

Rahman, A. 1989. "Credit for the Rural Poor." In *Institutions (Compendium Volume V), Bangladesh Agriculture Sector Series Review*. Dhaka: UNDP.

The Daily Janakantha. 2017. "Country's Poultry Industry is Fulfilling Cent Percent Demand." (In Bangla). May 1, 2017.

Saleque, M.A. 1999. "Scaling Up: Critical Factors in Leadership, Management, Human Resource Development and Institution Building in going from Pilot Project to Large Scale Implementation: The BRAC Poultry Model in Bangladesh." In *Poultry as a Tool in Poverty Eradication and Promotion of Gender Equity*, edited by Frands Dolberg and Poul Henning Petersen, 51-71. Frederiksberg, Denmark: DSR Forlag.

——. 2001. "Poultry as a Tool in Poverty Alleviation: Special Programme for the Rural Poor in Bangladesh." In the *Proceedings of the 2nd International Poultry Show and Seminar, WPSA Bangladesh Branch*, 66-76.

——. 2007. "An Effective Way to Integrate Small Farmers in the Value Chain: The Experience of BRAC." In the *Southeast Asian Regional Conference on Agricultural Value Chain Financing, Conference Proceedings December 12-14, 2007 Kuala Lumpur, Malaysia*, 51-66. Asian Productivity Organization and FAO.

——. 2009. "Current Status and its Challenges & Opportunity in the Emerging Market Environment." *Poultry Business Directory - 2009*: 13-24. Dhaka: Poultry Khamar Bichitra.

——. 2010. "Livestock and Livelihood-The Role of BRAC in Livestock Development in Bangladesh." Paper presented in the workshop on Review of Livestock Research Programmes and preparation of Future Research, organised by BRAC, Dhaka, Bangladesh.

Saleque, M.A., and A.S. Apu. 2013. "Production and Economic Performance of Small Scale *Sonali* Bird Farming for Meat Production in Bangladesh." In *Proceeding of*

8th International Poultry Show and Seminar, 2013, WPSA Bangladesh Branch, 20-24.

Saleque, M.A., and S. Mustafa. 1996. "Landless Women and Poultry: The BRAC Model in Bangladesh." Paper presented at Development Workers Course: Integrated Farming in Human Development, March 25-29, 1996, at Course Center Tune Landboskole, Greve, Denmark.

SA PPLPP. 2017. *South Asia Pro-Poor Livestock Policy Programme*. http://sapplpp.org/

Schleiss, K. 1998. "The Smallholders Livestock Development Project." In *ACIAR Proceedings*, 140-142.

Smillie, Ian. 2009. *Freedom from Want: The Remarkable Success Story of BRAC, the Global Grassroots Organization That's Winning the Fight against Poverty*. Dhaka: The University Press Limited.

World's Poultry Science Association. *Poultry in Bangladesh: Key Facts & Figures*. https://wpsa-bb.com/poultry at a glance/

Photo 3.1: A poultry worker vaccinating the chicks

Photo 3.2: Poultry rearer taking care of her baby chicks

Photo 3.3: A worker inside BRAC's poultry farm

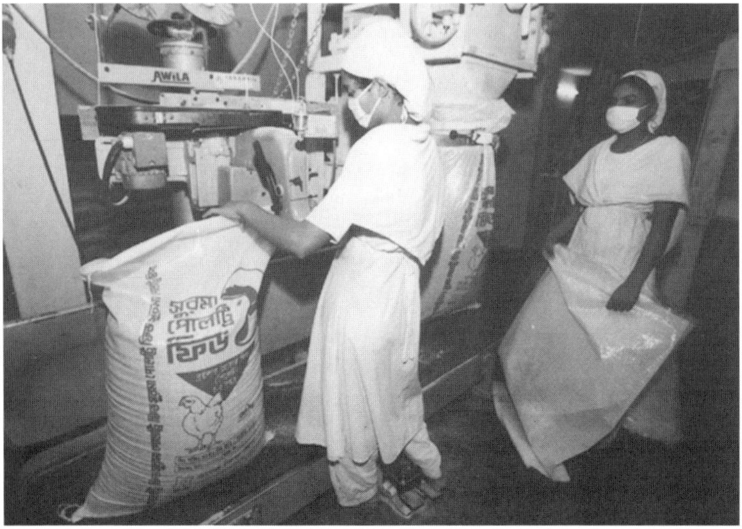

Photo 3.4: Staff working at a BRAC feed mill social enterprise

Chapter 4

Role of BRAC in the Growth and Development of the Livestock Sector

A. K. Fazlul Haque Bhuiyan

4.1 Introduction

Agriculture has been a powerful driver of poverty reduction in Bangladesh, accounting for up to 90 percent of the reduction between 2005 and 2010. More than 70 percent of Bangladesh's population and 77 percent of its workforce live in rural areas. Nearly half of all Bangladesh's workers and two-thirds in the rural areas are directly employed in agriculture and about 87 percent of rural households rely on agriculture for at least part of their income (World Bank 2016).

The livestock sector in Bangladesh is crucial for poverty reduction, nutrition improvement, and women's empowerment (Shahabuddin et al. 2011). Livestock contributes to food and nutritional security and income generation, and it forms an important livelihood base for millions of resource-poor livestock keepers. Rapid population growth, urbanisation, economic growth, and the associated increase in the demand for animal products have presented golden opportunities for expansion of the livestock industry.

Livestock in this chapter refers to and includes cows, buffaloes, goats, and sheep. The poultry sector is covered separately in Chapter 2. Given the protein needs of a rising population, there have been increased investments to increase the production of milk and meat. Despite this, Bangladesh is still deficit in milk and meat production as is illustrated in Table 4.1. The current production of these commodities needs to be at least doubled by the year 2021 in order to feed the country's growing population. Table 4.1 also indicates that although the deficit, as defined by the difference between demand and availability, is narrowing, demand continues to outstrip supply. Bangladesh also exports livestock-related products, including live animals, raw hides and skin, processed leather and leather goods, and in FY2014, these products ranked third in export earnings after the ready-made garments (RMG) and shrimps sectors (GoB 2015).

Table 4.1: Demand, production and availability of milk and meat in Bangladesh

Product	Demand		Production		Availability/head (ml/g)		Deficit (MMT)	
	2001	2016	2001	2016	2001	2016	2001	2016
Milk (MMT)	11.86	14.69	1.78	7.27	37.51	125.59	10.08	7.42
Meat (MMT)	5.69	7.05	0.78	6.15	16.44	106.21	4.91	0.90

Source: DLS, 2016.

The Government of Bangladesh has given top priority to livestock development in recent years to meet the growing demand for milk, meat, and egg production and create employment and generate income for the rural poor. However, on its own, the government was unable to address the needed interventions in the whole livestock sector. NGOs, especially BRAC, also realised the need and opportunities to work in this sector, which the Government appreciated and welcomed. This chapter discusses the contributions of BRAC in taking the livestock sector forward in Bangladesh.

4.2 Trends in Growth and Development of Livestock Sector

The population of the major livestock species comprises 23.79 million cattle, 25.76 million goats, 1.47 million buffalos and 3.34 million sheep (Figure 4.1) (DLS 2016). However, a disaggregated scenario of the growth of livestock in the recent period demonstrates satisfactory growth only for goats/sheep (around 4%); the growth of cattle/buffaloes is highly unsatisfactory with a rate of less than 0.5 percent over the same period (Ali and Hossain 2016). While Bangladesh has a high cattle density, the current production of milk and meat is quite inadequate to meet the current requirement (Table 4.1). The average weight of local cattle is also low, ranging from 100 to 150 kg for cows and from 150 to 250 kg for bulls that are, for example, approximately 25-35 percent kilograms less than the Indian varieties. Milk yields are also extremely low: 200-250 litres during a 10-month lactation period in contrast to 800 litres for Pakistan, 500 litres for India, and 700 litres for all Asia.

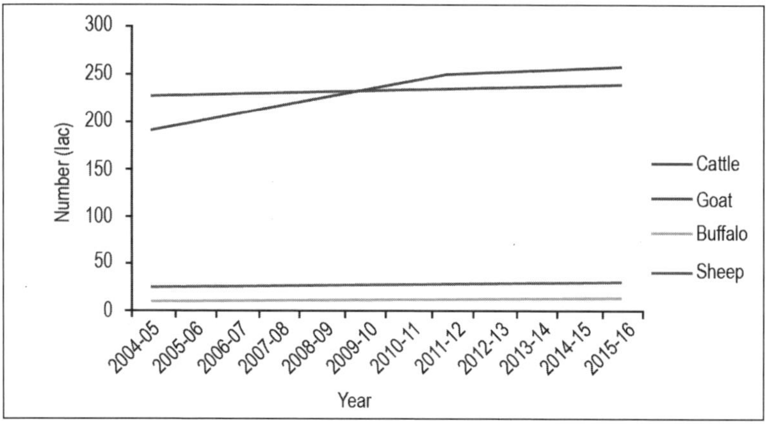

Source: DLS, 2016.

Figure 4.1: Livestock population in Bangladesh (in lac). I lac=100,000

Table 4.2 shows that the contribution of livestock to the national economy has declined over time. Some of the attributes of livestock such as providing employment and fuel remained steady. However, in this regard, Rahman et al. (2014) stated that the livestock sector's actual contribution has been consistently underestimated because the value added in draught power, threshing, sugarcane and oilseed crushing, local transport, dung for cooking fuel, and manure for fertilisation of crop fields were not taken into account.

Table 4.3 shows an increasing trend in the projected demand and supply of milk and meat in Bangladesh in 2020-21 compared to 2014-15 as reflected in the 7th FYP (Five Year Plan). The per capita consumption of all animal products has increased steadily. The rate of increase, however, is not uniform for all products: for meat, the rate of increase is relatively higher, but for milk, it is lower. Among meats, the consumption of chicken/duck has increased substantially, whereas the consumption of beef has declined to some extent during the same period. According to Bangladesh Economic Review (BER), significant differences are also observed between rural and urban areas in respect of consumption of animal products, with the urban areas ahead of the rural. Also, consumption inequality between rural and urban areas is higher for meat products, especially for beef, compared to other products, and such inequality has also increased in recent times.

Table 4.2: Contribution of livestock to the national economy (%)

Attribute	1997-1998	1999-2000	2000-2001	2015-2016
GDP	6.5	3.86	3.12	1.66
Agricultural product	-	12.90	16.13	14.21
Cultivation	95	95	75	75
Employment (full-time)	20	20	20	20
Foreign exchange earning	13	4.31	3.46	3.48
Protein source	20	25	25	25
Fuel	20	25	25	25

Source: DLS 2016.

Table 4.3: The projected demand and supply of milk and meat

Item	The nutritional demand and production (2014-15)		Projected nutritional demand and production (2020-21)	
	Demand	Production	Demand	Target
Milk (million MT)	14.48 (250ml/person/day)	6.97 (122ml/person/day)	15.22 (250ml/person/day)	9.29 (150ml/person/day)
Meat (million MT)	6.95 (120 gm/person/day)	5.86 (102.62 gm/person/day)	7.30 (120gm/person/day)	6.81 (110gm/person /daily)

Source: BER 2015.

The livestock sector currently employs around 20 percent of the rural work force and serves as a major source of protein. About 44 percent of high quality animal protein comes from livestock sources. Over the last five years, since the formulation of the National Livestock Development Policy, Bangladesh has progressed greatly in terms of milk and meat production. Figure 4.2 shows how milk and meat production increased between FYs 2001-02 and 2014-15.

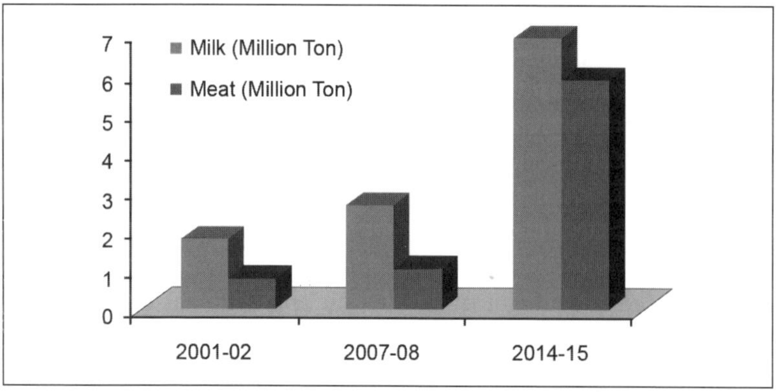

Source: BER 2015.

Figure 4.2: Comparison of milk and meat production over three fiscal years

It is evident from Figure 4.2 that milk and meat growth accelerated during the 6th FYP period (2011-2015). However, while the production of meat registered an impressive growth, the growth of milk production was relatively lower. One possible reason is that sustainable high-yielding dairy breeds or crossbreds are not yet available to farmers coupled with high rearing costs (feed, disease incidence, medicine, long generation interval, etc.).

According to BER (2014-15), the objectives for the livestock sub-sector include:

1. Promotion of sustainable improvements in the animal productivity of milk and meat, including products processing and value addition
2. Promotion of sustained improvements in income generation, nutrition, and employment opportunities for the landless, small, and marginal farmers and women in livestock rearing
3. Facilitation of increased private sector participation and investments in livestock production, livestock services, market development, and export of livestock products and by-products
4. Facilitation of the development of entrepreneurship for commercial livestock production

Both the Bangladesh Agricultural University (BAU) and the Bangladesh Livestock Research Institute (BLRI) conduct research for the development and improvement of the livestock sector. To effectively organise the functional aspects of the activities in the livestock sector, several BRAC technical personnel were educated and trained in various academic institutions, including BAU and BLRI. To encourage the development of livestock resources, the government provided subsidies to farmers who reared crossbred milking cows. The government also provided subsidies for vaccination and artificial insemination programmes. Both growth and target-oriented livestock programmes are being undertaken simultaneously for eradicating rural poverty.

According to Ali and Hossain (2016), livestock development in Bangladesh evolved over decades. While the initial thrust was on government-directed development and control, the focus subsequently shifted to private-sector-led development. In the early years, the development of livestock was initiated by the government through policy emphasis on disease control, research, and training, which subsequently encouraged and motivated the private sector participation.

After independence, the government encouraged the NGOs and the private sector to get involved in development work paving the way for the development partners, NGOs, and private sector to initiate livestock activities in Bangladesh. In the late 1970s, BRAC identified livestock rearing at the village homestead level as essential for poverty reduction, nutrition improvement, and women's empowerment. This triggered BRAC to step into livestock programmes, as is described in more detail below.

4.3 Evolution of the BRAC Livestock Development Programme

Current issues in the livestock sector include fostering commercial and semi-commercial diversified livestock farming, facing emerging diseases, development of climate-smart breeds and varieties, reducing dependency on external sources (high-yielding genetic materials such as breed, semen, liquid nitrogen), strengthening government regulations, instituting information technology (IT) and communication devices, providing frontline technical manpower at the grassroots level, technical knowledge management, strengthening market linkages, and bio-security measures. Ali and Hossain (2016) identified the following challenges facing the sector.

1. Wide yield gap among the traditional, intensive, and semi-intensive farming
2. Lack of availability of HYV livestock and lack of knowledge and technological know-how of maintaining high-producing genetic materials
3. Prevalence of animal diseases, exacerbated by inadequate coverage of animal health services. Animal diseases alone constitute half of the causes of death of all the livestock population
4. Policy and institutional reforms of the Department of Livestock (DLS) and its functional arms are of critical importance to induce changes necessary to meet the new challenges caused by globalisation, trade liberalisation, and WTO regulations
5. Quality assurance of artificial insemination is a critical factor constraining future development of livestock
6. Lack of an organised market for farm produce is a significant problem, particularly for smallholders
7. Lack of space and physical security of animal resources
8. Low investment in livestock research and its poor management

The overall goal of BRAC's livestock programme was to provide small farmers and women an entry point to diversify income earning and employment opportunities through training in livestock activities (Saleque 2010). The specific objectives were:

i. to generate income and alleviate poverty of the rural poor through livestock development
ii. to reduce the mortality of livestock
iii. to supply animal protein for the growing population

From1978 to 1982, according to Saleque (2010), BRAC disbursed loans to landless women for rearing cattle. The impact was not satisfactory due to low returns derived from the local breeds raised traditionally and high mortality. Veterinary services were either unavailable or inadequate (Anon. 1996-2000). Based on this experience, BRAC developed a comprehensive livestock model in 1985 that included the provision of training, distributing vaccines and medicine, undertaking crossbred stock development, and semen production and marketing.

The broad R&D programmes implemented by BRAC included artificial insemination(AI) and cattle development, dairy development and food production, livestock feed production, selection and group formation of farmers (institution building), training for capacity building, livestock rearing, provision of credit for livestock, technical support, marketing, socioeconomic intervention, and influencing the government livestock policy for the poor. Some of the programmes have already been accomplished, some are still in operation, and some are continuously being expanded.

4.3.1 Artificial insemination (AI) and cattle development

Ali (2017) reported that only 64 percent of breedable cows are covered by the present AI services in the country, indicating that there exists an opportunity to expand AI service in this subsector. Merely 1.6 percent of goats were inseminated using frozen semen, which was available only from BRAC's Buck Station (production centre for goat semen). Figure 4.3 gives details of AI coverage; BRAC is the main supplier in the private sector.

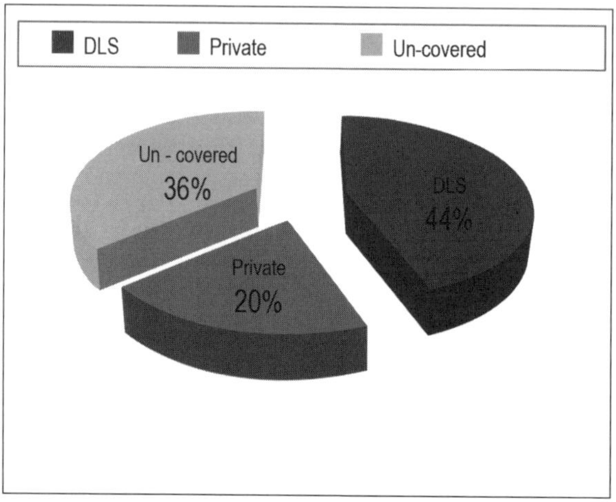

Source: Ali 2017.

Figure 4.3: National artificial insemination coverage of cattle

The national coverage of cattle AI, based on the number of doses of semen used in 2017 by the main breeding-service-providers, is presented in Figure 4.4.

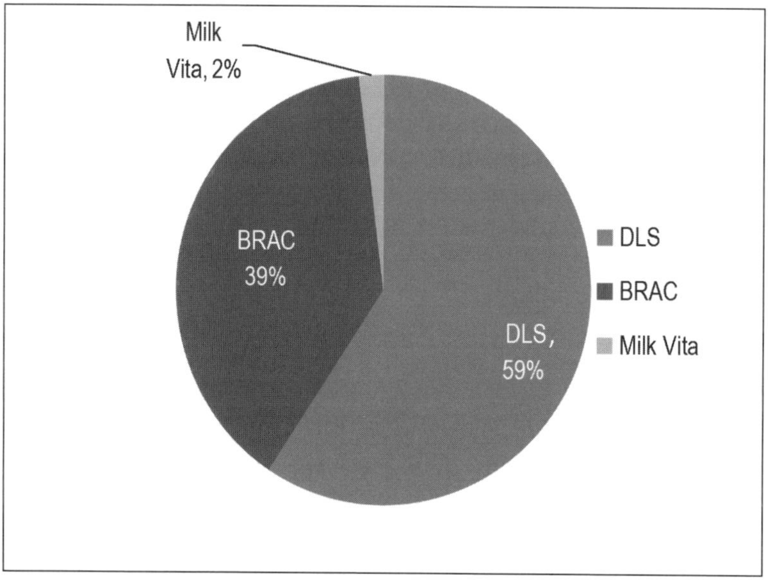

Source: Data collected from DLS 2017 and author's calculation.

Figure 4.4: Cattle AI coverage in Bangladesh in 2017

BRAC's Artificial Insemination programme began in 1985 as a partnership with the Government of Bangladesh to provide the rural poor with access to better quality breeds of cows. It was initiated in Manikganj district and expanded to other areas later. With only credit and training provision, the project did not make much headway as the cows produced on average only 1.25 litres of milk per day, which was not enough for the poor farmers to generate a decent income. BRAC figured that breeding higher-yielding dairy cows would help ameliorate this issue. At the time, only the government had access to high-quality bull semen; the rural poor seldom had access to it. BRAC initially trained 130 people as artificial insemination technicians; in 2017, it had over 3000 technicians (BRAC 2017).

Background

The government produced two kinds of semen: liquid and frozen. They supplied liquid semen and the proper insemination equipment to BRAC's trained AI workers to inseminate the cows of dairy farmers. But within secure power supply in villages, liquid semen lasted only two to three days, which limited BRAC's rural development endeavours. To address this situation, BRAC decided to set up a bull station for the production of frozen semen. Accordingly, in 1996, BRAC sent a team to study semen production and the AI activities of BAIF (Bharatiya Agro Industries Foundation) in Pune, India. BAIF is an NGO that is actively involved in cattle breeding and was the largest semen producer in India. Later, technical staff were sent to BAIF for practical training on laboratory operations as well as bull management. In 1998, BRAC established its own bull station as a programme support enterprise (PSE) and began producing frozen bull semen in 2000. To preserve the semen for a longer time in rural areas, BRAC provided liquid nitrogen to AI workers. In 2007, the artificial insemination project became self-sufficient and was transformed into a social enterprise.

Operations

BRAC established its bull station at Shambugonj, Mymensingh in 1998. It imported AI equipment from Minitube Company in Germany for the production of frozen semen. Initial technical support was provided by experts from BAIF, BAU, and DLS. BRAC procured breeding bulls from farmers in different areas of the country selected by involving qualified technical experts from DLS, BAU, and BRAC. BRAC also imported 100 percent Friesian and 100 percent Sahiwal semen from Canada and India respectively for the breeding of 50 percent crossbred bulls. In 2000, semen was produced and distributed on a test basis. To diversify its product line and reduce single product dependency, BRAC turned to goat-semen production in 2005. Both products were stored in liquid nitrogen and distributed to AI workers (currently called AI Service Provider or AISP) through the Central Container Areas (i.e., depots of frozen semen), now termed Area Sales Centres (ASCs).

When it was first built, the bull station held 35 bulls. In 2018, it increased its holding to 103 bulls, including 4 pure 100 percent Holstein Friesian from Australia and 19 Black Bengal goats. BRAC is also in the process of establishing its second bull station in Bogra with a 200-bull capacity to increase its semen production and AI activities. This bull station will have ovum pickup, embryo transplantation, and semen production facilities. BRAC is the pioneer of privately-owned large-sized bull-and-buck frozen-semen collection, with its processing, preservation, and distribution carried out through its centres and networks. Though there is a severe shortage of quality breeding bucks in the country, only BRAC has initiated frozen semen production, processing, and distribution of goat semen.

An MoU was signed between BRAC and DLS in 2007 to facilitate the implementation of AI activities of BRAC in different upazillas (sub-districts). Currently, all types of frozen semen get distributed to the depots from the bull station. BRAC Artificial Insemination now has 70 ASCs throughout Bangladesh. Artificial insemination workers (AISPs) purchase semen for an average of BDT150 and then sell it to farmers at BDT250-300,which includes both the cost of the semen and their services (Rouf 2017; personal communication). AISPs not only artificially inseminate the farmers' cows but also train farmers in cow healthcare (via water supplementation, feeding for proper nutrition, housing and management, disease prevention, and cattle breed selection).

The AISPs provide the insemination service to cows and goats on the villager's doorsteps, unlike the Government AI services, where farmers have to bring their cows to an AI centre, most of which are at the upazila level. At an early stage, BRAC came up with the innovative idea of placing three or four post boxes in prominent locations in a village so that clients who needed the service could drop a note with their names and addresses. With the expansion of cell phone usage, BRAC provides loans to the AISPs to buy a cell phone. The name and phone number of the relevant AISP are posted prominently throughout the village and in the local BRAC office. This information is also made widely available through the microfinance network (Matin et al. 2007). BRAC has also used popular media such as theatres and the internet (YouTube) for spreading information about the availability of AI services.

When a cow goes into heat, its farmer calls an AISP who performs the insemination within 12 to 18 hours. Farmers benefit from both male and female calves. High-quality breeds of male calves grow more quickly into larger than average size, and female calves eventually grow into a high-yielding cow. Having one calf a year is essential for farmers to make a profit from dairying. AISPs provide relevant technical information to farmers.

As of 2018, BRAC Artificial Insemination reached 62 of Bangladesh's 64 districts. In 2017, its workers artificially inseminated about 2.3 million cows. The AISPs provide other services in addition to AI, including FMD vaccination, mastitis test by CMT kits, fodder seed supply, cattle feed sale, mineral mixture (Mina-Mix), and primary health services carried out through health camps organised by veterinary doctors.

Selection and training

AISPs are selected from villagers with at least 12 years (Higher Secondary Certificate) of education. Initially, BRAC trained their AISPs at the government's Central Cattle Breeding Station (CCBS) and later at the Bangladesh Agricultural University (BAU) and other universities. Some selected features of the BRAC AI programme are given in Table 4.4.

Table 4.4: Selected features of BRAC's AI programme

Feature	Scale
Year of establishment of bull station (1999)	Semen production started in 2000
Number of production centres	1
Number of bulls kept for semen production	81
Form of semen used for AI	Frozen
Annual capacity of semen production (in lac doses)	20-22 (up to 2016), target of 28 (in 2018)
Annual production of semen doses (in lac) (2016)	22
Annual production of semen doses (in lac) (2017)	23
Price of semen dose (Tk per service)	Average 150, varies breed-wise
Number of cows inseminated during 2001-'05	527,578
Number of cows inseminated up to 2017	1,48,57,390
Number of calves born during 2001-'05	345,642
Number of calves born up to 2016	81,62,315
Conception rate (DLS approved)	61.5%
Number of AISP/volunteers working	2485 (up to 2017)
Number of regional sector specialists	43 (up to 2017)
Number of upazilas covered	450
Number of districts covered	62

Source: Saleque and Rouf -Personal communication, BRAC Head Office.

Table 4.5 shows the growth of BRAC's AI activities over the years.

Table 4.5: Growth of BRAC's AI activities

Year	Particular		Total
	Bull Semen Straw (Nos.)	Goat Semen Straw (Nos.)	
2000	17,128	0	17,128
2001	70,250	0	70,250
2002	43,201	0	43,201
2003	77,761	0	77,761
2004	1,21,486	0	1,21,486
2005	1,95,002	881	195,883
2006	2,75,422	29,791	3,05,213
2007	3,94,141	47,339	4,41,480
2008	5,26,545	24,411	5,50,956
2009	6,85,214	27,993	7,13,207
2010	11,08,637	38,130	11,46,767
2011	11,64,202	35,989	12,00,191
2012	13,01,280	33,042	13,34,322
2013	13,18,251	31,492	13,49,743
2014	14,21,285	22,968	14,44,253
2015	16,16,030	24,072	16,40,102
2016	19,38,493	29,787	19,68,280
2017	22,55,733	44,707	23,00,441

Source: BRAC AI Enterprise (Modified according to Saleque 2010).

Clients

BRAC Artificial Insemination initially targeted the rural poor, helping them generate income. Later, it adopted a community approach, in the sense that this service is now available irrespective of the socioeconomic condition of the clients. BRAC AI has become extremely successful, surpassing other providers. The general practice is for farmers to bring their cows to insemination centres, where the conception rate averages around 46 percent. The BRAC AISPs provide AI services at farmer's doorstep, and the conception rate averages over 65 percent. BRAC credits their success to the calm state of the cows. In general practice, a cow is exhausted from traveling in the hot sun. BRAC's quality bull-semen, paired with high conception rates, has drawn more farmers to use BRAC artificial insemination services.

Table 4.6 compares selected characteristics of different AI providers in the country. It confirms that the conception rate in BRAC programmes is higher than that of the other providers. Figures 4.5a and 4.5b compare information on the production and use of bull semen for the main breeding services in Bangladesh.

Table 4.6: Characteristics of AI service providers

Particular	Service provider			
	DLS	Milk Vita	BRAC	BAU
Year of starting	1969	1988	1985	1958
Area of operation (No. of upazilas) at present	451	14	410	6*
Breed used for semen production	Sahiwal, Friesian, local, & various combinations	Friesian and Jersey	Friesian Cross, Sahiwal Cross	Friesian Cross, Sahiwal-Red Sindhi Cross, Pabna, Red Chittagong
Type of semen used	Frozen- 60% Liquid- 40%	Frozen	Frozen	Liquid
Place of service	Centre based	Samity's place	At farmer's doorstep	BAU AI centre& Subcentres
Charge (BDT) for first service	Frozen - 30 Liquid - 15	Free	100	45
Charge for any repeat service	As above	Free	100	30
Conception rate (%)	46.5	47.4	61.5	60.0
No. of semen production centres:				
Frozen	29	1	1	0
Liquid	61	0	0	1
Service provider	Field Assistant/ AI Volunteer	Field Assistant & Inseminator	AISP	AI Technician

Note: *in Mymensingh District.

Source: Jabbar 2009.

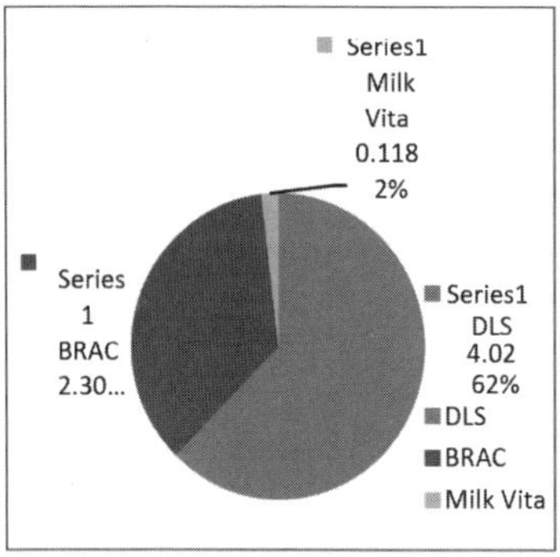

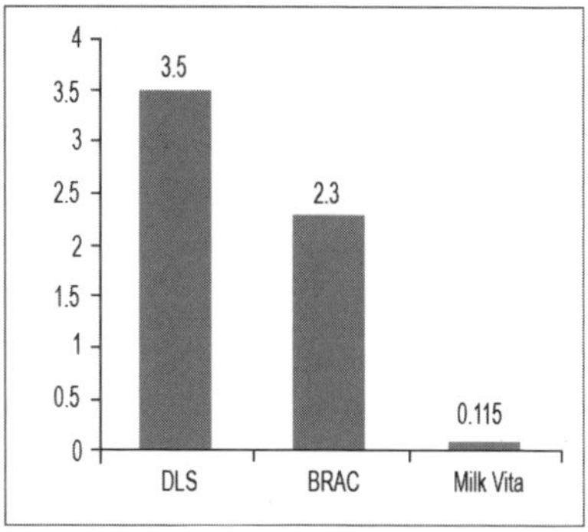

Source: DLS 2017 (Figures 4.5a and 4.5b).

Figure 4.5a: Bull semen production (million doses) in 2017

Figure 4.5b: Cattle inseminated (million Doses) in 2017

Feedback on BRAC's AI programme

Barua (2006) documented the feedback of the stakeholders of the BRAC AI programme. The feedback showed that AI implementers compete with other service providers in a discriminatory manner. Unfair price war, violation of bilateral deals, and existing breeding policy by the government have been identified as the major challenges faced by BRAC for transferring AI technology to the beneficiaries. Organisational and academic recognition are the main drivers of the AI volunteers — to work for BRAC as social entrepreneurs enhances their social and economic status. Despite the challenges, BRAC has been performing well compared to government and other service providers in the AI market due to the high conception rate, skilled AISP, doorstep service, close monitoring, and strict management.

4.3.2 Dairy development and food production

Foundations

A large number of BRAC's microfinance clients invested in cattle. In doing so, they were exposed to risk owing to poor breeding, limited veterinary services, shortages of cattle feed, and lack of market access.

Some of these challenges were addressed through social enterprises such as BRAC Artificial Insemination and BRAC Feed Mills. Still, the perishable nature of dairy products meant that it remained difficult for rural dairy farmers to reach the large urban markets, and the demand for milk in a single village was not enough to generate a sustainable profit. Dairy farmers also did not have access to proper refrigeration to store the unsold milk. As a response, BRAC initiated the BRAC Dairy & Food Project (BDFP) in 1998 to serve as a market conduit for dairy farmers gain better access to the market and receive fair prices throughout rural Bangladesh (BRAC 2016). BRAC received inspiration and technical support from Amul Dairy in India.

Mission of BDFP

The original mission of the BRAC Dairy and Food Project (BDFP) was to secure market access for dairy farmers, ultimately helping them generate better income. Over time, BDFP's goal has expanded to serving high-quality milk products to customers. Due to interrupted power supply and lack of refrigeration facilities, dairy products generally are not widely available in Bangladesh. Eighty percent of Bangladesh still relies on the "informal" milk market which delivers bulk amounts of raw milk to consumers. In essence, BDFP channels milk from rural areas into urban areas while channelling the revenue back into rural areas.

Operations and growth

The BRAC Dairy has not only secured fair prices for rural dairy farmers but has also expanded to offer cattle development and technical training, vaccination, fodder cultivation facilities, and other services. Through its 101 chilling centres, BRAC Dairy collects milk from farmers in rural areas and sells it nationwide under the Aarong Dairy brand. BRAC set up chilling plants in different places of the country to create opportunities for the poor and small holder famers in the dairy value-chain.

When BDFP was first started, it produced 140,000 litres of milk per day. As of 2018, it has the processing capacity of 250,000 litres of milk per day engaging approximately 1,500 employees, making it one of the largest BRAC enterprises. Aarong Dairy accounts for 22 percent of Bangladesh's total dairy market share and 24 percent of the national packaged dairy products market (BRAC 2015). BRAC Dairy collects milk from over 50,000 registered farmers, processes it into a wide range of different products, and markets them through a variety of retail channels. It focuses on producing premium quality products and promoting dairy nutrition knowledge. It is the third largest local milk processor in the country. In 2015, 110 automated milk collection units (AMCU) and some Rapid Milk Chillers (RMC) were introduced to improve the quality and efficiency of milk collection. It also introduced Laban, a new dairy drink. The current dairy products of BRAC Dairy include pasteurised milk, pasteurised low fat milk, ultra-high temperature (UHT) milk, butter, ghee, sweet curd, full cream milk powder, low fat milk powder, chocolate flavoured milk, mango flavoured milk, strawberry flavoured milk, strawberry yogurt drink, chocolate milk drink ,and Laban.

Every day, around 18 million litres of milk are produced in the country, but only 7 percent of it is sold to milk processing companies; the rest is sold in local markets. Every year, Bangladesh imports 65-70 thousand metric tons of powdered milk, equal to 1.7 million litres of liquid milk, worth BDT 200 crores to BDT 25,000 crores. Hence, there is a good opportunity for the local dairy industries to contribute towards filling this gap. The local processing industries would have to at least triple their output only to offset the imports.

4.3.3 Livestock feed production

BRAC initiated production of cattle feed in the country, and it has been producing commercial feed from its owned and rented feed mills since 2001. BRAC provides high-quality cattle feed at affordable prices for rural farmers. It also offers knowledge-based extension services to farmers to ensure efficient and appropriate use of the feed. The feed from its feed manufacturing plant is sold through its dealers and agents.

4.3.4 Training for capacity building

BRAC provides training to farmers as described below.

i. Cow rearer/beef fattener: Interested group members are trained as cow rearers and usually rear 2-3 cows. Cattle fattening is an important component of livestock rearing.

ii. Goat rearer: The goat rearers usually rear 3-5 goats.

iii. Fodder extension programme: This ensures the availability of fodder seeds/cuttings to farmers.

iv. Artificial insemination worker: As mentioned previously, the AISP works as a volunteer with a nominal fee. The semen is supplied by BRAC from its Bull Station.

v. Para-veterinarian and Vaccinator: BRAC selected one woman member and trained her as a paravet to cover 5-6 villages. Paravets were given 15 days training on feeding, rearing, and housing of livestock, and the basic treatment of livestock diseases. Trained veterinarians were responsible for the training of paravets. Upon successful completion of training, the paravets were responsible for the vaccination and health services of livestock in their operating area. They were allowed to charge a fee to the livestock owners for the rendered service and thereby earn some money. They provide vaccination for diseases like anthrax, black quarter, haemorrhagic septicaemia, foot and mouth disease, and rinderpest. The above functions were performed by the paravets until 2000 when BRAC changed the strategy to shift the responsibility to the AISP since they are in direct contact with the farmers.

BRAC trained over 500,000 cow and goat rearers up to 2000. Since then, most of the training and technical services to farmers are provided through the AISP in different areas of the country because they are also trained in livestock technical issues. The AISPs are guided by the veterinary doctors and animal husbandry experts. BRAC has initiated a health camp, mobile vet clinics, progeny shows, and awareness film shows in the field. It also introduced insurance and cash incentives for the AISPs.

4.3.5 Livestock micro financing and credit

BRAC's microfinance activities work through a unique "credit-plus" approach, addressing the special needs of various target populations such as rural women, youth and adolescents, landless poor, marginal farmers, migrant workers, urban poor, and small entrepreneurs. BRAC developed an integrated set of services including training in improved techniques, provision of improved breeds and technologies, ongoing supply of technical assistance and inputs, monitoring and guidance as needed, and marketing of finished goods. Learning from experience as the programme evolved, BRAC recognised that the poor do not constitute a homogenous group and therefore a uniform size of microfinance was not suitable for all categories of the poor. BRAC addressed this by offering differentiated financial services designed according to the needs of different people living at different levels of poverty (Saleque 2007).

Taking into account the poverty category, BRAC initially designed its microfinance programme into five principal products, each targeting a different market segment: CFPR/TUP (Challenging the Frontiers of Poverty Reduction/Targeting the Ultra Poor), IGVGD (Income Generation for Vulnerable Group Development), DABI, UNNOTI, and PROGOTI/MELA/ Women Entrepreneur Development Programme (WEDP. Loans are provided to trained livestock rearers (cattle and goat) to buy young and underweight cattle and goats at low prices. After buying them, they are provided deworming, vaccination, feeding, care, management, and disease-prevention services. When the animals are ready for sale after a certain period of rearing, they are sold at a good profit.

4.3.6 Technical support

Besides providing training, inputs, and other support, BRAC also provides technical support such as livestock-related technical advice, conducting refresher courses, collection of feedback, and regular monitoring of field activities. BRAC has well-trained technical professionals for providing training and technical support to farmers of different categories (Saleque 2007). Currently, technical support is provided to farmers directly (at their doorstep) by the trained AISP.

4.3.7 Influencing livestock policy for the poor

The South Asia Pro Poor Livestock Policy Programme (SA PPLPP) was established in 2006 with the objective of facilitating and contributing to the development of pro-poor livestock policy and programme implementation in three selected South Asian countries—Bangladesh, Bhutan, and India (SA PPLPP 2017)). SA PPLPP's interventions in these countries were implemented through programme partners: BRAC in

Bangladesh, the Department of Livestock Services in Bhutan, and BAIF Development Research Foundation in India. The programme mandate included the identification of good practices that had demonstrated sustainable benefits to smallholder livestock rearers, documentation of these practices, collating lessons learnt, and using these lessons to advocate for a more conducive policy and programme support environment for smallholder livestock rearers in the South Asia region. The programme is funded by the National Dairy Development Board and the Food and Agriculture Organisation of the United Nations. BRAC, the partner institute of SA PPLPP, is coordinating and representing the stakeholders of Bangladesh for the facilitation of pro-poor ideas. It has already documented some successes as Good Practices (GPs) in this regard, which have already been placed on the SA PPLPP website.[1]

4.4 Contributions of the BRAC Livestock Programme

4.4.1 Extension, production, R&D, and marketing

Extension

BRAC supports dairy farmers in their effort to become financially secure by buying cows and land. It developed services like artificial insemination, superior grass seeds, and veterinary services to improve the farmers' chances of success. BRAC credit support helped farmers to expand their operations. Farmers could not sell their produced milk fast enough, and they had no way to preserve it until BRAC Dairy was formed to connect farmers to markets. BRAC established 101 chilling stations to keep the milk fresh, and it uses strict methods to maintain quality. In 2017, BRAC collected 44.5 million litres of milk through its extensive network of rural dairy farmers. BRAC also processes the milk to produce a wide range of dairy products, which it sells through its retail and modern trade channels. As a result, products of 50,000 dairy farmers reach urban consumers fresh, fair priced, and of the highest quality. Operating since 1998, BRAC Dairy has become one of the largest social enterprises of the country with a 22 percent share of Bangladesh's total market for dairy products. The surplus generated by its livestock enterprises sustains its ongoing projects and the creation of new opportunities (BRAC 2015).The cattle development fund provided

1 www.sapplpp.org

subsidised artificial insemination services to 6,500 farmers, vaccinated 25,600 heads of cattle, delivered 8,000 kg of free fodder seed, and trained 2,000 farmers in animal husbandry methods. Through its AI programme, BRAC provided AI to 2.3 million cows in 2017 and 14.8 million cows since its inception. In this regard, BRAC claims 31 percent of the AI market share of 7.09 million breedable cows in the country. Table 4.7 summarises BRAC's performance in the dairy sector.

Semen production

In 1985, BRAC took the initiative to partner with the government to provide access to better quality cow breeds to people living in poverty in rural areas. It started distributing semen from its bull station in Mymensingh to depots around the country, with a network of 2,500 trained persons providing artificial insemination services for cattle to farmers. In 2017, (i) over 23, 00,000 cows were inseminated, with a success rate of 70 percent, (ii) 55 health camps were organised, where over 100,000 heads of cattle were vaccinated, (iii) the mastitis control programme was launched, and over 0.9 million tests were administered, (iv)153 new workers were trained, bringing the total to 2318.

Table 4.7: Summary of BRAC's AI, milk marketing, and vaccination programme

Programme		
Artificial Insemination (AI)	Milk Marketing	Vaccination/fodder seed distribution
No. of AI Technicians: 2318 (Active)	Share of market milk: 24%	No. of health camps organised: 180
Cows inseminated in 2015: 16,40,102	No. of Chilling Stations: 102	No. of cattle vaccinated: 150,000 doses, especially foot and mouth disease (FMD)
Cows inseminated in 2016: 19,68,280	Milk collection /day: 130,000 liters (Average)	Free fodder seed: In 2016: 10,000 kg In 2017: 15,000 kg
Cows inseminated in 2017: 23,00,441		
AI success rate: 70%		
Market Share: 31% of 7.09 million breedable cows		
The California mastitis test (CMT) used: 1,363 bottles (1,363 x 370)		

Source: Saleque and Rouf – Personal Communication, BRAC Head Office.

R&D

BRAC also invested in livestock R&D. In the 1980s, it supported a study to analyse the performance of different exotic, local, and crossbred cattle with respect to milk production, AI, and conception rate, as well as coverage of AI service in the country and scope for investment in the cattle AI programme. A study by Majid et al. (1998) was funded by BRAC and executed by BLRI titled "Investigation on the Strategy and Impact of Artificial Insemination Programme and Performance of Crossbred Cattle in Bangladesh." This work looked at the performance of crossbred cattle and the strategy, problems, and prospects of the AI programme. The findings of this study helped in designing the BRAC-initiated AI programme.

4.4.2 Influencing policies

BRAC is an active player in livestock development and extension. It has been involved in consultations and experience-sharing processes in formulating national livestock policies. BRAC has demonstrated to private sector companies that investment in livestock is a profitable business (Hossain et al. 2016) and private companies are now thriving and growing rapidly in the livestock sector.

4.4.3 Impacts of the BRAC livestock programme

About 50 percent of the total activities implemented by NGOs in Bangladesh are carried out by BRAC (Shamsuddoha 2009). BRAC collaborates with others to identify issues and problems and implement its programme to help livestock keepers and people engaged in livestock businesses. From its inception, BRAC's livestock programme has aimed to raise the incomes of poor people and disadvantaged women who would otherwise have been left out of the working sector. Instead, they are now earning and improving the quality of their lives. Many have also become entrepreneurs.

An assessment carried out in 2002 on some randomly selected farmers in two districts of the country, who participated in the BRAC Dairy Programme, found that BRAC's marketing and other support to smallholder farmers helped them to increase the number of cows per farmfrom1-2 cows to 3-5 cows per farm (Saleque et al. 2002). The average number of crossbred or local cows per farm increased from 1.53 and 1.35 respectively to 2.13 and 1.73. Milk yield also significantly increased from 2.75 litres to 6.22 litres, and the farmer's income was almost doubled. Thus the rural poor, especially women, were able to actively participate in the rural economy both as buyers and sellers of livestock goods and services. Moreover, they developed strong linkages with the government and also accessed the services of both the government and private sector. Growing market opportunities are stimulating the growth of livestock in the country. Training, technical support, and supply of inputs have led to increased incomes and employment for people of all categories (poor, women, and youth) and to the country's overall growth.

The Government encouraged NGOs and the private sector to engage in livestock development by liberalising its policy. Many NGOs adopted an increasing focus on livestock development for rural and urban poor people. Shamsuddoha (2009) found that some programmes were highly successful and expanded into major undertakings. In several instances, NGOs successfully recovered all of the operating costs from service charges on the credit provided. This represents a substantial development in the growth of self-reliance among Bangladeshi NGOs and the poor. Year-wise growth of employment through BRAC's poultry-livestock extension programme in 2006, 2007 and 2017 is shown in Table 4.8.

Table 4.8: Growth in employment through BRAC's livestock extension programme

Employment category	2006	2007	2017
No. of AISP	952	1900	2318
No. of cow rearers who received services	228,727	272,000	230,044

Source: Modified after Saleque, 2010 and BRAC AI Enterprise, 2017.

The livestock development activities of BRAC have created income opportunities and improved livelihoods for over half a million poor and smallholder famers in Bangladesh. In addition, BRAC provides technical services to about two million farmers through its AISP.

4.5 BRAC's Potential Future Role

Based on what BRAC has accomplished thus far, it has the potential to play a critical role in the future development of the livestock sector. Potential development and business opportunities arise from the huge gap between demand and supply, the increasing demand for milk and meat and their competitive price, the high price of imported powder milk, the scarcity of other protein sources, the scope for employment generation, the demand for quality services, and synergy with other BRAC enterprises. BRAC should focus not only on extension activities, but also pay more attention to R&D in the livestock sector. The greatest potential area for R&D is in livestock breed development. It has been observed that improved quality calves are in demand, suggesting that livestock owners are not satisfied with the quality (dairy merit) of existing stock. Using smart technology in livestock sector programmes needs attention. For example, it can be used in animal ID and recording animal traceability, early warning systems, e-business and marketing, animal and product purchase and sale, and sensitising and involving the younger generations in innovations in livestock, livelihoods, and food security through smart-farming (biology and IT-linked).

BRAC's cattle development programme through AI services needs to build long-term partnerships with appropriate breed-development players to increase the capacities for profitability and sustainability in the face of upcoming threats and challenges. Saleque (2010) suggested that further areas of R&D might include the use of conventional feed ingredients, appropriate use of maize stover as cattle feed, fodder cultivation in *char* areas and on other unused land, cultivation of short-term fodder crops in rotation, and development of techniques for preservation of feed and fodder during crisis/lean periods. Three potential areas where BRAC could invest in R&D are the development of techniques for assessing adulteration of different purchased ingredients, the incidence of various livestock diseases and measures for their control, and the disposal and alternative uses of litter and other waste products. Last but not the least, BRAC could take a lead role on the concurrent conservation and sustainable development of indigenous farm animal genetic resources (Bhuiyan 2014)—without using indigenous stock, one can not produce crossbred livestock! Moreover, the indigenous livestock is the appropriate breeding material for the rural people for whom and with whom BRAC mainly works. Thus, BRAC can work to ensure the current and future food security and livelihood of the poor in Bangladesh.

4.6 Collaborations and Partnerships

BRAC collaborated with several internal and external partners and organisations in various livestock-related issues, services, and R&D matters.

Details of the areas of collaboration, their tenure, and results or outcome are presented in Table 4.9.

Table 4.9: Livestock related collaboration and partnership of BRAC

Organisation	Area of collaboration	Tenure
Directorate of Livestock Services (DLS)	MoU with DLS in 2007 Technical and Input Support, Expert support	From 2007 to date
Bangladesh Livestock Research Institute (BLRI)	Technical Support, Sharing of Technology and Research	From 1985 to date
Bangladesh Agricultural University (BAU)	Training of AI Technicians, Professional Services	From 1999 to date
Chittagong Veterinary and Animal Science University	Technology Sharing	From 1998 to date
Sylhet Agricultural University (SAU)	Training of AISP, LSP Training	From 2012 to date
Patuakhali Science and Technology University (PSTU),	Training of AISP workers	From 2015 to date
Sher-e-Bangla Agricultural University	Training of AISP workers	From 2015 to date
Poultry and Livestock Association of Bangladesh	Member	To date
Bharatiya Agro Industries Foundation (BAIF), India	Training and Technical Support	From 1997 to date
South Asia Pro Poor Livestock Policy Programme (SAPPLPP)	Technical Support, Exposure Visits, Sharing of Technology	From 1997 to 2010
Donor Agencies: IFAD, USAID/ACDI VOCA, FAO, ADB, ATDP, DANIDA, USDA/Land o'Lake and others	Technology and Fund Sharing in Technology	From 1997 to date

Source: Saleque and Rouf – Personal Communication, BRAC Head Office.

4.7 Conclusion

Population growth, urbanisation, and the associated increase in the demand for animal products have presented golden opportunities to the livestock industry. Further development of the livestock sector and expanding livestock productivity should focus mainly on three elements: increasing the productivity of smallholder farmers, expanding commercial production, and ensuring better marketing facilities, especially for smallholders. The primary inputs required to sustain and enhance growth and development in the livestock sector are breed, feed, vaccine, and medicine. The government is giving due attention and support to livestock sector development through enabling policies and strategies. It encouraged NGO and private sector engagement in livestock development by liberalising its policies. BRAC used that window of opportunity to initiate livestock development programmes that included

- AI and cattle development
- dairy development and food production
- livestock and poultry feed production
- selection and group formation (institution building)
- training for capacity building
- livestock rearing
- livestock micro-financing and credit
- technical support, marketing, and socioeconomic intervention
- addressing the livestock policy for the poor

BRAC undertakes more than half of all the activities implemented by NGOs in the country. It implements its Livestock Development Programme primarily for rural and urban poor households. Through training, technical support, and supply of inputs to farmers, BRAC's work has led to increased incomes and employment for poor people, especially women and youth, and has thereby contributed to the country's overall economic growth.

There is a saying, "we cannot avoid the responsibility of tomorrow by evading it today." The sustainable development of Bangladesh demands both public and private investments in the livestock sector. Hence, the government should continue to encourage private investment in the livestock sector. But assuring the quality of breeding materials, feed, vaccines, and medicines through the legal and regulatory framework is necessary. On its part, BRAC has the scope to expand its livestock programme further to contribute to improved national nutrition.

References

Ali, M.S. 2017. "Breed development in Bangladesh: Role of DLS." Paper presented in the *Prani Sampad Seba Saptah 2017*, organised by DLSon 24-25 February, 2017, Dhaka.

Ali, Z., and I. Hossain. 2016. *Barriers to Development of Livestock Sub-sector in Bangladesh*. Dhaka: Bangladesh Institute of Development Studies. http://bids.org.bd/page/researches/?rid=36

Barua, P. 2006. *Analytical Documentation of the Artificial Insemination Programme of BRAC*. Dhaka: Research and Evaluation Division, BRAC.

Bhuiyan, A.K.F.H. 2011. "Implementation of the National Livestock Development Policy (2007) and National Poultry Development Policy (2008): Impact on Smallholder Livestock Rearers." Keynote paper presented at the South Asia Pro Poor Livestock Policy Programme (SA PPLPP) -BRAC Workshop held on 5th April 2011 at BRAC Centre Inn, Dhaka.

——. 2014. "Farm Animal Genetic Resources in Bangladesh: Diversity, Conservation and Management." In *Farm Animal Genetic Resources in SAARC Countries: Diversity, Conservation and Management*. Dhaka: SAARC Agriculture Centre (SAC).

BER (2014-15). *Bangladesh Economic Review: Ministry of Finance FY2014-15 and Seventh Plan Projection*. Dhaka: Government of the People's Republic of Bangladesh.

BRAC. 2015. *Annual Report, 2015*. Dhaka: BRAC.

——. 2016. *BRAC - Artificial Insemination*. https://brac.net/brac-enterprises/item/879-brac-artificial-insemination

——. 2017. *BRAC - Artificial Insemination*. https://brac.net/brac-enterprises/item/879-brac-artificial-insemination

——. 2017. http://www.bbarta24.net/others/14824

DLS (Directorate of Livestock Services). 2016. Dhaka: Author.

——. 2017. Dhaka: Author.

GoB. 2015. *Accelerating Growth, Empowering Citizens. Seventh Five Year Plan, FY2016-FY2020*. Dhaka: Bangladesh Planning Commission, GoB. http://plan

comm.portal.gov.bd/sites/default/files/files/plancomm.portal.gov.bd/files/aee61c03_3c11_4e89_9f30_d79639595c67/7th_FYP_18_02_2016.pdf

Jabbar, M.A. 2009. "Policy Barriers for Dairy Value Chain Development in Bangladesh with a Focus on the North West Region." Consultancy Report prepared on behalf of Unnayan Shamunnay for CARE Bangladesh.

Majid, M.A., T.N. Nahar, K.M. Hossain, and A.I. Talukder. 1998. "Investigation on the Strategy and Impact of Artificial Insemination Programme and Performance of Crossbred Cattle in Bangladesh." In *Research report of 1992/93 - 1997/98* of Animal Production Research Division, Bangladesh Livestock Research Institute, Savar, Dhaka, 1-53.

Matin, I., M. Sulaiman, and M.A. Saleque. 2007. "Imagining Microfinance More Boldly; Unleashing the True Potential of Microfinance." In *What's wrong with Microfinance*? edited by Thomas Dichter and Malcolm Harper, 23-34. Warwickshire, UK: Practical Action Publishing.

Rahman, S., I.A. Begum, and M.J. Alam. 2014. "Livestock in Bangladesh: Distribution, Growth, Performance and Potential." *Livestock Research for Rural Development* 26, no. 173. http://www.lrrd.org/lrrd26/10/rahm26173.html

Saleque, M.A. 2007. "An Effective Way to Integrate Small Farmers in the Value Chain: The Experience of BRAC." In *Southeast Asian Regional Conference on Agricultural Value Chain Financing, Conference Proceedings December 12-14, 2007 Kuala Lumpur, Malaysia*, 51-66. Asian Productivity Organization, NPC, FAO and APRACA.

——. 2010. "Livestock and Livelihoods: The role of BRAC in Livestock Development in Bangladesh. In *Proceedings of workshop on Review of Livestock Research Programme and Preparation of Future Research*. Dhaka: BRAC.

Saleque, M.A, K.S. Huque, and N. Sultana. 2002. "Marketing Intervention and Its Effect on Small Scale Dairy Development in Selected Areas in Bangladesh." *Bangladesh Journal of Livestock Research* 9, no. 1: 30-34.

SA PPLPP. 2017. *South Asia Pro-Poor Livestock Policy Programme*. http://sapplpp.org/

Shamsuddoha, M. 2009. "Development of Livestock Sector through Leading NGO in Bangladesh." *Fascicle of the Faculty of Economics and Public Administration* 9, no. 1: 36-44. https://ssrn.com/abstract=1434288

World Bank. 2016. *Bangladesh: Growing the Economy through Advances in Agriculture*. http://www.worldbank.org/en/results/2016/10/07/bangladesh-growing-economy-through-advances-in-agriculture

Photo 4.1: A goat rearer

Photo 4.2: A BRAC worker advising farmers on how to take care of their cows

Photo 4.3: A programme participant feeding her goats

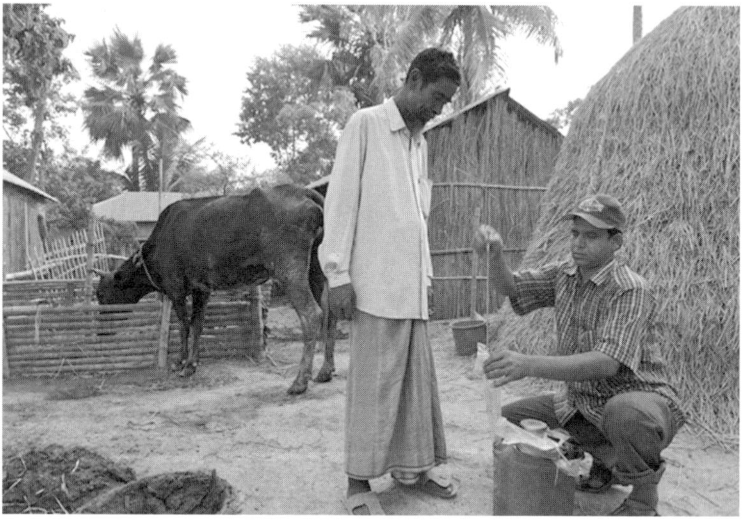

Photo 4.4: A BRAC worker preparing for artificial insemination of the cow

Chapter 5

Role of BRAC in the Growth and Development of the Fisheries Sector

M. Saifuddin Shah

5.1 Introduction

Fish and fisheries occupy a significant position in the culture and economy of Bangladesh—as expressed in the adage "a *Bangalee* subsists on fish and rice." Located in the subtropical part of the globe within the delta formed by three mighty rivers—the Ganges, the Meghna, and the Brahmaputra—Bangladesh is crisscrossed by 290 rivers of which 54 are transnational. There are numerous floodplains, lakes, ponds, *beels*, *haors*, *baors*, and brackish and marine waters. The inland fisheries diversity is one of the richest in the world, perhaps next to India and China. There are estimated to be 300 fresh and brackish water fish species in the country. With vast wetland areas created by the wide river-fed systems, and with abundant rainfall, year-round sunshine, and warm temperatures, the country enjoys a highly favourable climate for fish production.

The role of fish in food, nutrition, economy, employment, and the sociocultural heritage of the nation is enormous. Fisheries contribute 3.65 percent to the national GDP, and 23.81 percent to agriculture. It constitutes 1.97 percent of national exports. Sixty percent of the animal protein supply in the population's diet comes from fish. About 11 percent (or 16 million) of the total population of Bangladesh is dependent on the fisheries sector for their livelihoods, and of these, more than 1.4 million are women. The production of fish in the country is increasing every year. During the last decade, the annual rate of increase of production was 5.27 percent. In 2015-2016, the total fish production was 3.88 million metric tons (*Sangkolon*, National Fish Week, DoF, 2017).

The country's fisheries are divided into three subcategories: (1) Inland open water capture fisheries, (2) Inland closed water culture and /or culture-blended capture fisheries, and (3) Marine fisheries (mainly capture). During 2001-2015, total fish production in the country has increased from 1.89 to 3.88 million metric tons. Figure 5.1 shows the total production obtained during the last 15 years, while Figure 5.2 depicts the relative contributions of aquaculture, inland capture, and marine capture in the total production during the same period. The figure shows that the contribution of aquaculture production increased steadily during the period, but inland and marine capture production declined.

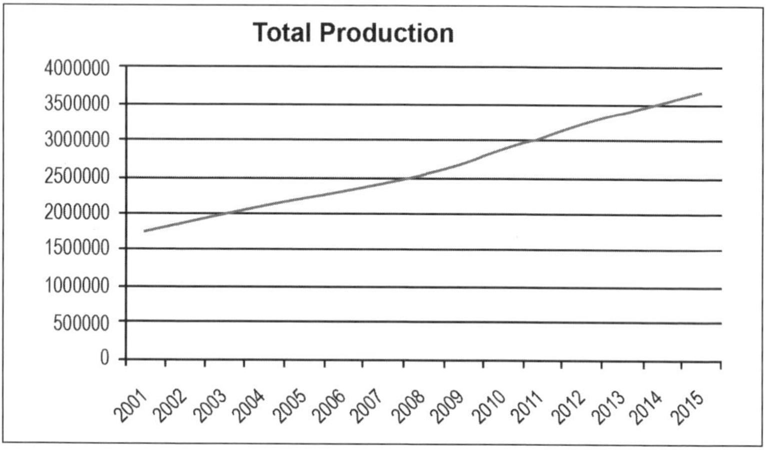

Source: DoF, 2017.

Figure 5.1: Total fish production in Bangladesh (2001-15) in MT

The Department of Fisheries (DoF 2017) apprehends that actual production will fall short of the targeted output of 4.56 million metric tons by the year 2020-21. Efforts need to be geared up by increasing production from both open-water harvest and closed-water aquaculture. Culture production would not be sustained in the long run without conserving the biodiversity of open-water fisheries because open-water populations provide an essential gene bank. The shrinkage of this gene bank would limit the scope for sustained aquaculture growth in the country. Increased aquaculture production can be achieved in either of two ways: by bringing more species into the culture system by taking up domestication selection programmes and by adopting more intensive use of inputs.

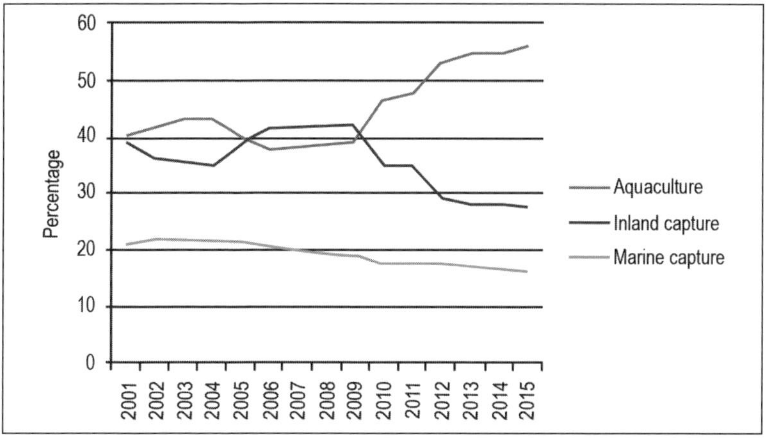

Source: DoF, 2017.

Figure 5.2: Contribution of production (%) from aquaculture, inland open water, and marine capture in total production

The gradual decline of capture fisheries production is due to a lack of attention being paid to conservation and management. Generally, the interests of capture fisheries and (crop) agriculture are counteractive. Floods are a welcome phenomenon for natural fisheries, but they are a curse for agriculture. Flood control and embankment of major rivers have seriously thwarted the breeding and feeding migrations of wild fish for many years. Sluice gates constructed at the mouths of channels connecting floodplains, *beels*, *baors*, and *haors* (see Table 5.1 for the definitions of the terms) were not provided with fish passes, nor are they managed so that fish can move between rivers and floodplains. The abstraction of water from rivers and other natural water bodies for winter irrigation also seriously affects wild fisheries. Increasing anthropogenic pressures on land and water resources amplified these problems, causing a severe decline in capture production.

Academic programmes in fisheries is now offered by many universities in Bangladesh and is a significant part of their curriculum. About 700 students graduate with a technical degree in fisheries every year. The

Department of Fisheries is the principal extension, management, and development agency of the government and a full-fledged Directorate. Of late, development efforts in the sector have been intensified with the activities of private entrepreneurs and prominent NGOs, especially BRAC. The role of Bangladesh Fisheries Research Institute (BFRI) and the Fisheries Departments of various universities is also important. The government initiatives for the development of the fisheries sector during the last two decades have been mainly donor driven. The main impetus has been given to the improvement and expansion of the aquaculture sector with an allocation of around 60 percent of the funding over the period 1986-2005 (AFSPAN: EC 2015).

Table 5.1: Definitions of selected water bodies

Haor

A haor is the term used in the north-east of Bangladesh for a wetland ecosystem in a floodplain depression. During the monsoon season, haors receive water from rivers in the area. Occasional high winds during the rainy season (June to August) generate large waves in the haor, which may cause considerable damage to homesteads. However, haors almost dry up in the post-monsoon period and become vast areas of green land during winter.

Baor

A baor is the dead arm of a river or an ox-bow lake in the Moribund Ganges Delta in the south-west of Bangladesh. The term is synonymous with beel and haor. Baors generally have water throughout the year.

Beel

A beel is the term used over most of Bangladesh for a floodplain depression that stays wet for most of the year.

BRAC's initial intervention in this sector was focused on the rehabilitation of poor fishers following the war of liberation.. Later, BRAC got involved in the sector in a major way through R&D and via extension activities. This chapter looks at the contributions and innovations of BRAC in promoting the fisheries sector in the country.

5.1.1 Growth, development, and key issues of fish production in Bangladesh

The fishery resource of Bangladesh is one of the richest in Asia. The areas of open waters and closed waters available for fisheries are

3.9 and 0.7 million ha respectively. While the contribution of open water production to the total production was 70-75 percent during the 1970s, it now stands at 28 percent. If marine capture is included, then the culture-capture ratio becomes 56:44. The decrease in capture production's share from such vast waters of rivers, *beels*, *baors*, *haors*, lakes, floodplains, coastal land, and other traditional water bodies like canals and roadside ditches is a matter of concern. On the other hand, due to various factors, including the large-scale diffusion of new technologies and the development of marketing, there has been a phenomenal growth in fish production in the aquaculture subsector.

The status of fish production from inland open water capture fisheries and from aquaculture is discussed below.

5.1.2 Inland open water capture fisheries

Open water fisheries development initiatives are principally linked with management and conservation. The lack of biological management, in particular, the factors described in the following paragraphs, can be reckoned as the causes of production decline from capture over the years.

Natural fish populations - Conflicts of interest with agriculture: An understanding of the environmental and biological impacts of the conflicts of interest of open water fisheries with other sectors is essential to provide context for the diminishing production from open waters. The open water fish species perform longitudinal and lateral migrations during monsoon for breeding and feeding. Embanking the major rivers for flood protection has stopped these migrations. The sluice gates made in the channels connecting the flood plains have seriously damaged the recruitment in the flood plains due to the obstruction of fish pass. The other conflicts are water use for winter crop irrigation, use of insecticides/pesticides, pollution, and siltation, as well as the construction of roads, bridges, and culverts, thereby blocking the passage of local fish migration.

Genetic basis of use conflicts, resource damage, and population bottleneck: Ecosystem fatalities combined with biodiversity damage in the form of species loss and intra-specific divergence loss lead a population to loss of adaptation. This is termed as a bottleneck situation for a population. A population in bottleneck condition gradually goes to extinction; the population passes through the stages of being vulnerable, endangered, and critically endangered before total elimination. The weakening fisheries biodiversity of the country may indicate that our species populations are experiencing a bottleneck situation. A population might reattain adaptive capability gradually through the re-creation of variation under conservation approaches.

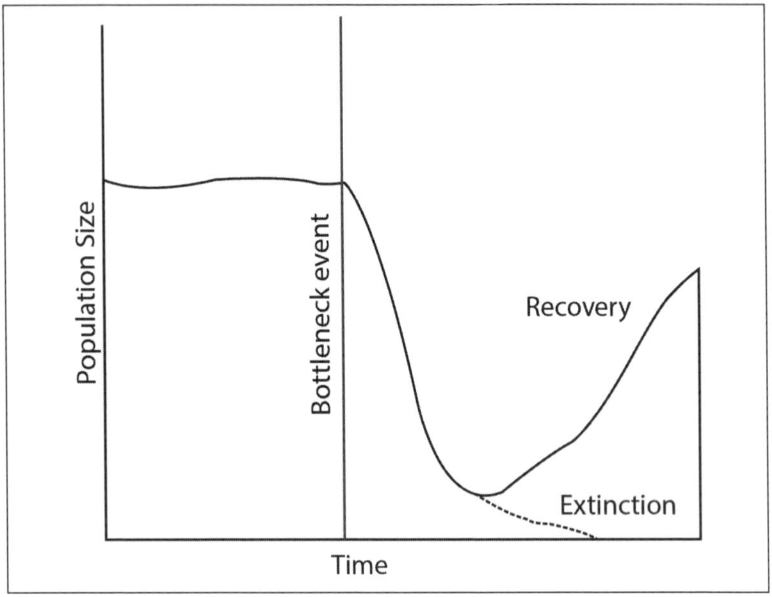

Figure 5.3: Population bottleneck

The biodiversity of an area is primarily the index of three things, the species diversity, intra-specific diversity within a species population, and ecosystem diversity. Open water biodiversity is considered the repository of the gene pools of the cultured stocks. Without achieving the skill to protect the open water fisheries biodiversity, aquaculture biology and production cannot be sustained in the long run.

Habitat restoration, clearance of migratory routes, and open water stocking: The decline of natural fish production has been mainly due to habitat degradation, among other related factors. The migratory routes of fish have been silted and blocked due to the construction of roads, culverts, bridges, industries, and others due to rapid urbanisation and development. There is 0.79 million ha of inland semi-closed waters of which there are about 1.0 million derelict *khas* ponds, *dighis*, blocked *khals*, dead rivers, *baors*, *beels*, and burrow pits in the country. These waters once were important fisheries resources. The reclamation of the waters is needed for the improvement of both fisheries management and culture. Artificial enhancement for natural fisheries rejuvenation management was done in the past but without appreciable impact. Programmes like *beel* nursery management by the DoF will not have an effect if the stocked fish do not have enough adaptive potential and cannot establish in the *beels* as self-sustaining breeding populations.

Management of sluice gates and sanctuaries: The sluice gates at the channels connecting the major rivers and the flood plains are constructed to mainly protect crops. But floods are mandatory for breeding and feeding migration of open water fish. Therefore, there need to be management options for allowing fish migration through the gates. The fisheries' interest in the flood plain has to be brought back in line with agriculture. The flood plains' deeper areas must be devoted to fisheries production where early flood water can be encouraged. Thus, the sluice gates management has to be aligned with the crop calendar in such a way that early flood is not harmful to the crops but allows breeding of the flood plain fish. The large-scale erection and management of sanctuaries in the rivers and flood plains are valuable alternatives to overcome the problem.

5.1.3 Aquaculture production

The phenomenal increase of aquaculture production during the last few decades is attributed to the diffusion of aquaculture technologies and market development at the grassroots level. Along with the intensification of farm management, new indigenous and exotic fish species have been brought into the management of the culture sector in recent times. At least 22 different indigenous species are being cultured in the country (Anon 2015). The Indian major carps *rohu*, *catla*, *mrigal*, and *kalibaus* are the principal species being produced in polyculture with Chinese grass carp, silver, big head, mirror, black, and common carps. Tilapia, *pangas*, *koi*, *sharpunti*, and *tengra* are monocultured on semi-intensive to intensive levels.

Issues that need attention for sustained growth and development of aquaculture production are briefly discussed below.

Culture intensification and genetic considerations: The total water area in the country being used for aquaculture is 3,71,309 ha (Figure 5.4). Of this, 80,577 ha are used for intensive culture (4-10 MT/ha), and 10,862 ha are used for highly intensive culture (10 MT/ha). Water areas used for semi-intensive and extensive culture are 220,862 ha and 58,076 ha respectively. These areas have very low production rates, which indicates that there is scope to increase production by bringing more areas under intensive to highly intensive culture levels with genetically improved strains.

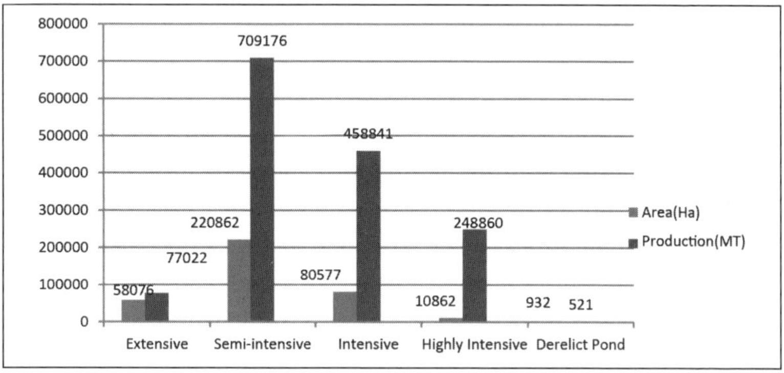

Source: BBS, 2015.

Figure 5.4: Pond aquaculture production under different systems of management with devoted water areas

Genetic quality of fish seed: Almost all of the present seed demand is being met by hatchery seed. Hatchery seed is prone to quality deterioration due to genetic consanguineous mating under the current brood management system. The seed requirement under intensive aquaculture will be very high. Meeting the requirement of good quality seed would be a daunting task since a large number of untrained/ semi-skilled people are involved in hatchery seed production. Thus seed quality assurance remains a key issue for the future expansion of aquaculture production in the country.

Feed, fertilizer, and water quality management of the brood ponds: The biology of brood management is crucial in hatchery production.

It is primarily determined by the genetic base of the broods and by food and nutritional management in the hatchery. The hatchery owners are not aware of the nutritional quality of the feed they use. It is linked with neither the nutritional demands of the fish species nor the stages of growth and development of the broods. The sources of feed are mainly agricultural by products. The addition of fish meal does not meet the required protein level. Very few hatchery owners mix any minerals in the feed. Some hatcheries apply commercial pelleted feed, the quality of which is often unknown. Feeding is closely linked to pond water quality. Fish size and the numbers of the broods have a crucial limit in nutrition management, but this is generally neglected under existing conditions.

Brood fish selection, record keeping, inbreeding, and genetic drift: Genetic quality determines the ability of fish to respond to good feeding, fertilisation, and water management. Often, the collection and establishment of brood populations are not done with care. Inbreeding is a frequent problem in hatcheries. Broods should be collected preferably from natural sources. In hatcheries, the recording of information on brood handling, transport and transfer, date and type of fish obtained, past origin, age and parentage of the fish is necessary to avoid inbreeding in seed production. Even if broods are collected from natural sources, often the number of fish collected is not many, and sampling inadequacy can lead to possible genetic drift.

Effective breeding number (Ne): N_e is an important concept in hatchery breeding. To prevent inbreeding, it is not enough to focus only on having a large number of brood. The number of males and females of a species used in a season and the number of breeding individuals contributing to the production of the next generation are both important to prevent the genetic base of the hatchery population from narrowing in future generations. In hatchery populations, the quality of the next generation produced is not determined by the total number of fish but by the number of breeding males and females taking part in the breeding process, by their sex ratio, the mating system applied, and variations in their family size. Many hatcheries use few broods, and even if there is large number of broods available, the sex ratio of the broods used in breeding is often highly skewed toward one sex, either male or female. Adherence to the principle of N_e can be achieved by using 1:1 sex ratio in breeding.

Hatchery facilities: The physical facilities of a hatchery often become limiting factors for avoiding inbreeding. An ideal breeding population is infinitely large. The hatcheries often cannot maintain a large breeding population of a species because of a lack of captive facilities. Many hatcheries do not have big pond areas. Carp hatcheries vary greatly in the number of brood holding ponds, the number of hatching jars, rectangular holding cisterns, deep tubewell capacity, and the number of people engaged.

5.2 Evolution of the BRAC Fisheries Programme

The rehabilitation of poor fishermen following the War of Liberation was one of BRAC's initial tasks in 1972. Its formal intervention in fisheries can be traced back as early as 1976 when the programmes in fisheries focused on creation of income-generating prospects for the rural poor by fish culture in excavated or re-excavated derelict ponds through technical and financial support. Hundreds of thousands of people participated in this programme. The gradual but phenomenal expansion of research, training, extension, and development activities in fisheries contributed significantly to the growth of the sector. Today BRAC is a principal actor in fisheries. The scale and diversity of its activities places it next to the Department of Fisheries. During the late 1980s, there was a drastic reduction in the supply of fish seed from natural sources. This led to a sharp increase in demand for quality seed of the major carps. BRAC came forward to establish its own hatcheries and also set up its first fisheries training centre in Rajendrapur in 1986. In 1996, there was a change in the BRAC fisheries programme strategy. BRAC set up four carps and eight prawn hatcheries under its Programme Support Enterprise (PSE) with the aim of supplying quality fish and prawn seed to its programme participants on a cost recovery basis. In 2008, the PSE evolved into a social enterprise with the bigger objective of supplying quality fish seed all over the country.

BRAC mainly operated carp and prawn hatcheries until 2006. However, in 2005, it established one tilapia hatchery in Magura and, in the same year, it became jointly involved with the Bangladesh Fisheries Research Institute in developing brood stock of Genetically Improved

Farmed *Tilapia* (GIFT). This was the turning point in BRAC's expansion of tilapia hatcheries and nurseries together with carp seed, prawn post larvae (PL) and food fish production. It is presently fully involved in the production of carp spawn, prawn PL, tilapia fry, and food fish, which are being run using a social enterprise approach. It operates three carp hatcheries, five prawn hatcheries, four tilapia hatcheries and five tilapia nursery centres located in ten districts: Moulvibazar, Bogra, Pabna, Magura, Khulna, Bagerhat, Barisal, Noakhali, Chittagong, and Mymensingh. The enterprise has now reached over 6,500 direct customers in 54 districts of Bangladesh. During 2016, it produced 4,795 kg of carp spawn, 11.18 million prawn PL, 100.90 million tilapia fry and 513.04 MT of food fish.

5.3 R&D Activities in Aquaculture

5.3.1 Supplemental feeding and fertilisation

In pond culture operations, inputs like supplemental feeding and fertilisation are the principal determinants of production. In 1989-92, BRAC carried out experiments in feeding and fertilisation in pond aquaculture with feeding and feeding plus fertilisation treatments. As expected, the feeding and fertilisation treatment yielded the best result in terms of production and profitability. This was the first-ever pond aquaculture trial with different options for the use of feed and fertiliser. Based on this research, the technology was disseminated widely throughout the country.

5.3.2 Sharpunti culture

The cost of aquaculture is mainly due to the cost incurred on feed, even in the culture of small fish species like *sharpunti*. The integration of duckweed feeding was experimented with in many small homestead ponds in Trishal, Mymensingh, and Tangail during 1993-95. The venture proved highly effective in generating income for the rural poor. A similar experiment was also done with rice-cum-fish culture in collaboration with BARI, BRRI, DoF, and SRTI in different parts of the country. Small fish culture in homestead ponds and feeding with rice bran was found especially suitable for the female members of households.

5.3.3 Carp seed production

The technology for artificial spawning of the Indian major carps was widely disseminated to hatchery operators, but optimisation of the technology took many years of hard work. However, spawning of *rohu*, *mrigal*, and *kalibaus* was optimised with comparatively little hard work and pain over time, but the selection of breeding optima for *catla* was difficult, and there were repeated failures. There was a similar experience with the grass carps and common carps at the initial stages. BRAC embarked on research to determine the breeding optima for the carp species in its Rajendrapur hatchery during 1998-2000. To improve the breeding performance of the species, a number of experiments were made with the hormone dose, the time of injection, the ratio of males and females in breeding, and water quality parameters. The protocols were eventually optimised, and the technologies are now being successfully practiced in all BRAC hatcheries.

Quality seed production

Under a memorandum of understanding, BRAC entered into a collaboration with the Worldfish Centre to work on the development of a logical breeding structure of cultured species. The aim was to produce genetically fast-growing strains of carp and tilapia and to disseminate the improved breeds to farmers and producers throughout the country so that local-level personnel could attain skills in selective breeding and genetic improvement. As a bid to control the inherent problem of loss of genetic variability, the concepts of pyramid and cohort breeding were incorporated. In 2003, the genetic improvement programme of *rohu* and *catla* was undertaken in the Moulvibazar hatchery. Three wild stocks of the species were collected from the Halda, Padma and Jamuna rivers, and they were crossbred to produce a synthetic base population of six families with higher genetic variation, which was incorporated in the breeding process. The resultant six families were pooled to form a communal stock. The same trial was repeated and progenies were maintained separately. In the second generation, broods were mass-selected for 20-25 percent fish from the stocks, with breeding between males and females from the alternate stocks. Besides this brood improvement programme, BRAC obtained improved strains of Chinese carps (silver carp, bighead, and grass carp) from the Parbatipur facility of DoF and Indian major carps, *rohu*, *catla*, and *sharpunti* from BFRI. Later, wild stocks of *rohu* and *catla* were also obtained from Worldfish. In order to maintain the genetic standard of the breeding populations of BRAC hatcheries, there is regular introduction of improved and unrelated germplasm in the hatcheries through the exchange of broods within the BRAC hatcheries and between other sources of broods in the country.

The pyramid breeding has not been applied in the breeding system of any species by any organisation in the country. However, cohort breeding is applied in monosex male tilapia fry production in Magura hatchery. The work was planned in two phases during 2008-2012 and 2013-2018. The first phase was completed on the stock enhancement of carp, GIFT *tilapia*, and prawn with fresh genetic material imported from other countries.

5.3.4 Prawn hatchery and post-larvae (PL) production

The R&D initiatives in prawn hatchery technology improvement by BRAC are highly significant. BRAC gradually improved their processes by trial and error studies on hygienic conditions and biosafety protocol, improvement in larval feed, and control of different physical and chemical hatchery parameters. The strictest adherence to the guidelines and improved monitoring procedures ultimately led to the achievement of the maximum survival of the PL with an average of 60 PL/litre. BRAC was the pioneer of prawn hatchery technology dissemination in the country.

5.3.5 Tilapia hatchery and cohort breeding

R&D activities conducted on tilapia (*Oreochromis niloticus*) have been very important. The experiments were carried out on two lines: extension of the breeding season through manipulation of temperature and fecundity through improving the brood fish rearing process. Season optimisation was obtained through achieving early and late maturity of tilapia corresponding with the seasonal water temperature in the hatchery. The pond and the surroundings of the hatchery were covered with polythene sheet, and an electric heater was to increase water temperature during winter. Also, open breeding of tilapia instead in hapas was conducted during warmer weather, and the sex ratio of broods was optimised for effective breeding. These experiments significantly helped to increase the performance of BRAC's tilapia hatcheries.

BRAC was the pioneer organisation in undertaking cohort breeding for genetic improvement of tilapia in its Magura hatchery in 2005. The monosex male production from larvae produced under cohort breeding is now the most significant programme for tilapia seed production in the country.

5.3.6 Koi, shing and magur culture

The indigenous stinging catfish (*Heteropnuestes fossilis*), commonly known as *shing*, is much in demand, both for its nutritious value and as a delicacy. Development of a culture package seed production, feeding, and fertilisation was deemed necessary. In 1991, artificial breeding of *shing* was tried with hormone injection. In the trial, fertilisation of eggs was possible through stripping of females and by mixing the eggs with milt from cut and macerated male gonads obtained by sacrificing males. However, the survival rate of the larvae was not satisfactory at that time. The technology of *koi* (*Anabas testudineous*) and *magur* breeding and seed production was not found to be successful for transfer to farmers. However, BRAC recently started Pabda and Gulsha production in its hatcheries in Pabna and Bogra.

5.3.7 Cage aquaculture

During 2006-07, cage culture of tilapia in the Dakatia River, Chandpur, was initiated in collaboration with the DoF to provide an alternative livelihood for fishers catching *hilsa* in the Meghna River, to reduce fishing pressure, and to conserve the natural resources of the Meghna River, especially during the banned period of *hilsa* fishing.

5.3.8 Sea bass induced breeding

The sea bass (*Lates calcarifer*) was considered to be the species with the most potential to be brought under aquaculture, and efforts for aquaculture development were deemed necessary. With this in view, induced sea bass breeding experiments were conducted in Teknaf,

Cox's Bazar, during 2000-08. Gonadal development in the broods could not be achieved; thus, the programme was discontinued.

5.3.9 Culture in the flow-through system

In another R&D effort, *tilapia*, *koi*, and *shing* production was tried in the flow-through system to reduce the space required, but with intensification of the system. However, while the production of *tilapia* and *koi* in the system was satisfactory, there was high mortality for *shing*.

5.3.10 Pearl culture in ponds

Pearl culture in rural ponds through implantation of foreign particles inside the local bivalve was thought to be a potential source of income for poor people. In Kolaroa, Satkhira, an experiment was carried out during 1990-94 in a few freshwater ponds where implantations were done, but the venture was ultimately not pursued because it was not profitable.

5.3.11 Prawn brood development in captivity

The development of prawn brood stock in captivity was experimented with, and berried prawn was produced in the trial. However, PL production from the system was not successful.

5.4 BRAC in Fisheries Management: Scaling of Experiences

As early as 1988, BRAC supported the government in supplying its hatchery-produced spawn for release in different parts of the country as a programme for open water stocking. Although not as a regular programme, the government had carried out open water stocking in the form of a *beel* nursery project in some *beels* and floodplains. From the late 1980s to 2006, BRAC was involved in open water fisheries projects in partnership with the Department of Fisheries and other development organisations. These included the Oxbow Lake Small Scale Fisheries Management Project (OLP II), the Community Based Fisheries Management Project (Phase II), and the Fourth Fisheries Project. BRAC took into account that the involvement of the fishermen is crucial when tackling conservation issues in open water fisheries management.

5.4.1 Ox-bow lakes fisheries management

Ox-bow lakes are semi-closed to closed water bodies in abandoned river meander loops. They are known as *baors* in south-west Bangladesh. The *baors* occupy over five thousand hectares and have an annual fish production of over 7,000 metric tons. Many poor fishers depend upon the *baor* fisheries for their livelihoods. In 1991, BRAC and the Department of Fisheries jointly executed the Oxbow Lakes Small Scale Fishermen Project (OLP II) with assistance from IFAD and DANIDA. Based on that experience, BRAC implemented its BRAC-*Baor* Programme (BBP) in 1993 parallel to the DoF-BRAC OLP II project. The OLP II project aimed to increase overall fish production in 22 selected *baors* in the greater Jessore area. The poorest users were thus able to participate in various fisheries development tasks, helping them increase their incomes and social status. Carp nurseries were included in the programme: 5-7 nursery ponds were excavated in each of the 22 *baors* to supply fingerlings for the stocking programme with support from the WFP. The participants were all female. The OLP II and BRAC-*Baor* programme had significant impacts in increasing fish production and incomes of the participating households. At the end of the OLP II project, the value of fishing assets of the participants had increased by 37 percent, and the average income per head had risen from BDT 4,090 per year in 1991-92 to more than BDT 11,000 in 1992-93. The BRAC-*Baor* project led to an increase in annual income of the participant households from BDT 3,476 in 1994 to BDT 7,285 in 1996. They had changed their status from being among the poorest, homeless, asset-less, and powerless members of society to those who were proud of their profession, had some property, and some say in their community (Hossain 1999).

5.4.2 Community based fisheries management

The Community Based Fisheries Management (CBFM) project was a countrywide project, completed in two phases during 1996-2001 and 2001-06. BRAC executed the project in 19 water bodies (seasonal and permanent lakes, floodplains, and rivers) with a total area of about 1600 ha covering 14 upazilas in Kishorgonj, Gaibandha, Rangpur, Bogra, and Naogaon districts. Through this project, BRAC mobilised the participants and trained them to increase their fisheries capacity.

The project involved 25,000 fishing households. They were provided information on fish catches, changes in fishing effort, species diversity, the impacts of fish sanctuaries, fishing habitat restoration, length-based fish stock assessment, fish population biology, fish consumption, household impacts, and the institutional framework for the management of open water fisheries. The project had funding from the Ford Foundation and DFID (UK). In the first phase, there were seven partner organisations; in the second phase, there were ten NGOs in project, in partnership with DoF, namely, Proshika, CNRS, CARITAS, *Banchte Shekha*, *Ghoroni*, CREED, SDC, FemCom, and BELA. BRAC played a coordinating role in the project.

As a result of management strategies like establishing fish sanctuaries, restoring fish habitats, maintaining closed seasons, and reducing destructive fishing practices, fish catches increased and benefits to leaseholders and middle agents fell relative to the share of returns to professional fishers. The introduction of management and habitat restoration through various CBFM activities (fisher-managed fisheries, community-managed fisheries, and women-managed fisheries) increased fish production by 64 percent and biodiversity in the project's water bodies by 28 percent. A total of 164 fish sanctuaries were established in 81 water bodies. Preliminary assessments at the time showed improvements in the population of 8 critically endangered, 16 endangered, and 12 vulnerable fish species in CBFM project sites. Fish consumption was also significantly higher (12 kg/HH^{-1}) in CBFM sites compared to other sites (10 kg/HH^{-1}). The training and information dissemination activities contributed to increased awareness and understanding of the importance of fish conservation and biodiversity by community people, including women. The CBFM project won the Outstanding Research Partnership Award from CGIAR in 2004.

Two special features of the CBFM programme are worth mentioning: microfinance management and gender mainstreaming.

Microfinance management

Although the principal focus of the project was on the management of water-body-dependent community fisheries, there was a complementary programme on microfinance implementation by eight microfinance institutions (MFI). The project had aimed to form community based organisations (CBOs) to channel the microfinance, but, except for CARITAS and CNRS, the other six NGOs ran it themselves. BRAC stood out as the best NGO in microfinance management in terms of loan recovery and portfolio quality.

Gender mainstreaming

In CBFM-2, the participation of women members in the *Beel* Management Committees (BMCs) and CBOs was encouraged in close association with their male counterparts. BRAC was successful in formulating and implementing plans in gender mainstreaming in the project. The issues of concern in the process were varied and wide-ranging. They included sharing of experiences between male and female members in the CBOs, building capacity and awareness of the female members, income generation activities with the female members, women members' role in resource management in existing scenarios, and monitoring the impacts of women's involvement in management. The issues also included fisheries gender networking, gender training, and indicators for future impacts assessment and for undertaking research studies on gender topics. The role of BRAC in the process of gender application management and encouraging women's participation in the project was commendable (CBFM 2007).

5.4.3 Fourth fisheries project

The Fourth Fisheries Project was the biggest development project ever implemented by the government. Funded by the World Bank, DFID, and GEF with the total budget of BDT 2,602.36 million (US$ 44.1 million) during 2000-2005, the project had five major components: inland open water management, fish culture extension, shrimp and coastal aquaculture, biodiversity conservation, and institutional strengthening in the fisheries sector. The project touched more than 500,000 fishers and fish farmers directly throughout the country in 56 water body sites in 33 districts. The interventions included fingerling stocking/artificial enhancement of open waters, establishment of fish sanctuaries, and restoration of habitats, as well as construction of fish pass/fish-friendly regulators in the sluice gates erected at the mouths of channels connecting water bodies and rivers. With the assistance of NGOs, the project used Community Based Fisheries Management (CBFM) through the formation of Fisheries Subcommittees (FSC) in villages, and Fisheries Management Committees (FMC) at the water body level. BRAC was one of over two dozen NGOs involved in 25 water bodies throughout the country, organising some 12,000 fishers from 360 villages into 318 FSCs and 31 FMCs. Out of the 31 FMCs, 26 were then registered with the Social Welfare Department. The project had deployed 97 field staff with a budget of BDT 50.6 million (CBFM 2007). It carried out such activities as the organisation of the Village Development Committees (VDC) which were then fed into the Fisheries Management Committees, helping the VDCs to set up systems of data collection in a participatory manner. BRAC also provided guidance in the identification and selection of local NGOs to be involved in the project in consultation with villagers and DoF personnel.

At the implementation stage, the project mobilised and organised the beneficiaries to form Fisheries Community Based Organisations (FCBOs) and helped them enhance their capacity in preparing and implementing Management and Activity Plans (MAPs) and participation in monitoring project activities. BRAC also provided training to the VDCs and FMCs in management administration, including setting up and maintaining their organisation by themselves, keeping a record of the proceedings of discussions, decisions, and activities, basic financial management, information retrieval systems, and identification of development activities. Particular emphasis was given to sustainable livelihoods and poverty alleviation of dependent beneficiaries.

When the impact of the Fourth Fisheries Project was evaluated, the project was found to have far-reaching outcomes. Fish yields per hectare had been doubled in three years of project implementation. In every project site, one to seven fish species that were reported to have been extinct or endangered had reappeared with the establishment of sanctuaries.

Also, the longer-term-use right (ten years) given to the beneficiaries resulted in significant enthusiasm for conservation of the resources in a sustainable manner through the proper observance of management measures like season, size, and gear bans.

5.5 BRAC's Potential Role in Future Development of the Sector

Though the fisheries sector has experienced a steady development in registering production increases at an annual rate of over five percent during the last ten years, there are still some issues where BRAC, based on its experience, can continue to support the fisheries sector.

5.5.1 Open water fisheries sustenance

The sustenance of open water fisheries via loss of fisheries biodiversity is a concern for the lasting development of fish production in the country. BRAC can play a meaningful role in sustainable management and conservation of open water fisheries through its experience in mobilising stakeholder communities.

5.5.2 Fast growing strain development by genetic selection

Problems experienced with hatchery-produced fish seed described in Section 3 indicate that continuing efforts are needed to identify and select genes that will lead to faster fish growth, improved body size and shape, disease resistance, and fecundity. BRAC can play a vital role in this research.

5.5.3 Aquaculture intensification

Aquaculture intensification can be achieved both by bringing new indigenous or exotic species into culture and by increasing the level of inputs used. Serious trials need to be undertaken on the increased use of inputs like feeding, fertilisation, chemicals, the density of stocking, and species combinations. Presently, out of 0.37 million ha of closed waters, 0.081 million hectares are being utilised highly intensively, and 0.012 million hectares are at intensive levels of culture. There is evidently a large water area which can be brought under intensification and for which a package technology is needed. This will require high-quality commercial farm managerial capability and require a large amounts of genetically improved fish seed of the cultured species. Here also, BRAC can play a prominent role.

5.5.4 Carp-prawn polyculture

There is scope for BRAC to promote the polyculture of prawn with carps, despite recent problems experienced with prawn seed production and hatchery technology. However, there are still many critical aspects to work on for a fuller understanding of prawn culture. For example, there is the familiar issue of morphotypes formation in male prawns under different stocking densities and sex ratios of stocked prawns, stocking densities vis-a-vis harvest size in the continuous harvesting system, and seeking possible mechanisms for all-male prawn PL production.

5.5.5 Quality assurance in fish and shrimp feed

The cost of buying feed is the largest production expense for aquaculture. Increased production from intensified aquaculture will largely depend on the availability of trusted sources of prime quality feed. The majority of the feed brands currently in the market are not trustworthy (Ahmed 2017; Personal Communication). BRAC could play an important role in assuring the supply of quality fish feed, for example, by creating and supplying its own feed brand.

5.5.6 Fish as food security

There is a great demand for fish in Bangladesh, and production in culture-based systems is increasing rapidly. Most fish is consumed in the domestic market; only about two percent is exported, of which almost half is frozen shrimp. Some value-added shrimp items are also exported, but to date, there has been no value addition to any domestically marketed fish. The quality of the fish sold in domestic markets is always uncertain as the fish are often treated with formalin to prevent bacterial contamination. Also, red dyes are often poured on the gills of dead fish to falsify the freshness of the gills. Recently, the practice of selling live Indian major carps has been noticed in the Dhaka markets. The fish are reportedly transported in canvas water tanks fitted on trucks. Since there is no artificial aeration, many of the fish die before they are sold. It appears that this practice is based on customers' preference for live fish to avoid the presence of formalin in the fish they buy. Much remains to be done to improve fish quality through the improvement of handling, cooling, packaging, and transportation. BRAC could play an important role in these activities.

5.6 Conclusion

Fisheries is a thriving sector in the agricultural economy of Bangladesh with vital roles in food, nutrition, income, and employment. Though the contribution of capture production has been diminishing over the decades, total fish production has increased at an average rate of over five percent per year during the last fifteen years. This increase has principally been realised from aquaculture. However, the decline of open water fisheries biodiversity threatens the sustainability of hatchery breeding populations. The narrative of fisheries development described in this chapter illustrates the importance of having technical fisheries people in the sector to promote and sustain aquaculture and fisheries development. The process has been strongly supported in recent times through the active participation of classified entrepreneurs, development partners, and NGOs. BRAC is the principal NGO in fisheries in the country, and its contribution to the sector is next to that of the Department of Fisheries.

Ever since its inception in 1972, BRAC has continuously expanded the horizon of fisheries and aquaculture. Together with its role in open water fisheries management in association with other development partners, the research and development initiatives of BRAC have brought about innovations in many adaptive aquaculture technologies, creating significant impacts on fish production, income, and employment in the country. BRAC has formalised the use of feed and fertilisers in pond fish culture. It introduced the idea of involving women in low-cost small fish culture in homestead ponds. BRAC has been a pioneer in research, extension, and training in hatchery and seed production of carp, tilapia, and prawns, which has revolutionised the growth and development of aquaculture in Bangladesh. It changed its initial PSE strategy for supplying quality fish seed to its participants in ongoing programmes to its present Social Enterprise form, thus serving the whole country. Concerns regarding genetic seed quality prompted BRAC to embark on brood bank establishment and variation conservation through taking up breeding strategies like pyramid breeding in carp and cohort breeding in monosex GIFT tilapia. These programmes continue to sustain increased aquaculture production in the country. Attempts to introduce cage aquaculture, induced breeding of sea bass, *koi*, *shing*, and *tilapia* culture in the flow-through system, and pearl production in ponds were not fruitful because they did not have proven packages for the detailed processes involved.

BRAC has had a significant role in rural poverty alleviation and socioeconomic upliftment through innovations in aquaculture. As the biggest NGO, BRAC has an important role to play in formulating national fisheries policy, and it can be involved in other areas of fisheries and aquaculture needing attention, either alone or in coordination with other organisations.

References

AFSPAN (Aquaculture for Food Security, Poverty Alleviation and Nutrition). 2015. *Aquaculture for Food Security, Poverty Alleviation and Nutrition.* https://cordis.europa.eu/project/rcn/101755/reporting/en

BBS (Bangladesh Bureau of Statistics). 2015. *Statistical Pocket book of Bangladesh.* Dhaka: Bureau of Statistics, Ministry of Planning, GoB.

CBFM. 2007. *Community Based Inland Open Water Fisheries Management and Development (CBFM) Project (Phase-2), Project Closure Report, September 2001-March 2007.* Dhaka: BRAC Development Programme, BRAC.

DoF. 2017. *Yearbook of Fisheries Statistics of Bangladesh 2016-17.* Dhaka: Fisheries Resources Survey System (FRSS), Department of Fisheries.

Hossain, M.M. 1999. "An NGO as the Custodian for Fisher Groups in Culture Based Semi-Closed Water Bodies: The Experience of BRAC." In *Sustainable Inland Fisheries Management in Bangladesh,* edited by A.J. Middendorp, P.M. Thompson, and R.S. Pomeroy, 255-258. Makati City, Philippines: International Center for Living Aquatic Resources Management (ICLARM).

Sangkolon. 2017. *National Fish Week.* Dhaka: Department of Fisheries (DoF).

Photo 5.1: A BRAC worker conducting field training on fisheries

Photo 5.2: Crossing gender boundaries in fishing

Photo 5.3: Happiness knows no bounds after a big catch

Photo 5.4: A big catch makes the day

Chapter 6

Replicating BRAC's Experiences Internationally

Md. A. Saleque

6.1 Introduction

Agriculture is the primary source of nutrition, employment, and income for 70 to 80 percent of the population in developing countries (FAO 2014). The health and wellbeing of more than two billion people depend on the success of smallholder farmers (IFAD 2011). In most parts of Africa and Asia, farms are small, with nearly two-thirds of them having less than one hectare. Access to inputs is a major issue as quality seeds, feed, fertiliser, equipment, credit, and training are in short supply. The success of these farms and the people who work on them—and the billions who depend on them—require effective, reliable, and sustainable solutions that can be implemented on a large scale. As the population increases, so does the demand for food. Thus, agriculture is an essential part of the economy in all African countries that can contribute towards eradicating poverty and increasing incomes (Blein et al. 2013).

BRAC is perhaps the only NGO from a developing country that has gone global, with a presence in eleven countries in Asia and Africa. With its long history of success in Bangladesh, BRAC extended its development model to Afghanistan in 2002 (Chowdhury et al. 2006) and then gradually to other countries: one in North America, six in Asia and five in Africa. BRAC has since phased out its programmes in Sri Lanka and Haiti.

One of the programmes that BRAC has successfully replicated internationally is the Agriculture, Food Security and Livelihood Programme (AFSL). AFSL is being implemented in five countries in Africa (Uganda, Tanzania, Sierra Leone, South Sudan, and Liberia) and one in Asia (Afghanistan). It has been introduced recently in Myanmar and Nepal.

Table 6.1 shows the year in which the AFSL programme was initiated in these countries. BRAC International's[1] (BI) engagement in these countries is based on decades of experience in Bangladesh in promoting innovative and effective solutions for smallholder farmers. In each country, it builds upon its proven approaches, while introducing newer innovations and taking into account the local context and on-the-ground realities. The AFSL programme under BRAC International works closely with other BRAC programmes in health, education, microfinance, and adolescent empowerment. It aims to improve food security, nutrition, income status, and the resilience of people in rural communities by promoting and developing productive and environmentally sustainable farming practices. These include training, investments in agri-businesses, supporting community-based service providers, establishing demonstration farms and promoting farming techniques and proven technologies, financial services, production and supply of improved farming inputs, formation of producer groups for more effective cooperation, and development of more efficient market linkages across the value chain.

This chapter gives an overview of the AFSL programme in BI countries in terms of the challenges facing this sector and how BRAC has addressed them, contributing to improved economic, nutritional, and social progress in these countries.

Table 6.1: BRAC International's countries of operation

Country	Initiation of BRAC Operations	Initiation of the Agriculture Food Security and Livelihood Programme
Afghanistan	2002	2003
South Sudan Tanzania Uganda	2006	2007
Pakistan	2007	None
Sierra Leone Liberia	2008	2008
Philippines	2012	None
Myanmar	2014	2018
Nepal	2015	2018

1 BRAC programmes outside Bangladesh are managed through BRAC International (BI) which is registered in the Netherlands.

6.1.1 Agriculture in BI countries: Selected statistics

Table 6.2 shows the arable land, production of rice, maize, eggs, and meat in the countries with BRAC programmes. The average arable land used in these countries varies from 5 percent in Liberia to 34 percent in Uganda.

Table 6.2: Arable land production and yield in BRAC International's operating countries (2016)

Country	Arable Land[a] (% of land area)	Maize		Rice (Paddy)*		Eggs	Meat
		Production (MT)	Yield (MT/ ha)	Production (MT)	Yield (MT/ ha)	Production (thousands)	Production (MT)
Afghanistan[b]	12	311,646	2	356,565	3	398,420	291,660
Bangladesh	60	2,445,576	7	52,590,000	5	8,338,680	672,773
Liberia	5	n/a	n/a	309,144	1	131,000	36,834
Myanmar	17	1,830,631	4	25,672,832	4	11,295,284	3,078,982
Nepal	15	2,231,517	3	4,299,079	3	1,294,166	372,412
Sierra Leone	22	12,554	0	1,560,363	2	258,000	50,580
South Sudan	n/a	107,000	1	n/a	n/a	n/a	407,225
Uganda	34	2,663,025	2	246,551	3	725,000	470,122
United Republic of Tanzania	15	5,875,560	1	2,985,581	2	1,780,000	529,533

Note: *Paddy, not clean rice.

a. "Arable land is the land under temporary agricultural crops (multiple-cropped areas are counted only once), temporary meadows for mowing or pasture, land under market and kitchen gardens and land temporarily fallow (less than five years). The abandoned land resulting from shifting cultivation is not included in this category. Data for "Arable land" are not meant to indicate the amount of land that is potentially cultivable" (FAO 2018).

b. Of all the listed countries in Table 6.2, Afghanistan is the only country where wheat production exceeds that of maize or rice; wheat production in 2016 was 4,555,110 MT (FAO 2018).

Source: FAO, 2018.

6.2 Overview of the AFSL Programme in BRAC International

Creating an enabling environment for smallholder farmers and other poor individuals with access to tiny household plots of land has become the cornerstone of AFSL's work. Through its years of work in alleviating poverty and building sustainable livelihoods, BRAC has developed a deep understanding of the barriers these farmers face. It has geared its approach towards helping people increase their incomes, build their resilience, and improve food security. In terms of the Sustainable Development Goals (SDGs), the BRAC AFSL approach addresses two core goals: SDG 2 - zero hunger and SDG 12 - responsible consumption and production, while also supporting SDG 1 (end poverty) and SDG 8 (decent work and economic growth). In addition, SDGs 3, 5, and 13 are affected where their focus areas overlap (good-health and wellbeing, gender equality, and climate change respectively).

BRAC's follows two distinct approaches in the AFSL programme as below:

a. Direct delivery approach; and
b. Market development approach.

6.2.1 Direct delivery approach

One of BRAC's hallmark approaches has been direct implementation. This direct service delivery approach is especially appropriate for countries where existing markets are grossly underdeveloped, such as in Liberia and Sierra Leone. In these environments, BRAC plays a hands-on role in training farmers, supplying inputs, and creating cadres of self-employed entrepreneurs. As a form of micro-franchising, this entrepreneurship-based delivery system is complemented by marketing and model farmers who train other farmers through the use of demonstration plots. Their work is further complemented by BRAC's social enterprises, which include a poultry hatchery, seed farms, and a feed mill, which provide a foundation for future market development. In these countries, there are a few input suppliers (e.g., seed enterprises) who import the inputs from different countries rather than promote to stimulate domestic production. There is little or no mechanisation, and most farmers produce simply for their own consumption. Even if they produce a surplus, buyers often do not exist.

6.2.2 Market development approach

In more developed markets, BRAC plays less of a direct role and places greater emphasis on facilitating other value chain players and incorporating components of a "Making markets work for the poor" (M4P) approach[2]. Here too, BRAC engages smallholders, directly focusing on women farmers and leveraging its strength as a provider of technical training and microfinance services. It also facilitates the building of farm-to-market connections. This involves working with other market actors such as small- and medium-sized enterprises. This approach provides both an initial push, and it also enables the long-term sustainability of a new, pro-poor market system. It is based on the recognition that no single service provider—be it BRAC, the government, or any other NGO or private sector actor—can catalyse the large-scale change needed for the development of agriculture. It requires existing private enterprises (including hatcheries, agro-vets, seed farms, and fertiliser dealers) to improve and expand their services in a way that ultimately benefits the smallholder farmer.

BRAC has combined direct service delivery with M4P activities (called hybrid M4P) with success in Tanzania. This approach has the potential to be replicated in Uganda and other sub-Saharan countries where markets are moderately developed.

In both the Direct Delivery and Market Development approaches, BRAC builds partnerships with relevant NGOs, government, and private actors by strengthening their capacities and sharing experiences and lessons with them. Within the public arena, the role of government has been changing. Many government agencies are being expected to "do more with less" (Gray and Stites 2013). Additionally, as the nature of problems evolve and often become more complex, the government agents find that to implement public policy, they need competencies that lie beyond the scope of their agencies. Here too, there may be specific potential roles for external agencies. For example, BRAC is currently participating in the Government of Liberia's development of a national framework for agriculture, playing a central role in drafting new livestock policies. BRAC plays an active role in engaging, informing, and influencing governmental decision-making on pro-smallholder farmer policies in the countries where it operates.

---

[2] Making Markets Work for the Poor (M4P) approach seeks to change the way that markets work, so that poor people are included in the benefits of growth and economic development to create a systemic change for the agricultural value chains.

6.2.3 Programme focus

Following the approaches mentioned above, BRAC supports smallholder farmers by improving food security, income, resilience, and nutrition through different interventions that develop productive and sustainable agriculture-based livelihoods. It emphasises and focuses on four areas: (1) strengthening market systems by building sustainable, pro-poor value chains; (2) improving agricultural production and agriculture-based nutrition through extension services on agronomic practices, growing nutrition-dense vegetables and livestock rearing; (3) promoting climate-smart agriculture; and (4) involving more women and youth in the agriculture and livestock value chain.

Strengthening market systems by building sustainable, pro-poor value chains

BRAC has always focused on the creation and promotion of value chains and integrating smallholder farmers in them to increase their production and income. Additionally, BRAC introduces new farming technology to increase the area of arable land as well as reduce post-harvest crop losses and livestock mortality. It also connects smallholder farmers to input and output markets. BRAC recognises that to achieve a broad and sustainable scale of coverage, it has to partner with existing market actors, strengthening their work in a way that ultimately benefits the smallholders through better, more accessible, and more affordable services. This facilitator role focuses on catalysing systemic market development by helping to create linkages within the complex networks of small companies that constitute the rural value chain.

Supporting enhanced nutrition

It is essential to focus on agriculture hand in hand with nutrition to address malnutrition. This is especially relevant in both Asia and Africa, where malnutrition remains common, and stunting rates have increased 23 percent since 1990, according to a 2015 report of UNICEF, the WHO, and the World Bank (World Bank 2015). Through its interventions, BRAC is promoting the growth of nutrition-rich crops and poultry rearing in its operating countries. (see section 3.0 on "Country-Specific Approaches and Activities").

BRAC's nutrition-sensitive agriculture activities entail targeting poor households, promoting gender equity, and providing nutrition education so that household resources are used to improve household members' nutrition, especially that of women and young children. Over the years, BRAC has been making its mark in the field of nutrition-sensitive agriculture, or "agri-nutrition." With a proven model, BRAC promotes training and capacity development of vulnerable, poor, and smallholder farmers by providing start-up support, access to finance, nutrition awareness campaigns, mother forums, and dietary diversity through its agri-nutrition projects in different countries.

Climate-smart agriculture

To address the complex impacts of climate change, BRAC has undertaken a number of interventions, including —

a. Strengthen the capacity of farmers and relevant stakeholders;
b. Introduce climate-smart agricultural technologies;
c. Promote improved climate-resilient crop/livestock varieties;
d. Promote alternative adaptation options; and
e. Raise awareness and build partnerships to address climate change in agriculture-dependent communities.

BRAC introduces and expands the production of environment-friendly and environment-resilient crop varieties (such as drought-tolerant and pest-resistant crops and short-duration crops)and improved poultry (e.g., *Kuroiler*) and livestock breeds, in areas where they are most needed. To enhance resilience, BRAC focuses on building the capacity of farmers to adapt to climate change while reducing their exposure to short-term risks.

Women and youth

Women and youth face an extraordinarily large share of challenges in the rural marketplace. BRAC has found that investments directly targeting women yield a higher social and economic return than other investments. Young people entering the job market face multiple social and financial pressures, including family pressures, early childbearing, unemployment, transactional sex, a lack of relevant vocational training, and rural-urban migration. This is especially true for adolescent girls, who often rely on subsistence farming while navigating the difficult terrain of adolescence (Bandiera et al. 2017). BRAC focuses on women and youth in its AFSL programme by targeting at least 65 percent of women and youth in every project and keeping the particular needs of women and youth in mind while designing its intervention. For example, training offered at the field level allows women participants to bring their children. Traders and market actors are encouraged to visit producer groups at the community level and to sell and buy products there to overcome the barriers women farmers face in connecting to the market. Youth interventions are often tailored to match their abilities and interests. Educated youths are often more interested in entrepreneurship, and they are thus often trained to become market actors in agriculture value chains.

6.2.4 Programme interventions

The AFSL programme engages with a wide range of agricultural sub-sectors such as crop agriculture, horticulture, cash crop, poultry, and livestock. All of BRAC's work is geared to help smallholder farmers and other poor individuals, while tailoring specific interventions according to local market contexts and conditions.

Improved agronomic practices and application of agricultural technologies

These interventions cover capacity development of model/lead farmers, general farmers, and village extension workers and establishment of crop and poultry demonstration plots/farms. The lead farmers further disseminate the knowledge and technical know-how gained from BRAC training within their producer groups. BRAC works closely with private sector actors for demonstration and technology transfer.

Improved input and output market access through developing entrepreneurs

BRAC strengthens the capacities of existing agro-vet/agro-dealers, traders, and other entrepreneurs in the selected value chains through training and by stimulating their businesses in the supply chain. In this regard, BRAC forms farmer producer groups (FPGs) headed by lead/model farmers and establishes strong relationships between the SMEs and producer groups. BRAC also partners with private sector companies to ensure the supply of reliable inputs and purchase of the farmers' products.

Agricultural finance

Access to mainstream microfinance is very limited for smallholder farmers. BRAC has developed specialised loan products with payment cycles and other conditions appropriate to the seasonality of the farmers' livelihoods. BRAC has developed two agri-loan types for its programmes in Tanzania and Uganda (see section 3.0). Group loans, ranging between USD 100 to USD 500, are provided to smallholder farmers who are part of a farmer group. Individual loans, between USD 1000 to USD 5000, are provided to individual SMEs. For example, the LEAD project in Tanzania has an investment fund component that aims to co-invest with agro entrepreneurs (SMEs) and aid in the development or improvement of products and services that serve smallholder farmers.

Supply of inputs

BRAC ensures the provision of inputs such as seeds and day-old chicks, which are chosen based on the context of the country. If the inputs are not available, or the available inputs are not of good quality, BRAC provides them from its own supplies. For example, BRAC has seed farms in Liberia, Sierra Leone, and Uganda, which provide good quality seeds to local farmers, and a poultry farm and feed mill in Liberia (see section 3.3 for details). If quality inputs are already available in the market, BRAC creates links between the supplier and farmers so that they can access quality inputs. Inputs such as medicine, vegetable seed, fertiliser, pesticides, and tools are often received via the private sector.

Digital technology promotion

Information and communications technology, particularly the increasing prevalence of mobile phones, presents an exciting opportunity to lower delivery costs for BRAC while expanding smallholder reach and access to information like agronomic best practices and technical support. By enabling access to critical market information, technology reduces the information imbalance between smallholder farmers and more powerful value chain players. For example, BRAC has been piloting a Feed Calculator project in Tanzania with Single Spark, a social business based in the Netherlands, for low-cost feed formulation, reducing costs, and increasing returns.

BRAC aims to increase the use of mobile technology in three areas: (1) mobile money (starting with mobile repayments and disbursements of micro-loans), (2) digital data collection and analysis, and (3) digital delivery of information like weather, market prices, disease, and pest outbreaks, and training content. BRAC has been piloting subsets of these innovations (for example, in the Japan Social Development Fund project in Uganda), and there are many opportunities to devise innovations and deploy them more broadly across operations.

Research and development

BRAC conducts rigorous trials to determine the suitability of crop and vegetable varieties in its operating countries, selecting varieties with shorter maturity, drought tolerance, and higher yield. BRAC collects the breeding material of maize, rice, cassava, and vegetables from research institutes or the respective government and conducts trials in its farms in Uganda, Liberia, and Sierra Leone (see details in Section 3.0). It also promotes locally-adapted poultry and livestock breeds (e.g., *Kuroiler* chicks) as they are more sustainable in the longer term.

Social enterprise

BRAC established social enterprises in a few countries where quality inputs such as seed, day-old chicks (DOCs), and feed are not available. In Liberia, there is a clear scarcity of domestically produced quality DOCs and feed, but there is no poultry hatchery and feed mill to produce and supply these inputs to farmers. Most of the DOCs and animal feed are imported from neighbouring countries. This does not ensure quality and is not cost-effective as there are high transport costs and high mortality rates of DOC. To address this problem, BRAC set up a Poultry Hatchery and Feed Mill in Liberia (Saleque and Imran 2016a). Similarly, after realising the challenges and the need for improved, quality seeds, BRAC set up agriculture research and seed testing centres in Uganda, Liberia, and Sierra Leone to produce and supply rice, maize, vegetable, and bean seeds to farmers. These centres also conduct research on local/hybrid seed varieties and do comparative analyses with other available seeds to identify the best-performing ones. In Uganda, BRAC has also set up a Tissue Culture Laboratory to produce disease-free orange-fleshed sweet potato (OFSP) vines and banana plantlets.

Key programme participants

Most of the participants under the BRAC AFSL programme are poor and smallholder farmers. Table 6.3 lists the different categories of farmers and others involved in BRAC's agriculture, food security, and livelihood programmes.

Table 6.3: Programme participants

Participants	Description
Lead/model farmers	Lead/model farmers are progressive farmers who are selected from the communities to motivate other farmers to use improved technologies. They receive 3-5 days of intensive training and play a key role in organising producer groups; they make linkages with input suppliers and buyers, community agriculture and poultry promoters, and relevant market actors, creating a platform for buying and selling products.
Demonstration (demo) farmers	Demonstration farms are established to test modern farming and rearing practices and to disseminate and share results amongst neighbouring farmers. Demonstration farmers are selected from lead farmers or CAPs/CPPs (see below). By practicing and adopting new technologies, they inspire other farmers in the community.
General farmers	General farmers receive 2-3 days of training and get information from neighbouring lead and demo farmers. They are part of producer groups, allowing them to make production plans and bulk purchases of inputs and to increase their bargaining power with buyers.
Producer/Farmer groups	Farmers groups are formed with 12 to 20 members, including one lead/model farmer and other general farmers, to exchange technical know-how, increase farmers' bargaining power, and establish linkages with local, regional, and national buyers, market actors, and millers. Farmer groups are also linked to input suppliers to access quality inputs.

Continued

Continued from Table 6.3

Description	Description
Community Livestock Promoters (CLPs)	CLPs are the primary actors who provide extension services and technical advice to livestock farmers at the community level. They are progressive farmers or entrepreneurs selected from local communities who receive 5 days of training and bimonthly refresher training from BRAC. They promote the use of quality inputs (e.g., feed, vaccines, feeders, drinkers, and feed) by linking poultry producer groups with agro-vets. They are also linked with government extension workers, where possible, to connect farmers to government services.
Community Agriculture Promoters (CAPs)	CAPs are the primary actors who, like CLPs, provide extension services and technical advice to agriculture farmers at the community level. They receive 5 days of training and bimonthly refreshers. They promote the use of quality inputs by linking farmer groups with agro-dealers.
Agro-vets/ agro-dealers	Agro-vets and agro-dealers are existing local entrepreneurs. By integrating and training them, BRAC facilitates a systemic change in the input supply and service delivery systems by allowing farmers to access input and output markets. BRAC provides 2 days of technical and business training to them.
Traders/ wholesalers	BRAC has identified traders and wholesalers to whom smallholder farmers are linked. These traders and wholesalers are the middlemen of the value chain who help smallholder farmers reach end markets and play a crucial role in overall market development. BRAC provides a 2-day long technical and business training to them.

BRAC's extension model for agriculture, poultry, and livestock

BRAC has developed its extension model based on its experience in different countries. The model is applied based on the country context. BRAC implements the AFSL programme through its branch offices, which cover around 1000-1200 farmers in 15-20 communities, depending on the country context. One Programme Assistant (PA) is based at the branch level and made responsible for supervising 10-15 community agriculture/livestock promoters (volunteers), each of whom are further responsible for providing services to 7-10 model farmers (MF) and 50-75 general farmers (GF). To use the market development approach, in addition to this model, each PA also supports 10-15 market actors, who are also directly linked with CAPs/CLPs. Community Agriculture Promoters (CLPs) specialise in quality seed, seed germination, seedling production, distribution, and marketing. Model farmers focus on production technology, insect and disease management, irrigation, and demonstrations. CLPs specialise in poultry vaccination, selling feed, and medicine.

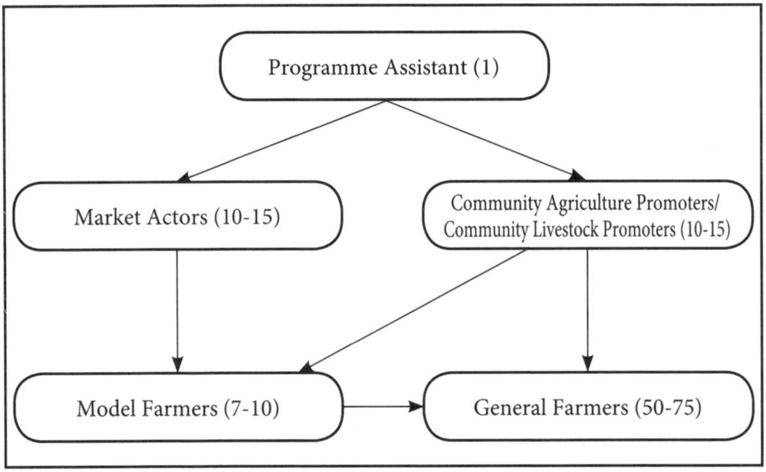

Figure 6.1: BRAC's extension model for agriculture, food security and livelihood

6.3 Country-Specific Approaches and Activities

The previous sections provided an overview of BRAC's overarching strategy for its agriculture, food security, and livelihood programme in Africa and Asia. The following section describes country-specific activities in Tanzania, Uganda, Liberia, Sierra Leone, South Sudan, and Afghanistan.

6.3.1 Tanzania

Tanzania is one of the poorest countries in Sub-Saharan Africa. It ranked 151 out of 187 countries on the United Nations Development Programme (UNDP) Human Development Index in 2016. Some 13 million Tanzanians live in poverty. Eighty-five percent of the population live in rural areas and rely on agriculture for their livelihoods, their source of income, and food security (Saleque 2017a). Agriculture and livestock are the backbone of the Tanzanian economy and accounted for 31 percent of the GDP in 2016 (World Bank 2016). The agriculture sector is dominated by smallholder farmers, most of whom operate at subsistence level and face challenges in expanding their production to the commercial scale. These constraints range from barriers to production (e.g., limited access to land and capital, poor knowledge of modern farming technology, imperfect markets, lack of transportation, inadequate access to quality inputs), barriers to trade (unintegrated agricultural input and output markets, poor transport links, and an absence of effective market communication), and barriers to finance, (because farming is perceived to be too risky).

Highlights (2008-2017): Tanzania

- 9,144 farmers producer groups formed
- 125,828 agriculture farmers and 71,928 livestock and poultry rearers received training
- 447 agro-entrepreneurs (agro-vets and agro-dealers, traders, etc.) developed
- 689 CAP and 1962 CLPs/CLPPs and 100 Livestock Artificial Insemination promoters (LAIPs) received training
- 777 horticulture nursery owners received training
- 17,663,427 nursery saplings distributed to farmers
- 2070 demonstration farms (agriculture-1520 and poultry-550) established
- 122,340 livestock inseminated
- 53,830,055 doses of poultry vaccine used
- 2 loan products developed
- 27,000 farmers received agriculture loan, and 50 entrepreneurs received SME loans

BRAC has been working in Tanzania since 2006 but started its AFSL programmes in 2007 through a project supported by the Bill and Melinda Gates Foundation (BMGF). The goal of the project was to increase production and income by providing training to farmers and ensuring the supply of agricultural inputs, quality seeds, fertilizers, pesticides, feed, tools, and access to markets for more than 100,000 farmers and other members of the community. Support from BMGF enabled relevant foundational agricultural extension services, agricultural research and development, and seed production. The project phased out in 2011.

Taking into account the learning from this first project, BRAC designed its next project, "Helping poor farmers in Tanzania," funded by DFID from April 2012 to March 2015, to increase productivity. The project raised the skills, capacities, productivity, and incomes of 14,050 small and marginal farmers (65% women) in crops, vegetables, nursery, poultry, and livestock. It focused heavily on developing community service providers and trained 300 CAPs, 400 CLPs, and 100 Artificial Insemination (AI) workers (BRAC 2015a). The project provided comprehensive support, including high-quality inputs, capacity building, technology transfer, demonstration, installation of irrigation pumps, and market linkages.

After implementing two projects following a direct delivery approach, BRAC realised that to support overall economic growth and ensure the sustainability of its intervention, it needed to go beyond direct delivery and work with the private sector actors. Therefore, in concert with DFID, it co-designed the "Livelihood Enhancement through Agricultural Development (LEAD) Project," a modified M4P model that was implemented over four years (April 2013-March 2017). Through this project, BRAC began piloting a modified approach to market development in Tanzania. LEAD incorporated elements of the "Making Markets Work for the Poor" (M4P) approach, which seeks to change the way that markets work, so that poor people are included in the benefits of growth and economic development to create a systemic change in the poultry and maize value chains.

The LEAD initiative had four objectives:

1. Connect smallholder farmers to markets
2. Establish a strong community-based supply chain providing technical services and inputs
3. Support smallholder investment in their farms by offering agri-finance loans
4. Stimulate the growth of small- and medium-sized private agricultural enterprises (SMEs).

LEAD represented an important two-fold shift in the way BRAC approached its role in the agricultural supply chain.

- With LEAD, BRAC began a transition to a "facilitator" role, rather than the more active "implementer" role it played in earlier interventions. BRAC recognised that to reach a transformative scale, it would have to partner with existing market actors, strengthening their work in a way that ultimately would benefit the smallholder through better, more accessible, and more affordable services. This facilitator role focused on catalysing systemic market development by helping to create linkages between the complex network of small- and medium-sized companies that constitute the rural value chain, including seed suppliers, chick hatcheries, feed producers, and livestock veterinary service providers. At the same time, some services were still implemented directly, such as loans to farmers via BRAC's microfinance unit and training to smallholder farmers, since private sector actors were not interested in playing such a role. The LEAD project also connected these smallholder farmers to input and output markets and organised farmers into more sustainable, formal groups. Farmers were linked with agro-dealers, traders, and other market actors and were encouraged to sell their produce to non-local markets through collective and contractual sales.

- LEAD introduced an investment fund to stimulate small- and medium-sized enterprises (small private sector, dealer, traders, and market actors) to supply quality inputs and provide services to smallholder farmers. BRAC provided capacity development training and business development training as well as credit support (40% grant and 60% loan).

The LEAD programme tapped into both supply and demand forces, working at several levels to improve farmers' practices and use of technology, facilitating linkages to markets and finance, and stimulating private investment in the agricultural value chain. Smallholder farmers participating in LEAD received training in agronomic best practices (e.g., using drought-tolerant maize, incorporating climate-smart practices like intercropping) and new technologies on the market. They gained access to high-quality inputs such as seed and feed from vetted dealers and finance to grow their production output. LEAD included two financial products for smallholders and micro-entrepreneurs: a loan for general maize and poultry farmers (which typically is paid in monthly instalments, with 6- or 12-month tenures), and a loan for agro-vet and agro-dealers. BRAC also partnered with the One Acre Fund NGO in Tanzania to design and deliver specialised loan products (which included inputs) to smallholders.

LEAD served 106,000 smallholder farmers (65% women), formed 8,021 producer groups, disbursed USD 8.4 million in agri-finance loans to 27,000 farmers and USD 722,375 in investment fund loans to 50 SMEs, and facilitated 80 value chain workshops. It also trained and supported 89 local agro-dealers and 50 investment fund entrepreneurs to provide services to outreach farmers and also helped to develop their businesses to meet farmers' inputs and services and output needs. The LEAD project also introduced the adoption of post-harvest processing equipment such as the maize sheller, Purdue Improved Crop Storage (PICS) bags, and drying technologies. Due to increased growth and lower feed costs, farmers were able to secure, on average, 1.8 times higher profit for chickens raised on smartphone app-supported feed formulas (BRAC 2017e). A comparison of baseline and end-line assessments shows that the project led to significant gains in farmers' income and productivity (BRAC 2017e). Because of the success of the project, BRAC has adopted this modified M4P model as one of its core intervention models and plans to expand it in other BRAC countries, with necessary contextualisation.

6.3.2 Uganda

Agriculture is the core of Uganda's economy and the primary source of employment, engaging 73 percent of the country's labour force, primarily in rural areas. It comprises 24 percent of total GDP (World Bank 2016). The sector remains one of the critical determinants of the improvement of household livelihoods and the socioeconomic transformation of the country.

Starting from a modest launch in 2006, Uganda is the site of BRAC's largest and fastest scale-up in Africa. Its programmes have included microfinance, small enterprise, crop agriculture, poultry and livestock, health, education, youth empowerment, adolescent livelihoods, and the Karamoja Initiative (a holistic programme addressing complex challenges in this disadvantaged subregion). BRAC Uganda has been operating agricultural programmes since 2007, reaching approximately two million people, and it has undertaken a variety of initiatives to stimulate the market in a sustainable manner.

BRAC Uganda recently completed a six-year agricultural extension service delivery project funded by Master Card Foundation (MCF), which was implemented across 100 branches in 64 districts. The project aimed to enhance the livelihood opportunities of smallholder farmers and their families by providing comprehensive support such as capacity building to general farmers, model farmers, adolescent girls, youth entrepreneurs, community agriculture promoters (CAPs), community livestock and poultry promoters (CLPPs), and artificial insemination (AI) workers. BRAC provided training and ensured the supply of agricultural inputs (quality seeds, day-old *Kuroiler* chicks, vaccines) and credit support, as well as access to markets. The project ultimately supported more than 366,710 farmers. With additional support from the Japan Social Development Fund (JSDF), project support was extended to 386,000 farmers. CAPs were trained to buy the improved seed and sell it to farmers. Similarly, CLPPs sell feed, tools, and provide vaccination services to their community. Model farmers were trained so that they could provide training and information to other farmers regarding advanced agricultural and livestock practices (Fishman et al. 2017).

Highlights 2008-2017: Uganda

- 6,060 farmers producer groups formed
- 149,660 agriculture farmers and 237,250 livestock and poultry rearers received training
- 502 agro-entrepreneurs (agro-vets and agro-dealers, traders, etc.) developed
- 1080 CAP, 1500 CLP/CLPP, and 84 AI worker received training
- 386 horticulture nursery owners received training
- 1308 MT seeds distributed to farmers
- 1,952 demonstration farms (agriculture-466 and poultry-1366) established
- 19,200 farmers involved in Vitamin-A enriched OFSP production
- 31,766,680 doses of poultry vaccine used
- 946,572 nursery saplings distributed to farmers

Years of work with the rural farmers and close interaction with their communities helped BRAC realise that increasing income and production alone is not sufficient to fight the high rate of malnutrition in the country. Achieving nutrition standards requires a multi-sectoral and integrated approach. BRAC designed "An Innovative, Integrated Approach to Enhance Smallholder Family Nutrition," a project which was implemented in four districts (Kalungu, Rakai, Ibanda, and Sheema) of South-Western Uganda with funding from JSDF through the World Bank. The project aligns with the Uganda Nutrition Action Plan (UNAP), whose ultimate goal is to reduce malnutrition among women of reproductive age, infants, and young children. This three-year project was launched in July 2014 to introduce vitamin A-rich orange-fleshed sweet potato (OFSP), which has the potential to significantly reduce childhood malnutrition in the region. The project combines best practices in agriculture and health support to improve nutrition in mothers and young children. It has supported 19,200 poor and smallholder farmers in 180 villages in 17 sub-counties under four districts. The programme resulted in an increase in the consumption of nutritious OFSPs, resulting in an overall expansion in the intake of nutrient-rich foods. Through this project, BRAC also piloted the use of digital technology to make information easily available to farmers and to increase the efficiency of project implementation.

The Community Connector (CC) project was a five-year (2011–2016) USAID-funded project that worked with vulnerable households in 15 districts of Uganda to reduce poverty by improving nutritional status and sustainably strengthening agricultural livelihoods. A number of activities were implemented to address household behaviour on nutrition, hygiene, diet quality and diversity, and child spacing. The activities included community dialogue sessions, Family Life Schools, educational drama performances, radio programmes, household visits, children's malnutrition assessments, primary school nutrition clubs, and the multiplication of fruit trees and amaranth seeds. Training in agricultural technologies, farming as a business, and establishing links to markets was also provided, complemented by micro-enterprise training and grants. Over the life of the project, CC worked directly with 97,246 households made up of 539,118 people.

BRAC's earlier work in Uganda focused on the farmers' capacity building and linking them with extension services. However, these interventions were not obtaining the desired improvement in farmers' incomes because quality seed remained one of the major challenges in

Uganda. Only ten percent of seeds were supplied from formal sectors. Based on this local need, BRAC set up a seed enterprise in Uganda's Nakaseke District (Central Region) in 2009 to provide quality seeds and their timely delivery to smallholder farmers. BRAC Uganda formally created BRAC Uganda Social Business Enterprise Ltd, a legal entity, for the seed production farm and processing unit in 2011.

In 2015, BRAC Uganda Social Business Enterprise installed an improved and highly-automated seed processing plant to process maize, vegetable, and rice seed with a capacity of producing up to 12 tons of maize seed per day. Further, BRAC has a seed farm of 50 acres, also in Nakaseke, where it conducts trials of different varieties of crops, including OFSPs. In addition, it has three production hubs for growing seeds through contract farming. BRAC's seed processing plant also has a newly developed Seed Quality Control Lab to test seed purity, moisture, and germination percentage. The seed social enterprise buys the seeds from contract growers, processes them at the seed processing plant, and then sells them to farmers through agro-dealers and BRAC-trained CAPS. In 2017, the seed enterprise produced and sold 580 metric tons of seeds (rice, maize, vegetable, and beans). This facility enables BRAC to put research into practice and provide the highest quality inputs for local farmers at comparable and competitive prices (see Highlights). BRAC has introduced 11 varieties and has marketed three maize varieties, one rice variety, two bean varieties, and five vegetable varieties, and also identified three varieties of cabbage, bean, and pumpkin for 2017.

BRAC also set up a tissue culture laboratory in July 2015 to produce disease-free, OFSP vines, plantain (*matoke*), Irish potato, and more.

6.3.3 Liberia

Agriculture and livestock play essential roles in alleviating poverty, increasing income, and improving food security for poor and smallholder farmers in Liberia. Eighty-three percent of the population of the country lives below USD 1.25 a day, and food insecurity affects 16 percent of households (World Food Programme 2015).

Both the government and development partners consider these to be priority sectors. But Liberia is still a net importer of food and essential agricultural commodities. While there are a handful of vegetable seed companies, quality remains a major issue, and no private seed companies exist for selling rice and maize seeds. Farmers tend to borrow seed from neighbours or keep some of their own grain to plant the following year. However, farmers are willing to buy quality seed if they have the opportunity. The livestock subsector is relatively unproductive, contributing only 14 percent of the agricultural GDP and relying heavily on imports due to a poorly developed domestic sector. Cattle, goats, and sheep are imported from Guinea, Cote D'Ivoire, and Mali, and the poultry sector is similarly reliant on imports of day-old chicks that have around a 25 percent mortality rate in transport, thus driving up costs.

Highlights 2008–2017: Liberia

- 1,650 farmers producer groups formed
- 10,008 agriculture farmers and 13,735 poultry and livestock rearers received training.
- 263 CAP and 567 CLP/CLPP received training
- 129 agro-entrepreneurs (agro-vets and agro-dealers) developed
- 224 horticulture nursery owners received training
- 25.5 MT seeds distributed to farmers
- 368 MT feed and 80,734 day-old chicks sold to farmers
- 1,780 demonstration farms (agriculture-91, poultry-900 and livestock-779) established
- 696,221 doses of poultry vaccination used
- 7 water pumps installed
- 195 households received cash for work facilities
- 26 nutritional awareness campaign organised

BRAC started its poultry and livestock programme in Liberia in 2008 with SEDF and Omidyar Network support. The programme addressed the problem of poor crop and livestock production and productivity through the capacity development of farmers and by ensuring the supply of essential inputs and creating market linkages. The programme was designed to raise farm productivity and income and increase rural employment. It included a wide variety of small-scale production systems in rural and peri-urban areas.

Since the nutritional status and food security of the population is very low and many farmers still struggle with subsistence farming, BRAC's projects focused more on food and nutrition security programmes. "Reducing hunger in the rural areas of Liberia" was BRAC's second AFSL project in Liberia. Funded by DFID and implemented from April 2012 to March 2015, the project aimed to reduce hunger in the rural areas of Liberia by providing training and inputs to poor landless women to establish kitchen gardens (2500 farmers) and small-scale poultry farms (240 farmers) in their homesteads and link them with market actors.

Simultaneously, BRAC implemented the "Increasing food security in poor, rural areas in Liberia through livestock production, processing and marketing" project, which was supported by the EU from 2012 to 2016. The project worked to increase the income of project beneficiaries through capacity building and by providing support to 12,650 farmers in the poultry, goat, pig, and cattle value chains in 20 branch offices in 6 BI counties. Additional capacity building and support targeted 400 community service providers, local traders, government staff, and market actors. The project established seven pig breeding farms and four slaughterhouses and smokehouses and also trained staff in hygienic slaughtering and meat-handling practices. BRAC adopted a technical assistance role in this project, which then acted as a steppingstone for BRAC as it then supported the Liberian Ministry of Agriculture in developing its livestock policy for the government (BRAC 2016).

In 2014, when the Ebola Virus Disease (EVD) afflicted the country, BRAC had to suspend its regular operations for three months due to government-imposed emergency restrictions on movements and gathering. BRAC's beneficiaries were affected in many ways, including migration, loss of farm resources, and closure of markets. In the aftermath, BRAC focused its interventions towards recovery and resilience building of farmers. It launched the "Building Resilience against Ebola" project funded by the Google Foundation from April 2015 to June 2016. The goal of the project was to support community mobilisation in preventing the spread of Ebola and bolster the recovery process via health and livelihood/agriculture/livestock support in the post-Ebola period. The project supported 2,740 poor and smallholder farmers (240 backyard poultry rearers and 2,500 kitchen gardeners). The emergency livelihood support included feed support to model poultry rearers, training and input to kitchen gardeners, and social mobilisation and advocacy against Ebola (BRAC 2017a).

The combination of large amounts of unused land (Liberia has only 5% of its arable land under cultivation; see Table 6.2) and the demand for increased food production led BRAC to come up with a different set of interventions, which were implemented under the "Food Assistance for Asset" project funded by WFP from February 2017 to June 2017. The project supported over 6,000 vulnerable beneficiaries in clearing vegetation and developing community or government-owned land for crop and vegetable cultivation. The project also supported the maintenance of feeder roads and the construction of drainage. The beneficiaries received food for their work for 90 days. Through this project, the beneficiaries received short term (food for work) and long term (crop cultivation in fallow land) benefits (BRAC 2017a). The project created a pathway to engage the most vulnerable, landless households in agricultural production.

Combining its experience and learning from different projects, BRAC designed the "Supporting the poor and food and nutrition insecure to react to crises and strengthen resilience in Liberia" project in 2016, funded by the European Union. Under this project, BRAC Liberia is working in both the crop and livestock farming sectors, targeting 7,500 poor and vulnerable farmers (65% women) in six severe and moderately food insecure counties (Grand Cape Mount, Bomi, Margibi, Grand Bassa, Montserrado, and Bong). This project builds resilience against food crises, enhances access to sufficient and nutritious food by addressing temporary/permanent market failures, improves access to balanced dietary intake in post-crises situations, and develops capacity at regional, national, and local levels on effective resilience-building initiatives and mechanisms.

BRAC poultry farm and feed mill

BRAC felt the need to set up a local poultry hatchery and feed mill enterprise to boost the poultry sector and decrease the dependency on importing key inputs. Most DOCs and animal feed were imported from neighbouring countries. As already mentioned, this did not ensure quality and was not cost effective as there were high transport costs and high mortality of DOCs. Therefore, BRAC Liberia established the Poultry Hatchery and Feed Mill in Buchanan, Grand Bassa County, funded by Chevron Foundation and the European Union. BRAC became the first NGO to establish a seed farm, a poultry hatchery, and a feed mill in Liberia. Its operation began in March 2014 (Saleque and Imran 2016a; 2016b).

BRAC has developed 500 poultry model farmers while demand for locally produced DOC and feed has been growing gradually. The production capacity of the poultry hatchery is 125,000 DOC per year, and the feed mill capacity is 672 metric tons (MT) per year. Currently, BRAC's poultry hatchery is supplying DOC to 90 percent of farmers. However, this production is lower than its capacity due to limited market demand in Liberia as well as small commercial farm size (Saleque and Imran 2016a).

BRAC seed farm

The local challenges and the need for improved quality seeds encouraged BRAC to set up the first Agriculture Research and Seed Testing (ARST) centre in Liberia in 2010. The ARST produces high-quality maize and rice seeds and multiplies yellow cassava cuttings. The breeding materials are collected from the Liberian Central Agricultural Research Institute (CARI) and other research institutes. Rice and maize seeds and cassava cuttings are sold directly to smallholder farmers through CAPs. Cassava farmers are also linked directly to millers, who process and sell the milled cassava, and rice farmers are similarly linked with rice millers. Recently, the BRAC seed research centre also started producing vegetable seeds. The seed centre also conducts research on local and hybrid seed varieties to find out which seeds perform best. Using that knowledge, BRAC then multiplies the selected seeds and sells them. The initiative has been appreciated by different agencies, and BRAC has an advantage by being the pioneer in this industry (Saleque and Imran 2016b). The seed farm produced and sold about 19.5 MT of rice seed, six MT of maize, and distributed over 3,000 vitamin cassava cuttings to farmers up to 2017.

6.3.4 Sierra Leone

BRAC began operations in Sierra Leone in 2008. It has since pursued projects to promote poultry, livestock, and agriculture development, develop swampland for improved rice cultivation, develop the pig value chain, increase food security and recovery following the Ebola epidemic, operate seed testing and multiplication farms, and strengthen the resilience of extremely poor women and their families following disasters. Through its programme, BRAC provides training to farmers, establishes demonstration farms, produces and distributes quality seeds, provides inputs and tools to farmers, and conducts nutrition awareness campaigns.

Highlights 2008-2017: Sierra Leone

- 768 farmers producer groups formed
- 19,231 agriculture farmers and 2108 poultry rearers received training
- 200 CAP and 216 CLP/CLPP received training
- 8 demonstration farms (agriculture-1 and livestock-7) established
- 17,000 chicks distributed to farmers
- 409,020 doses of poultry vaccine used
- 7 pig breeding farms, 75 model pig farms, 750 pig rearers, and 4 slaughterhouses developed.
- 10 blocks of IVS of over 100 hectors of land developed.
- Seed farm produced and sold about 10.6 MT of rice, 1 MT of maize, and distributed over 1000 vitamin cassava cuttings to farmers.

With support from the SEDF and Omidyar Foundation during 2008-2011, a project was launched that aimed to increase the income level of farmers/rearers (especially women), which would subsequently increase their asset-base. The programme focused on capacity building of farmers and the supply of quality inputs for farming to increase the productivity of rural farmers.

The "Reducing hunger in the rural areas of Sierra Leone" project was funded by DFID for three years. The project aimed to reduce hunger in rural areas by providing training and supplying inputs to 3,000 poor landless women to establish kitchen gardens and 400 small-scale poultry farms in their homesteads and linked them with market actors. This project increased family food intake and improved the nutrition and general health of children (Khakshi et al. 2015). About 200 CAPs and 200 CLPPs were also trained under this project.

As in Liberia, Sierra Leone was also affected by the Ebola virus disease outbreak. The "Building Resilience against Ebola" project in Sierra Leone was supported by Google from June 2015 to March 2016. The goal of the project was to support community mobilisation to prevent the spread of Ebola and to bolster recovery via health and livelihood, agriculture, and livestock support in the post-Ebola period. The project supported 500 poultry rearers and 3,000 kitchen gardeners to resume production, which had been devastated during the Ebola epidemic. The project also supported the initiation of rice and maize seed production in the BRAC seed farm for distribution among farmers, which was critical during the post-Ebola phase.

In addition, BRAC implemented the Food Security and Livelihoods Project supported by Oxfam/Disaster Emergency Committee (DEC) from May 2015 to October 2016. The project aimed to ensure food security and livelihoods in the Koinadugu district. The project provided technical support and organisational strengthening training for ten women's agricultural processing groups. Cash transfers for food were provided to extremely poor households in 23 Ebola-quarantined communities in Koinadugu, a remote and inaccessible district. One thousand two hundred households were provided with conditional cash grants to purchase groundnut, rice, pepper seeds, fertilizer, and agricultural tools as start-up capital.

The "Reducing poverty and hunger by increasing incomes and improving livelihoods" project, funded by DFID and implemented from May 2015 to October 2017, aimed to sustainably reduce poverty and hunger by increasing the incomes and improving the livelihoods of pig farmers. The project supported farmers by improving their knowledge, skills, and access to affordable high-quality inputs (e.g., feed, vaccines, and medicines). The project also developed community service providers and linked them with pig rearers and other market actors. The project established five pig breeding farms for production and supplied quality pigs to 75 model farms, 750 general farmers, and other community people. It also established four slaughter/smoke-houses for meat processing (BRAC 2017d).

The Inland Valley Swamp (IVS) project, supported by the WFP and JICA, was implemented from October 2015 to April 2016 in ten communities in Port Loko district. The project developed 106 hectares of IVS land to improve rice cultivation by using improved technology, and it developed links with Agriculture Business Centres (ABCs) for the processing of rice. In addition to training, this project supported 530 direct beneficiaries through cash for work and land leasing initiatives to develop the livelihoods of vulnerable farmers. The project also formed ten village savings and loan associations (VSLA) for generating community and household assets. The average rice yields nearly trebled from one MT to nearly three MT per hectare after two years of project intervention (BRAC 2015c).

Seed testing and multiplication farm

BRAC established a Seed Testing and Multiplication Farm of 63 acres at Lunsar, Port Loko district in 2012 to test and multiply highly productive varieties of crops as well as to demonstrate improved farm management. It produces high-quality rice and maize seeds and also multiplies yellow cassava cuttings. The breeding materials are collected from the Sierra Leone Agricultural Research Institute (SLARI) and other research institutes. Recently, the BRAC seed farm also started producing vegetable seeds. It tests the local and hybrid seed varieties to find potentially best-performing seeds. Using that knowledge, BRAC then multiplies and sells this seed. BRAC is recognised as the pioneer and first mover in this sector, and the initiative is appreciated by various agencies. Since its inception, the seed farm has produced and sold about 10.6 MT of rice seed and one MT of maize, and it has also distributed over 1,000 vitamin-A-rich cassava cuttings to farmers.

6.3.5 South Sudan

BRAC began its work in South Sudan in 2008. Eighty percent of the population lives in rural areas with agriculture, forestry, and fisheries the primary livelihood activities for a majority of households (African Development Bank 2013). Two and a half decades ago, the country was a net exporter of agricultural products to regional markets, but recurring conflicts and war have turned the country into a net importer of food. BRAC's work in the agriculture and livestock sector of South Sudan mainly focuses on providing emergency livelihood support to the displaced population along with building their capacity to adopt improved agricultural techniques and technologies.

Highlights: South Sudan

- 3,760 farmers producer groups formed
- 20,837 agriculture farmers, 100 poultry and livestock rearers, and 920 CAP received training
- 60 MT seeds distributed to farmers
- 32 MT feed distributed to farmers
- Fishing and vegetables kits distributed to 12,077 households
- 52 demonstration farms (agriculture) established

In an effort to design an effective approach for the extremely poor population of South Sudan, BRAC has collaborated with the WFP In a project that offered an integrated package of food distribution, skill development, and savings and credit opportunities to support the resettlement of 530 displaced poor of South Sudan.

BRAC executed the "Improving Techniques and Technology for ensuring Food Security through Agriculture in South Sudan Project," funded by Oxfam Novib, from 2013 to 2015. This project aimed at improving techniques and technology in agriculture to ensure food security. The project provided training to 240 farmers (40 demonstration farmers and 200 ox-plough farmers), 280 kitchen gardeners, and 100 poultry rearers, and it established two collective demonstration farms (CDF) on 21 acres of land involving 40 community farmers (30 female and 10 male). Farmers learned about the best practices and modern techniques for the cultivation of maize, sorghum, cassava, vegetables, groundnuts, and upland rice. They were able to practice modern farming techniques in the farms and to increase their yields as well as preserve good quality seeds for the next year's cultivation (BRAC 2017b).

From 2014 to 2016, BRAC implemented two "Emergency Livelihood Response Projects' supported by FAO. The main activity of this project was the distribution of foundation seeds to support the implementation of seed multiplication activities through farmer groups. The first project distributed crop seeds directly to 2,300 farmers, while the second project distributed fishing and vegetable kits to 12,077 households;

it also organised trade fairs in Central and Eastern Equatorial states (BRAC 2017b).

Highlights 2003-2017: Afghanistan

- 19,984 farmers received training
- 3,000,000 nursery saplings distributed to farmers
- 2 MT of seeds distributed to farmers
- 200 adolescent girls received training in vegetable gardening

6.3.6 Afghanistan

Afghanistan is the first country to which BRAC expanded its operation outside of Bangladesh in 2002 (Chowdhury et al. 2006). The Agriculture, Food Security, and Livelihood Programme was one of BRAC's key focus areas in the country in its first few years of operation. Some of the projects conducted by BRAC in Afghanistan over the years are described below.

The "Agriculture Development Project," funded by WFP, was implemented from 2004 to 2008. The project aimed to improve livelihoods through the adoption of modern technology and sustainable agriculture practices throughout the country. Through training, the project developed the technical skills of 12,682 farmers in the crop, vegetable, livestock, and poultry sectors with a special focus on vulnerable women and women-headed households. The project also developed 2,286 agro-entrepreneurs and linked them with other market actors. It supported smallholder farmers, including the provision of input supply (i.e., seed, fertiliser, pesticides, DOC, vaccine), demonstrations, technology transfer and adaptation, livestock clinics, developing market linkages, and other activities. Along with technical training, BRAC provided microfinance support to the beneficiaries who had no cash to purchase cows, sheep, goats, or other agricultural assets. The project reached a cumulative total of 19,984 farmers (BRAC 2017c; 2008).

BRAC also executed the "Kitchen gardening and horticulture nursery project" funded by the World Food Programme from 2004 to 2008. The objectives of the project were to increase the income and employment opportunities of village women, to mobilise and organise poor women to produce vegetables through kitchen gardening, increase the nutritional status of poor families, and promote effective homestead land-use to increase agricultural production. In this project, around 250 female beneficiaries from six districts of two provinces were trained in kitchen gardening and received support for horticulture nurseries. Farmers produced 3,000,000 saplings and distributed them to neighbouring farmers. Similarly, during the agriculture and livestock project in 2008, BRAC introduced loans that helped many farmers start or continue their businesses for better livelihoods.

More recently, in 2016 and 2017, BRAC implemented the "Promoting collective vegetable gardening by adolescent girls for reducing malnutrition" project funded by Leveraging Agriculture for Nutrition in South Asia (LANSA). The objective of the project was to improve the nutrition levels of adolescents and their household members by promoting vegetable cultivation and consumption among 200 adolescent girls and their household members. The pilot project took place in eight communities, with 25 adolescent girls selected per community for collective farming of different vegetables such as tomato, potato, cucumber, onion, cabbage, cauliflower, radish, and spinach. The core objective of the training was to explain the practical aspects of vegetable cultivation, in addition to emphasising the importance of vegetable consumption for better health. Girls also received information about the types of vitamins and minerals contained in the vegetables that are useful for reducing malnutrition. A large majority of girls in the intervention groups participated in gardening, demonstrating their interest in the interventions, and many girls displayed increased levels of nutrition-related knowledge by the end of the project (Alim et al. 2017).

6.4 Impacts and Learning

BRACI's AFSL programme has covered over 600,000 poor and smallholder farmers and reached over three million people in six countries outside Bangladesh. Table 6.4 shows the numbers of model farmers, general farmers, and community service providers in each country. Figure 6.2 shows the cumulative growth over the years 2011-17.

Table 6.4: Number of farmers and community service providers

Country	No. of Model Farmers				No. of General Farmers				Community Service Providers			Total Population Reached by BRAC
	Agri-culture	Poultry	Live-stock	Total	Agri-culture	Poultry	Live-stock	Total	CAP	CPP	Total	
Tanzania	5,137	4,007	0	9,144	120,691	62,305	5,616	188,612	689	1,962	2,651	969,004
Uganda	2,060	2,000	2,400	6,460	147,600	232,250	600	380,450	1,080	1,500	2,580	1,818,477
Liberia	0	900	750	1,650	10,008	8,390	3,695	22,093	200	500	700	121,089
Sierra Leone	378	130	260	768	18,853	900	818	20,571	200	216	416	125,900
South Sudan	3,760	0	0	3,760	17,077	100	0	17,177	920	0	920	125,622
Afghanistan	n/a	n/a	n/a	n/a	18,082	n/a	1,902	19,984	n/a	n/a	n/a	145,883
Total	11,163	7,037	3,410	21,782	332,311	303,945	12,631	648,887	3,089	4,178	7,267	3,305,976

Source: BRAC MIS, 2017c.

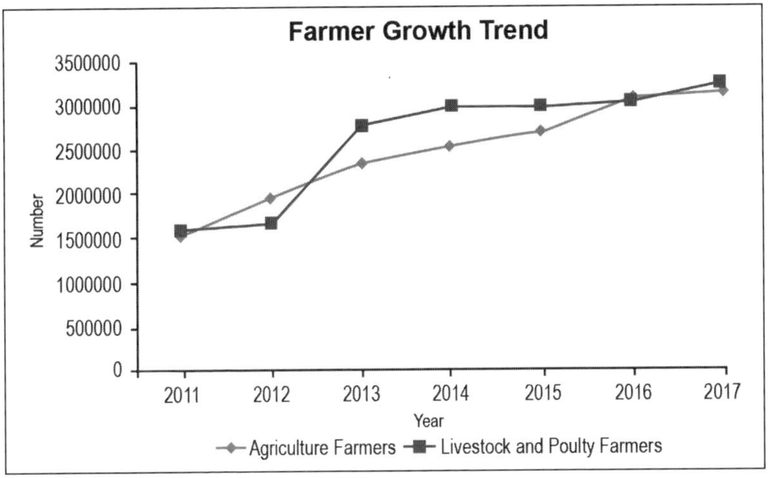

Source: BRAC MIS, 2017c.

Figure 6.2: Growth trend of general and model farmers in the BI countries

6.4.1 Major successes: A narrative

Successfully replicated BRAC models: The AFSL programme has successfully replicated BRAC's core programme models, which were tried and tested first in Bangladesh and then in different countries across the world with necessary contextualisation. This supported the overall south-south cooperation agenda with which BRAC international started its operations. It has once again proved that the cost-effective models developed by BRAC in Bangladesh are equally effective and relevant in addressing poverty, food insecurity, and other challenges in different countries.

Expanded from direct delivery to facilitator and technical assistance role: Although the AFSL programme started its operation by replicating tested models, it went beyond that and developed new models with a stronger focus on market system development. BRAC shifted itself towards a facilitator role, rather than only the implementer role, as seen in the DFID-funded LEAD project in Tanzania. Through the success of its interventions, BRAC has also established itself as an effective and trusted technical assistance provider, which is reflected in the support that BRAC provided to the government of Liberia in developing its National Livestock Policy.

Supported countries in their time of crisis: Most of the countries where BRAC operates internationally are frequently affected by disease outbreaks, conflicts, and natural disasters. The AFSL programme stood beside rural farmers in times of these crises, helping them to recover and build their resilience in future crises. The most recent example of this kind of work was in Liberia and Sierra Leone which experienced the worst Ebola crisis in recent history. BRAC supported over 6,000 farmers during and in the post-Ebola period with special assistance packages.

Developed innovative models as per country context: Keeping its proven intervention packages at the core of its work, BRAC developed different innovative models of intervention to suit the particular needs of farmers in individual countries. In Uganda, which has an alarmingly high malnutrition rate, BRAC tailored its core programme activities to promote the production of nutrition-rich bio-fortified crops. In Tanzania, where the government focuses on the transformation of agriculture from subsistence farming towards commercialisation, BRAC adopted a modified Making Markets Work for the Poor (M4P) approach, which combines BRAC's core interventions with more advanced market development work. In West Africa, where poverty, food, and nutrition security is the main concern, BRAC adopted food for work, cash for work, and nutrition-sensitive agriculture as the key programme approaches.

Established social enterprises to support the overall system: Capitalising on its experience of running many successful social enterprises in Bangladesh, BRAC decided to set up social enterprises in some countries based on their needs and context. These include the first and only poultry hatchery and feed mill in Liberia to encourage the private sector to invest in the poultry sector, pig breeding farms and slaughterhouses in Sierra Leone and Liberia to promote hygienic meat production and sale, and a seed enterprise and tissue culture lab in Uganda for the production of high quality seed.

6.4.2 A decade of results and impacts

BRAC International's over ten years of work in Africa and Asia have yielded specific evidence on its effectiveness. Some examples are given below:

- The four-year LEAD project in Tanzania, as mentioned earlier, led to significant gains in farmers' income and productivity. The median monthly income of participating maize farmers rose five-fold, while egg production rose by a factor of 5.5 (Hamisi and Tariquzzaman 2017). The LEAD team also established close relationships between farmer producer groups and buyers by supporting collective sales, sales to non-local markets, and contract arrangement with buyers. The percentage of maize farmers selling via contractual arrangement grew from two percent to eight percent, while the percent of poultry farmers doing so grew from three percent to fifteen percent (for eggs). In addition, maize farmers selling to non-local markets doubled from five percent to ten percent.
- After three years of the Global Poverty Action Fund (GPAF) Programme in Tanzania, a randomised control trial showed that farmers experienced exceptional increases in crop productivity (71% for maize) and number of livestock (125% for poultry) compared to a control group, with an 85.5 percentage point gain in income from the sale of agriculture products (Hamisi and Okello 2015).

- In Uganda, BRAC's agri-nutrition programme, which focuses on expanding intake of nutrient-rich foods, resulted in an enormous increase in the consumption of the nutritious orange-fleshed sweet potato, from four percent of individuals in the control group to 24-70 percent of those in various intervention groups (Okello and Mpiira 2017).
- The final report on the Community Connector (CC) project (FHI 360 and Community Connector 2016) found that by the end of the project, there were substantial improvements in food hygiene behaviour, Water, Sanitation and Hygiene (WASH) behaviour, dietary diversity for children, and meal frequency (three or more meals) for children. The value of beneficiaries' household productive assets increased by 35 percent compared to the baseline. At the end of the project, 81 percent of individual farmers were using at least two of the sustainable agriculture technologies promoted by CC. Households that adopted the CC-promoted agricultural enterprises had an eight percent increase in disposable income and a 21 percent increase in savings.
- An impact study was conducted in 2015 on a Kitchen Gardening and Poultry Rearing intervention. The median food consumption score is an indicator used in food security analysis that incorporates dietary diversity and nutritional value. The study found that the score of targeted households increased by 18.3 percent in Sierra Leone and 10.3 percent in Liberia over three years (Khakshi et al. 2015). It was also found that, in Liberia, participating farmers' income increased 72 percent (from USD 364 to USD 626) over three years (Khakshi et al. 2015).
- An assessment of the LEAD project in Tanzania found that 72 percent of participating farmers perceived the agri-finance loan to be useful, while an average of 77 percent of households indicated an agricultural loan helped them to purchase inputs on time, increasing their production and income (Bukulu et al. 2017).
- A 2016 study of LEAD's investment fund found that participating entrepreneurs nearly doubled their average monthly income

from USD 1,672 to USD 3,327 within one year. The number of buyers and sellers also increased significantly from 2,458 before receiving funding from BRAC to 4,821 (a 96% increase) after receiving funding (Saleque 2017b).

- A study in South Sudan indicates that demonstration farming had a positive and significant effect on reducing household food insecurity. For instance, the Household Food Insecurity Access Scale score of the treatment group after intervention was 9.20 points, whereas it was 10.03 points for a matched control group. Similarly, the probability of severe food insecurity is 12 percentage points lower for the treatment group compared to the matched control group, a significant result (Barua and Chowdhury 2015).
- In Afghanistan, the knowledge that girls gathered on agri-nutrition encouraged almost all the girls (99%) to participate in agricultural activities, particularly vegetable cultivation in treatment areas. Participation increased by 34 percentage points in treatment areas compared to control areas (Alim et al. 2017).

6.4.3 Key challenges

Frequent crises and suspension of project activities: Many countries where BRAC International's AFSL programme operated have experienced frequent conflicts, disease outbreaks, and other disasters. This has disrupted project delivery and the achievement of the desired impact. For example, in 2014, the project activities had to be suspended in Sierra Leone and Liberia because of national restrictions on movements and public gatherings due to the Ebola outbreak. Following the outbreak, some project beneficiaries were forced to migrate to safer zones, and many faced losses of farm resources and assets. Due to the unstable situation in South Sudan, project follow-up and data collection were done through mobile phones.

Human resources: Although many BI projects started operation under the leadership of BRAC's technical experts from Bangladesh, local staff were the key to delivering frontline activities. Over time, the key positions were filled by local staff. However, the unavailability of qualified people locally has been and remains a great challenge for many of the country offices. For example, while implementing the LEAD project, lack of skilled and experienced local staff with adequate knowledge of the M4P approach was a significant challenge. Therefore, training on M4P was arranged for one hundred staff. Additionally, as the hatchery and feed mill is the first and only one in Liberia, local staff had no experience in this sector. BRAC gradually developed the capacity of local staff to operate this enterprise.

Poor infrastructure and government legislation: Most countries where BRAC International's AFSL programme operates are either underdeveloped or affected by conflict. As a result, there is very poor market infrastructure to support the production and productivity of smallholder farmers. Underdeveloped markets are a critical issue in Liberia and Sierra Leone, as they rely heavily on the import of goods. High input costs pose a great challenge. Storing vaccines is also challenging due to the lack or irregularity of power supply, so BRAC uses thermos-stable poultry vaccines. Most financial institutions were found not interested in providing agricultural loans to smallholder farmers due to high risk. As a result, BRAC intervened and developed agricultural finance in Tanzania and Uganda.

6.4.4 Key lessons learned

Across the countries of operation, farmers face similar challenges, and some core activities are required to address those challenges: Through its work in various countries, BRAC has learned that farmers across the low-income countries of the world face similar challenges, and some core activities like training, access to finance, and access to post-harvest technology are equally effective in all contexts. Training played a significant role in the adoption of modern practices, particularly when developed alongside market facilitation activities (which support and activate market engagement). Finance provision is key to rural agricultural development. Agricultural finance provides a liquidity boost to farmers to stimulate and deepen their market engagement. The innovation of PICS bag technology for post-harvest loss mitigation helped smallholder farmers to access reliable markets that offered good prices, which incentivised farmers to invest in production and post-harvest technologies. Moreover, targeting and supporting the right entrepreneurs with an investment fund can be very successful, particularly when brought together and applied with in-depth local knowledge and careful studies of local market gaps and value chains.

Participation of multiple actors is a key factor in sustaining the impacts of the projects: The participation of private-sector producers and suppliers of agricultural inputs and their linkage with local retailers creates synergy and effectiveness in technology promotion. It also significantly increases the likelihood of continued and sustainable rural value-chain development. The involvement of the government in projects implemented by NGOs and building their capacity to scale up those interventions are also crucial for improving the overall agriculture sector performance of any country.

Multi-sectoral interventions are required to address the challenges of the 21st century: BRAC's earlier interventions solely focused on the performance of the agriculture sector. It designed its interventions to address the sector's specific challenges. But in recent years, food insecurity, malnutrition, and the effect of climate change have forced BRAC to adopt a multi-sectoral approach. Through its work in Uganda and Liberia, BRAC has proved that multi-sectoral interventions combining health/ nutrition, agriculture, and disaster preparedness are often more cost effective and successful in addressing the 21st century's complex challenges.

Programmes need to constantly evaluate themselves and innovate to stay relevant: Despite the great success of BRAC's models in improving agricultural production and food security in Bangladesh, these models required upgrading and contextualisation in other countries. The programme models also need to change in each country over time, and here, implementation research plays an important role. BRAC constantly evaluates the performance of its programmes and innovates to keep itself effective and relevant to the needs and nature of its beneficiaries. In the coming years, with the rapid growth of digital technology, it is even more important for programmes to develop new delivery models and evaluate their performance to find the best solutions.

Women and youth need specialised interventions to ensure their full participation in the agriculture value chain: Across all countries, women and youth constitute a large percentage of the agriculture labour force. However, their participation in the overall value chain is limited compared to their male counterparts. These groups need specially focused, tailored training and support to ensure their equal participation. Some form of positive discrimination or affirmative action is required. With proper support, they will play a vital role in the transformation of the agriculture sector.

6.5 Conclusion

The agriculture interventions of BRAC International focus on helping people reach their full potential. It explores the root challenges that lead to cycles of inter-generational poverty and devises comprehensive, multi-faceted programmes to address them. BRAC has had over a decade of experience working in Tanzania, Uganda, Liberia, Sierra Leone, South Sudan, and Afghanistan and has reached more than three million people of different categories, including vulnerable poor smallholders, especially women and youth. Using innovations in terms of products, services, and technology, it develops and promotes the use of productive, environmentally sustainable farming practices to improve the food security, nutrition level, income status, and resilience of people in rural communities.

The diverse activities of BRAC work together to form a holistic approach towards lifting people out of poverty through agriculture. BRAC now has an array of proven models that can be replicated and expanded to reach more places and people. It has already experienced many successes through its projects, including significant improvements in household productivity, income, hygiene behaviour, nutrition, and food security. BRAC continually seeks to improve its operations by taking advantage of new technologies, research, and approaches, persistently measuring their effectiveness, and always challenging itself to do more, and better.

References

African Development Bank. 2013. *South Sudan: An Infrastructure Action Plan*. Tunis-Belvedere, Tunisia: AfDB.

Alim, M.A., M. Gulam, M. Hijran, M.A. Hossain, and M. Sulaiman. 2017, January. "Nutrition Promotion and Collective Vegetable Gardening by Adolescent

Girls: Feasibility Assessment from a Pilot in Afghanistan." *Asian Journal of Agriculture and Rural Development, Asian Economic and Social Society* 8, no. 1: 40-49.

Bandiera, O., N. Buehren, R. Burgess, M. Goldstein, S. Gulesci, I. Rasul, and M. Sulaiman. 2017. "Women's Empowerment in Action: Evidence from a Randomized Control Trial in Africa." LSE/World Bank. https://www.ucl.ac.uk/~uctpimr/research/ELA.pdf

Barua, P., and R.A. Chowdhury. 2015. *Impact Evaluation of Demonstration Farming on the Food Security among Smallholders in South Sudan Using PSM Method.*

Blein, R., M. Bwalya, S. Chimatiro, B. Faivre-Dupaigre, S. Kisira, H. Leturque, and A. Wambo-Yamdjeu. 2013. *Agriculture in Africa - Transformation and Outlook.* NEPAD (New Partnership for African Development). http://www.un.org/en/africa/osaa/pdf/pubs/2013africanagricultures.pdf

BRAC. 2008. *Afghanistan Annual Report.* Kabul: BRAC Afghanistan. https://www.slideshare.net/anwark76/brac-afghanistan-annual-report-2008

——. 2015a. *GPAF project completion report.* Tanzania.

——. 2015b. *GPAF Project Completion Report.* Liberia and Sierra Leone.

——. 2015c. *Japan Bilateral Project Report on IVS.*

——. 2016. *BRAC Liberia EU Project Progress Report.*

——. 2017a. *BRAC Liberia Agriculture and Livestock Progress Report.*

——. 2017b. *South Sudan Agriculture and Livestock Progress Report.*

——. 2017c. *MIS Report.*

——. 2017d. *Pig Value Chain Project Completion Report.* Sierra Leone.

——. 2017e. *LEAD Completion Report.* Tanzania.

Bukulu, J., H.F. Hamisi, and S. Tariquzzaman. 2017. *Agri-Finance Report, Livelihood Enhancement through Agricultural Development (LEAD) Project in Tanzania.*

FAO. 2014. "Nutrition-Sensitive Agriculture." http://www.fao.org/3/a-as601e.pdf

——. 2018. "FAOSTAT, Crops, Livestock Primary, Suite of Food Security Indicators." http://www.fao.org/faostat/en/#data, accessed 16/04/2018

FHI 360 and Community Connector. 2016. *Final Report, Community Connector, the Integrated Nutrition and Agriculture Project.*

Fishman, Ram, Stephen Smith, Vida Bobić, and Munshi Sulaiman. 2017. "How Sustainable Are Benefits from Extension for Smallholder Farmers? Evidence from a Randomized Phase-Out of the BRAC Program in Uganda." Working Paper, IZA Institute of Labour Economics. doi:10.13140/RG.2.2.16494.00327

Gray, B., and J.P. Stites. 2013. *Sustainability through Partnerships: Capitalizing on Collaboration.* London, Ontario: Network for Business Sustainability.

Hamisi, H.F., and P.O. Okello. 2015. *Endline Report for the Global Poverty Action Fund (GPAF) Programme.* Maendeleo, Tanzania: BRAC.

Hamisi, H.F., and S. Tariquzzaman. 2017. *Completion Report for the Livelihood Enhancement through Agricultural Development (LEAD) Project in Tanzania.* Maendeleo, Tanzania: BRAC.

IFAD. 2011. *Viewpoint: Smallholders can feed the world.* Rome, Italy: Author.

International Food Policy Research Institute. 2005. *Women: Still the Key to Food and Nutrition.* Washington DC: IFPRI.

Khakshi et al. 2015. *Impact Assessment of Food Security Intervention through Kitchen Gardening and Poultry Rearing in Sierra Leone and Liberia, August 2015.* BRAC Sierra Leone and BRAC Liberia: Research and Evaluation Unit.

Okello, Patrik Olobo, and Robert Mpiira. 2017. *An Innovative, Integrated Approach to Enhance Smallholder Family Nutrition: Increasing Vitamin A Intake Using Orange Flesh Sweet Potatoes, Midline report of JSDF project in Uganda.*

Saleque, Mohammad Abu. 2017a. "Investment Fund a Key Booster to the Missing Middle: An Insight to BRAC Learning from the LEAD Project." https://www.researchgate.net/publication/318912806_'Investment_Fund'_a_key_booster_to_the_Missing_middle_An_insight_to_BRAC_learning_from_the_LEAD_project

——. 2017b. "Livelihood Enhancement through Agricultural Development (LEAD) Project of BRAC– An Innovative Model for Improving Livelihood of Smallholder Farmers." https://www.researchgate.net/publication/317836557_Livelihood_Enhancement_through_Agricultural_Development_LEAD_project_of_BRAC-

Saleque, M.A., and K.H. Imran. 2016a. "Assessing the Technical and Financial Viability of BRAC Poultry Hatchery & Feed mill enterprise in Liberia." BRAC Assessment Report (unpublished).

——. 2016b. "Assessing the Technical and Financial Viability of Seed Enterprise in Liberia." BRAC Assessment Report (unpublished).

The World Bank. 2015. *A Sweet (Potato) Solution to Malnutrition.* http://www.worldbank.org/en/news/feature/2015/12/16/a-sweet-potato-solution-to-malnutrition.

——. 2016. *Agriculture, Value Added (% of GDP).* World Bank National Accounts Data.

World Food Programme. 2015. *Emergency Food Security Assessment, June 2015, Liberia.* https://www.wfp.org/publications/liberia-emergency-food-security-assessment-june-2015

Photo 6.1: Harvesting eggplants in Tanzania

Photo 6.2: A happy poultry rearer in Liberia

Photo 6.3: A farmer feeding her semi-scavenging birds in Tanzania

Photo 6.4: Kitchen gardening in Sierra Leone

Chapter 7

Learning from the Past: Looking to the Future

Hugh Brammer

7.1 Introduction

BRAC continues to work in all sectors of Bangladesh's agricultural economy and play an important role in maintaining national self-sufficiency in food production. Over time, BRAC has gradually changed its strategies towards more enterprise-oriented models that are designed to provide extension services through different social enterprises. For example, BRAC Seed and Agro Enterprise produces, processes, and markets high-quality seeds through an extensive network of farmers, dealers, and retailers and markets micronutrient-rich fertilisers. Through the Nurseries, BRAC produces and markets high-quality timber, fruit, and ornamental tree saplings. BRAC has made similar enterprise-oriented interventions in the poultry, livestock, and fisheries sectors, and it has recently started a pilot Apiculture enterprise.

In its programmes in Bangladesh and internationally, BRAC focuses on four strategic objectives: strengthening pro-poor market systems, making agricultural systems more resilient to climate extremes, improving food and nutritional security, and empowering women and youth along the rural enterprise chain. Up to 2018, BRAC had reached about two million farmers in Bangladesh and elsewhere through its innovative, cost-effective, and evidence-based interventions.

This chapter examines possible future activities for BRAC that could generate skills and employment to reduce poverty further. Some of the suggested methods would be appropriate for application or adaptation in several developing countries.

7.2 Looking to the Future

7.2.1 The challenge

Bangladesh's rapid population growth and the accelerating rate of urbanisation present the Government of Bangladesh, its development partners, and NGOs with prodigious challenges. Similar challenges exist in many other developing countries. BRAC must address these challenges and avail of the opportunities inherent in them.

Perhaps the greatest challenge is addressing the human welfare problems generated by the increasing rate of urbanisation. In Bangladesh, it is estimated that the population of the capital city Dhaka alone, already 14.5 million in 2015, could grow to 27.3 million by 2030 (Bird et al. 2018). Inevitably, the majority of urban immigrants will be poor people, and they will need support to find shelter, food, water, and employment. The pressure on Dhaka must be relieved by promoting the expansion of other cities and towns and by seeking to generate more employment in rural areas.

In the agriculture sector, there are two main ways in which BRAC could assist the Government of Bangladesh. In the first place, there is a need to support the rapidly increasing demand for food of the growing urban population by promoting crop, livestock, poultry, and fisheries production in peri-urban areas using the methods described in the earlier chapters of this book. Employment in rural areas needs to be generated to reduce the rate of urban migration. In the following subsections, some of the possible interventions that could stimulate employment in the regions, towns, and villages throughout Bangladesh are described. They provide ideas that might be relevant for application in other countries that face similar problems of rural poverty and rapid urbanisation.

7.2.2 Agricultural mechanisation

Many agricultural procedures in Bangladesh are already almost fully mechanised: ploughing, irrigation, threshing, and rural transport. The increasing unwillingness of school-educated persons to engage in the physically demanding field work of transplanting and harvesting rice is creating labour shortages and increasing wage rates for these operations in some areas. In order to continue increasing rice production at affordable costs to meet the increasing demands of the country's growing population, the mechanisation of these remaining agricultural operations should be promoted and supported. BRAC could play a key role in both these aspects.

Suitable models of small machines for direct-seeding, transplanting, and reaping rice (and other field crops) exist that are suitable for the small size of farms and fields in Bangladesh. BRAC could assist in promoting the use of these machines by training young people in their use and maintenance, thereby generating rural employment that could simultaneously reduce the rate of urban migration and assist in increasing food production. BRAC could also explore the possibility of setting up local factories to manufacture appropriate machines, possibly by tapping on Chinese experience in the design and manufacture of small agricultural machines.

7.2.3 More efficient use of irrigation water

Present methods of flood-irrigating rice waste both water and energy used to operate irrigation pumps. These methods are therefore unnecessarily expensive for farmers. They also lower the water table in some areas to below the levels that can be reached by domestic hand pumps and shallow tube wells used for irrigation; in some coastal regions, they are also increasing the risk of drawing in saline water. There is an urgent need to promote more economical methods of irrigation in the widespread floodplain areas where groundwater is contaminated with arsenic.

BRAC could assist in three activities to promote more efficient and economical methods of irrigation.

- The System of Rice Intensification (SRI) described in Section 3.1 needs to be promoted in the extensive floodplain regions where shallow groundwater is arsenic-contaminated (as described in the annex to Chapter 1). Much less water is used in this system of rice cultivation than in either the flood-irrigating rice method or the Alternate Wetting and Drying (AWD) method. Besides, deep tube wells (DTWs), that are expensive to provide and operate, are needed in areas where shallow groundwater and soils are most heavily contaminated with arsenic to tap uncontaminated water below ca 150 m. The adoption of SRI could increase the area that could be irrigated compared with conventional flood-irrigation and would therefore reduce costs to farmers.

- More efficient methods of water distribution within tube well command areas should be promoted. There can be considerable loss of water in distribution channels extending to the outer parts of command areas, especially in DTW command areas and on the more permeable soils used for dryland crops such as wheat and maize. Irrigation channels need to be lined, or portable, flexible pipes should be used.
- The use of solar-powered irrigation pumps deserves widespread promotion. This could significantly reduce the costs of irrigation.
- The adoption of more economical methods of irrigation could also reduce Bangladesh's greenhouse gas emissions: of carbon dioxide by reducing or avoiding the use of pumps powered by diesel fuel or electric power; and of methane by adopting the SRI method of rice cultivation in place of flood-irrigation.

7.2.4 Reducing arsenic contamination of food

In areas where arsenic-contaminated groundwater is used for domestic water supply and irrigation, there is an urgent need to reduce arsenic contamination of food produced by crops grown on arsenic-contaminated soils and cooked in arsenic-contaminated water. The primary need is to assess the scale of food contamination in different areas.

In the first place, it would be useful to equip BRAC's soil testing laboratories to analyse the arsenic contents of water, soils, and food, and to train staff in the appropriate methods of analysis and interpretation of results. At the same time, BRAC's health field-staff could be trained to take samples of foods commonly eaten, starting with rice, for laboratory analysis. Since farm livestock and poultry are also fed arsenic-contaminated crop residue, weeds, and kitchen waste and drink arsenic-contaminated water, there is an additional need to study the effects on meat, milk, and egg quality. Studies to find practical ways of reducing contamination of all such foods could be conducted in consultation with universities that are experienced in conducting soil and crop arsenic studies.

The information gained from such studies is urgently needed, not only in villages where crops and food are found to be arsenic-contaminated but also in urban areas where potentially-contaminated food crops (especially vegetables) are marketed. Such studies are urgently required in areas where crops have been irrigated with highly-contaminated water since STW irrigation was introduced 30-40 years ago. The people in these areas have been eating arsenic-contaminated food the longest and the soils have probably become highly contaminated. The information produced by such studies should be handled carefully so as not to create undue public alarm.

7.2.5 More efficient use of fertilisers

The traditional methods of broadcasting fertilisers in fields are very wasteful and thus unnecessarily expensive for farmers (and for the country if potash and phosphorus fertilisers that have to be imported). There are also potential adverse environmental hazards in the case of excessive use of nitrogen, which can be leached into adjoining *beels* and groundwater. BRAC could assist in promoting the more efficient use of fertilisers in three ways.

- Promoting placement of fertilisers in the soil instead of broadcasting them. There is scope for trials with appropriate fertiliser combinations and rates of application on different soils and crops. Small-scale fertiliser-placement machinery exists and needs to be adapted for different soils and crops.
- Pelleting fertilisers (called super granules). Pelleted compound fertilisers would facilitate fertiliser the placement described above; their use would also help to reduce wasteful leaching of nitrogen from soils. Drying and pelleting manure from poultry farms would also be useful; such manure would be especially useful for vegetable growers in peri-urban areas. However, the use of manure from poultry farms that use antibiotics should be banned because of the risks to human health from eating vegetables that have absorbed the antibiotics from the manure.
- Showing farmers how to carry out simple fertiliser trials in their fields and how to use the results. As described in the Chapter 1 Annex, there can be considerable differences in soil

fertility between different soils in a village, and even between neighbouring fields. That diversity can make recommendations derived from conventional fertiliser trials made in one field in one village in a region meaningless for individual farmers who may have several fields on different land types and soils in their village. The suggested method of fertilising needs to be tested in multiple regions and adapted as necessary. BRAC could do useful pioneering work in propagating this amongst farmers. If the method is found to work satisfactorily, BRAC could promote its widespread use via television and radio as well as through its field programmes.

The three methods described above should be tested for application in other countries where BRAC works.

7.2.6 Farmer groups

The method described in the last bullet above is adapted from the FAO Farmer Field School extension method, originally designed and promoted for pest management in rice. In this method, farmers are the local "experts," and extension staff are mainly facilitators responsible for organising activities and providing new technical information. This method deserves testing by BRAC for its applicability in Bangladesh. However, "school" is an inappropriate name for such groups: it implies a top-down approach. It is impossible for extension "officials" to visit every group in a village or upazila regularly. In a village, groups with a common interest (*samity*) could be formed — for example, farmers in an STW irrigation command area. They could learn from each other's experience, and watch or listen to television or radio farming programmes on a regular basis and discuss amongst themselves the relevance of the information for their specific conditions or needs.

7.2.7 Packaging of fruits and vegetables

Further urbanisation will increase the demand for fruit and vegetables in cities and towns. There is presently considerable wastage in transporting and marketing fruit and vegetables. BRAC could both reduce such wastage and promote fruit and vegetable production in other parts of the country by establishing packaging, bottling, and canning factories in production areas (preferably avoiding the use of plastics and other materials that could pollute the environment when discarded). This proposal deserves testing, both for technical practicality and for market demand for preserved products.

7.2.8 Increase livestock, poultry and fisheries production

Continuing efforts need to be made to identify, test, and introduce innovative measures that can increase meat, eggs, and fish production to meet the increasing demand for such food items as population and incomes grow. As described in Section 7.2.4, there is an urgent need to study the extent to which meat, milk, and eggs are contaminated by arsenic in areas where groundwater and soils are contaminated with arsenic and to seek appropriate avoidance or reduction methods.

7.2.9 Assisting populations in disaster-prone regions

Insofar as the country's rapid population growth is not matched by movements of people to urban areas and employment abroad, it seems likely that the numbers of poor families living in rural areas could increase. The number of poor families will probably remain large and may increase in disaster-prone regions such as riverine and estuarine *char* areas and the most flood-prone and cyclone-prone regions and subregions described in the annex to Chapter 1.

River and estuarine *char* areas deserve particular attention. Settlement and land use are particularly problematic in the areas listed below:

- On river *chars*, because of the temporary nature of land areas, exposure to damaging floods, the risk of fields and crops being buried by sand or raw silt deposits, and remoteness of many areas from government and commercial services and markets
- In estuarine *char* areas, by the erosion of long-settled and farmed land on the old islands Bhola, Hatia, and Sandwip; the raw sediments and salinity of new *char* land; exposure to cyclone and storm surge hazards; and remoteness of many areas from government and commercial services and markets.

Therefore, intensive efforts are needed in *char* areas to provide people with skills that will enable as many of them as possible to find employment in more secure habitable areas, including in rural towns. Methods of seasonal crop and livestock production that are suitable for the specific conditions in these hazardous regions and which need minimal permanent human residence need to be investigated and promoted. With its higher sensitivity to social conditions and greater flexibility of operations than government departments, BRAC could play a valuable role in exploring and testing alternative opportunities in different disaster-prone regions.

7.2.10 Education

Bangladeshi readers of the annex to Chapter 1 may discover that there is much that they did not know about the physical geography and climate of their country. Similarly, they may not know or understand much about the country's agriculture and the relationship of land use to local physical and social environments (described in chapters two through six). People must be educated in these subjects so that they may better understand development opportunities and constraints at both the national and local levels to enable better use and management of the country's environmental resources. Such knowledge would also provide them with a better understanding of the implications of climate change and sea-level rise.

The pupil's knowledge of physical geography, climate, and agriculture of Bangladesh must be enhanced. BRAC could play an influential role in promoting such basic knowledge by preparing textbooks at the appropriate educational levels, based on the books referred to in the Chapter 1 Annex and official reports. BRAC is already involved in promoting education in Bangladesh and could use its expertise in supporting the teaching of these subjects.

7.2.11 Climate change and sea-level rise

There is no evidence that global warming has changed the climate of Bangladesh to date (described in the Chapter 1 Annex). Bangladesh lies in a region of the world where annual temperatures have changed at much less than the global average rate. Of more concern to Bangladesh is the high rate of temperature increase in the Arctic regions. The increase in the rates of the polar-ice-cap melting and the thawing of permafrost can increase the rate of sea-level rise over time. It is in Bangladesh's interest to take responsibility and decrease its own emissions of greenhouse gases.

As was described in Section 7.2.3, the adoption of more efficient irrigation methods and SRI cultivation could reduce carbon dioxide and methane emissions. BRAC could explore methods for the use of solar power and wind that could reduce the use of diesel in rural transport and power generation. Studies are needed to explore practical methods that could reduce wind and hail damage to solar panels and windmills that can occur in *kal-baishakhi* and cyclones.

Reference

Bird, J., Li Yue, H.Z. Rahman, M. Rana, and A.J. Venables. 2018. *Toward Great Dhaka: A New Urban Development Eastward.* Directions in Development, countries and regions. Washington, DC: World Bank Group.

Annex

List of Individuals Interviewed

BRAC

Name	Designation	Department/Organisation
Abdul Bayes	Director	Research and Evaluation Division
AQM Shafiqur Rouf	General Manager (GM)	AI Enterprise
Ahmed Mushtaque Raza Chowdhury	Vice Chairperson	BRAC
Sirajul Islam	Programme Head	Agriculture and Food Security (AFS)
Md. Jobaidul Karim Masud	Head	Seed and Agro Enterprise
Mohammad Anisur Rahman	Director	Dairy and Food Enterprise
Md. A. Saleque	Advisor	Agriculture, Food Security and Livelihood, BRAC International (BI)
Md. Azizul Haque	Deputy General Manager Research and Production	Seed and Agro Enterprise
Md Musharraf Hossain	Deputy General Manager	Fisheries Enterprise
Mizanur Rahman	Ex-Sector specialist	Livestock programme
Mohammad Ali	Ex-General Manager	Dairy and Food Enterprise
Md. Mokarrom Hossain	Ex Programme Manager	Fisheries Enterprise, BRAC
Mr. Sudhir Chandra Nath	Ex- Programme Head	Seed and Agro Enterprise
S. N. Kairy	Chief Financial Officer	BRAC and BI
S. Nandi	Ex-Sector Specialist	Fisheries Programme
Tamara Hasan Abed	Managing Director	Enterprises

Outside of BRAC

Name	Designation	Department/Sector
Golam Hossain	Ex-Director General	Bangladesh Fisheries Research Institute (BFRI)
Md. Azizur Rahman	Ex-Deputy Director	Department of Livestock Services Gov't of Bangladesh (GoB)
Mokammel Hossain	Ex-Director General	Department of Fisheries, GoB
Hamidur Rahman	Director General	Department of Agriculture Extension, GoB
Kazi Fattah	Ex-Director General	Department of Livestock Services, GoB
Moshiur Rahman	Managing Director, President	Paragon Group and Bangladesh Poultry Industry Central Council
Muazzam Husain	Formerly Professor and Head	Department of Agriculture Economics, Bangladesh Agricultural University
Safiqul Islam	Chairman	Prawn Hatchery Owners Association
Shykh Seraj	Director	Founder Director and Head of News Channel i
Talukdar Saiful Islam	Ex-Deputy Director	Artificial Insemination, Department of Livestock Services, GoB

Index